PELLISSIPPI STATE
LIBRARY SERVICES
P O Box 22990
Knoxville, TN 37933-0990

The
The Long Prison Journey of Leslie Van Houten

The LONG PRISON JOURNEY of LESLIE VAN HOUTEN

Life Beyond the Cult

KARLENE FAITH

NORTHEASTERN UNIVERSITY PRESS
BOSTON

Northeastern University Press

Copyright 2001 by Karlene Faith

All Rights reserved. Except for the quotation of short passages for the purposes of criticism and review, no part of this book may be reproduced in any form or by any means, electronic or mechanical, including photocopying, recording, or any information storage and retrieval system now known or to be invented, without written permission of the publisher.

Consistent with California law, the subject of this book, Leslie Van Houten, will not benefit from it financially. The author's royalties will be shared with community programs for street kids.

Library of Congress Cataloging-in-Publication Data
Faith, Karlene.
    The long prison journey of Leslie Van Houten : life beyond the cult / by Karlene Faith.
      p. cm.
    Includes bibliographical references and index.
    ISBN 1-55553-481-3 (cloth : alk. paper)
    1. Van Houten, Leslie, 1949–   2. Manson, Charles, 1934–
3. Women prisoners—California—Biography.   4. Women murderers—California—Biography.   5. Ex-cultists—California—Biography.   I. Title.
HV9468 .F35 2001
364.15'23'092—dc21
[B]   2001030470

Designed by Diane F. Levy
Composed in Bembo by Binghamton Valley Composition, Binghamton, New York. Printed and bound by The Maple Press, York, Pennsylvania. The paper is Sebago Antique, an acid-free sheet.

MANUFACTURED IN THE UNITED STATES OF AMERICA
05 04 03 02 01   5 4 3 2 1

Dedicated to Jane Van Houten

Contents

Acknowledgments	ix
Chronology	xiii
INTRODUCTION	xv

Part 1: The Journey

ONE: GETTING ACQUAINTED	3
TWO: LIFE BEFORE THE CRIME	27
THREE: THE CRIME AND FIRST TRIAL	39
FOUR: REMINISCENCES AND TRANSITIONS	57
FIVE: A NEW TRIAL	97
SIX: TEMPORARY FREEDOM AND A THIRD TRIAL	119
SEVEN: DOING TIME	135
EIGHT: REFLECTIONS	155

Part 2: Leslie's Letters

NINE: MARKING TIME	167
Notes	191
Works Cited	199
Index	203

Acknowledgments

MY FIRST APPRECIATION goes to Leslie's good friends and mine, Sue Talbot and Nancy Stoller. Over many years, their loyalty and vigilance have been reassuring. Special thanks to Nancy for her careful reading of the manuscript at two different stages, and her wise suggestions for improvements.

As explained in the Introduction, Anne Near played a major role in helping me formulate my thinking about the Manson crimes. Anne's dialogic skills and keen editorial hand have guided my approach to this book two decades after our collaboration. I am deeply grateful for Anne's friendship and for her work on this project. I'm also grateful to Holly Near for her varied assistance and support over many years.

Special thanks to Linda Grippi, Leslie's good friend since their high school days, for her valuable, reliable assistance and warmhearted reassurances throughout the writing of this book. Thanks to friends Debra Miller, Sue Talbot, Sally Savitz, and Frances Reid for camaraderie and exchanging court-watching notes during Leslie's second trial, in 1977.

Thanks to journalist Ann Japenga and criminologist Nils Christie, for their encouragement, long ago, to embark on this project. Loving appreciation to Pamela Sleeth, for her expert and generous guidance in helping me come to a clearer understanding of cult phenomena. Thanks to lawyer Ellen Barry, for her sustained commitment to the human rights of prisoners and their children and for facilitating information gathering. Special thanks to friend and colleague Simon Verdun-Jones, for giving me a place at Simon Fraser University, where I've worked since 1982, and for his steady support.

Special thanks to Jane Van Houten, for her wisdom, enduring patience, cheerful disposition, and boundless compassion.

I'm grateful to my numerous family members and friends who took the time to learn about Leslie and to support her release.

In the course of writing this book, I had the good fortune to be approached by Aili Malm, an SFU graduate student in criminology. Her offer of assistance resulted in the sorting of over twenty-five years of letters from Leslie; Aili also assisted with last-minute research, referencing, and manuscript preparation. My keen thanks to her for her gracious generosity of time, skill, and good humor.

My nephew Scott Anderson is a computer whiz; he was indispensable to this project, as he has been in previous work whenever computer questions arose. For additional computer assistance, his partner, Kate Mangan, came to my rescue. Thank you, Scott and Kate.

Special appreciation goes to Jeanne Gallick, who was my partner in organizing the University of California tutorial program in 1972 in the women's prison. She lent her bright spirit and many talents to an uncommon teaching situation. Her companionship and support from the outset made the project possible. Thanks, too, for her evocative comments on an early draft of the manuscript.

Others who read all or parts of the manuscript at various stages or who discussed the project with me, whose critiques or encouragement were immensely helpful, included Beverley Beetham Endersby, Robert Spitzer, Laraine Goodman, David Estrin, Bonnie Berry, Cath Moody, John Moody, Carolyn Bell, Dorothy Dittrich, Liz Straker, and a number of anonymous reviewers. I am grateful to each of them.

It was Bonnie Berry who suggested Northeastern University Press for publication and who made the initial contact on my behalf with Sarah Rowley, Editorial Assistant, and Bill Frohlich, Director and Editor in Chief. Thank you, Bonnie, from my heart, and thank you, Sarah, Bill, and Ann Twombly, Production Director, for moving swiftly and efficiently through the manuscript preparation process. Sarah, Claire Renzetti, the Series Editor, and Diana Donovan, the copy editor, provided me with excellent suggestions for changes. My thanks to all of you. Any flaws or errors in the work are clearly my own responsibility. Except as noted, all the opinions expressed herein are my own.

Finally, I offer everlasting thanks to Leslie Van Houten, for all the ways she reveals her deep humanity and respect for life. Those who know the details of her crime only as presented by the media will see this statement as paradoxical—if not perverse, even blasphemous. These contradictions are part of the reason I believe we need to pay attention to her. I am grateful to have known Leslie as a friend since 1972. I have endeavored to do her justice without fanning or dismissing the enduring grief of Leno and Rosemary LaBianca's families.

Vancouver
February 2001

Chronology

Date	Leslie's Age	Event
August 23, 1949		Leslie Van Houten born
August 10, 1969	19	Leno and Rosemary LaBianca murdered
October 1969	20	Arrested in Inyo County on suspicion of theft
December 1969		Connected to the LaBianca murders; transferred to Sybil Brand Institute (jail) in Los Angeles
June 1970– April 1971		Remained at the Sybil Brand Institute through pretrial and trial
April 19, 1971	21	Sentenced to death and thereafter transferred to death row at the California Institution for Women to await execution in the San Quentin gas chamber
February 1972	22	California State Supreme Court abolished death penalty (reinstated 1976); Leslie's sentence converted to life in prison
June 1972		U.S. Supreme Court outlawed capital punishment nationally (for four years)
1974	24	Leslie completely disassociated from Charles Manson
1976	26	Transferred to the main prison at California Institution for Women

1976		Lawyer Maxwell Keith succeeds in overturning original sentence; Leslie returned to Sybil Brand Institute to await second trial
January 1977	27	Second trial begins
September 1977	28	Second trial ends with deadlocked jury
December 27, 1977		Leslie freed on bail
March 1978		Third trial begins
July 5, 1978		Leslie returned to Sybil Brand Institute to await sentencing; convicted on two counts of felony robbery-murder and returned to California Institution for Women
early 2001	51	Remains in prison

Introduction

This is a book about Leslie Van Houten, who, three decades ago, gained infamy as one of the "Manson girls." She was nineteen years old when she participated in murder. She has been imprisoned since October 1969, except for six months in early 1978 when she was out on bail, before and during her third trial. I met Leslie in 1972, when I was tutoring and doing research at the California Institution for Women (CIW).

In February 1972 the California State Supreme Court abolished the death penalty, so Leslie's sentence of death was reduced to life in prison. Virginia Carlson, the warden at CIW, wanted to institute programs for these new "lifers," and asked me to tutor the three women who were still being held on death row. Then known as the "Manson girls," Leslie Van Houten, Susan Atkins, and Patricia Krenwinkel had been convicted with Charles Manson (and Charles "Tex" Watson, who was convicted separately) for the 1969 murders of seven strangers in their homes.

Charles Manson spent much of his life in reformatories and prisons for common street crimes (burglary, car theft, forgery, pimping). In 1967, in his mid-thirties, he was free on parole; in 1968 he was the unlikely spiritual guru of a cult, and in 1969 he orchestrated two nights of brutal murder, including the highly publicized mass murder at the home of Sharon Tate, where five people were killed.

Fear gripped the Los Angeles area as details were reported ad nauseam.

The accused, in addition to Manson, were three of the many young girls and one of the young men who had been living in a commune led by Manson, referred to by the press as "the Family." Leslie Van Houten was not present at the Tate murders. She did, however, accompany two other Manson disciples on the second night of murder. This book does not minimize the horror of what happened to Rosemary and Leno LaBianca in the wee hours of August 10, 1969. But my first aim is to clarify the events that led to Leslie's and the others' participation in that tragedy and Manson's effects on them. More personally, I offer a portrait of the Leslie I have known, from a time before Charles Manson lost his power over her to the present. This version of the life of a "Manson girl" differs from other versions, in that I learned the stories firsthand over decades.

During the thirty years following the murders many changes have occurred in Leslie's life. In the mid-1970s she completely separated from Manson's power. She then began the hard work of realizing what she'd done and of doing penance. She matured quietly and gracefully through young adulthood and middle age, making a life within her prison community. Those who believe she should have been put to death for her crime are understandably angry that she, unlike her victims, has had the opportunity to mature at all, even if in the harsh conditions of prison. I argue that, unless punishment is meant to be limitless, it is time for her to be paroled.

Most of what is known about Leslie by those over age fifty (in the year 2000) is what they saw sensationalized in the press or on TV at the time of the crime and the first trial, and from a mass-market book written a few years later by Vincent Bugliosi, the prosecutor of four of the five Manson defendants. This age group might remember stories about a trio of girls who jeered at the judge; girls who, on the command of Manson, like robots, shaved their heads to show solidarity. Most of what is known about Leslie by those who are younger than fifty is simply a vague image of one of the so-called Manson girls who murdered for Charlie, an image based on Manson lore and mythology that has been transmitted from one generation to another, often on the Internet.

In prisoner education and human rights work over the years since the early 1970s, I've encountered thousands of women and hundreds of men in various U.S. and Canadian prisons. Hundreds of them have struck me as unusually gifted or strong in character. Leslie Van Houten is an especially remarkable person, both because of who she is today and because of how she got that way. I make this assertion while understanding why many readers might protest any affirmation, of any kind, for any reason, of anyone involved with Charles Manson.

Anne Near

For years, Leslie and I talked about doing a book together. By 1980 I'd been gathering notes for seven years, and Leslie had ideas on how we might structure her story. Yet I was confounded about how to begin until I began talking with my friend Anne Near, whose perspective I valued. Her full life has included being a wartime factory worker; a demonstrator at peace marches; a rancher and rancher's wife; a record company comanager; a mother of four and grandmother of five; a human rights, community, and arts activist; a mentor to many; and an author.[1] (Now retired, Anne turned eighty-four in 2000.)

Anne and I had been transcribing my interviews with women in prison. She rightly questioned the value of working on Leslie's story because Leslie was unlike most other women in the prison—she came from a middle-class background and her life seemed to have been idyllic until her adolescence. Also, her sensationalized crime was altogether unusual. A woman accused of murdering strangers has been a rare phenomenon in the history of crime.[2] It is not difficult to understand the circumstances of crimes such as theft or drug possession, or even domestic murder, but it is difficult to understand how a woman could attempt to murder a stranger.

The year before I began teaching and doing research at CIW, I had taught at Soledad state prison.[3] At Soledad, I felt perfectly at ease with men who had murdered, while believing I was "the kind of person" who could never kill anyone. But when I first started working at CIW in 1972, I heard stories of situations that could have happened to any woman. Leslie's conviction, however, was for something profoundly out of the ordinary.

Though in 1980 I had been acquainted with Leslie, Susan, and Patricia for eight years, I hadn't talked with them about the crimes since 1973. And except for a few of their family members and mutual friends, I rarely spoke with anyone on the outside about them. Because I valued Anne's opinions and because she was interested in my work with women in prison, we engaged in a series of taped dialogues about crime, women, punishment, and prison life. Anne's questions eventually helped me focus on how to draw meaning from the horrific events that had brought Leslie and the others to prison. Anne's insights were key to my coming to terms with what seemed incomprehensible.

We discussed Leslie's crime and its effects, her trial, her two retrials and her six-month release on bail, my experience of Leslie in and out of prison, and what we thought the Manson crimes meant in the context of the world at large. Anne helped clarify my thinking about the "Manson girls" and the times in which they lived.

In the 1960s teenagers and young adults, throughout North America and beyond, were faced with their powerlessness against possible annihilation from the Cold War and their lack of the right to vote against fighting a war in Vietnam, which was costing more and more lives. In the United States, the voting age was lowered from twenty-one to eighteen in July 1971, as a response to Vietnam veterans who complained about being old enough to kill but not old enough to vote. Searching for spiritual meaning, many studied Eastern thought as explained in Western terms—with or without a guru (teacher)—looking for *nirvana* (perfect peace). Leslie's spiritual quest and her trust in her guru were not unusual for the time. She joined Manson's cult and she was brainwashed. Manson's followers were led from being independent, promising young people to being obedient disciples who lost their ability to think for themselves.

The conversations with Anne were immensely clarifying to me, but it was many more years before I gained enough distance to proceed with this book. An emerging scholarly literature on cult programming offers support for the view that Leslie and the others in the Manson "family" were victims of brainwashing by the man they had adopted as their guru.[4] In the years before I talked with Anne, I had seen the so-called Manson girls begin to realize they were no longer members of a special "family." In talking with Anne Near, I came to appreciate how, before they met Manson, these women had been oversocialized to be utterly "feminine"—at the extreme end of a continuum of male dominance and female compliance.

Much has transpired in all our lives since my conversations with Anne in her farmhouse kitchen in northern California, but the words still ring true. I came to see Leslie, Susan, and Pat as victims of a tortured boy who became a murderous, controlling man, a man with a penchant for seducing and exploiting trusting, vulnerable young women. A charismatic negative force, he transformed their lives in ways that could not have been anticipated by anyone who knew them.

Keeping in Touch with Leslie

In one form or another, my contact with Leslie has been fairly steady, beginning in 1972. Since 1982, having returned from California to my native Canada, I have been able to visit Leslie only rarely. Our communications consisted primarily of sporadic correspondence until 1995, when we began speaking on the phone from time to time.

Leslie has to stand in a long line to sign up for each call she makes, and then wait with all the others to see if her name will be called. She doesn't always make the list because too many others are ahead of her; time to make calls is limited. When she does make the list she has many people to call, including her mother, Jane, and her friend Linda Grippi, who, since high school, has been like a sister to her. When she does call me, our twelve-minute-maximum conversations are monitored and taped, and we're frequently interrupted by a recording to remind me (first in English, then in Spanish) that I'm speaking with a California state prisoner, that our conversation is being recorded, and that if I want to cut off the call I should hang up immediately and no one at that "inmate facility" will ever be able to call my number again. Between and through these recorded interruptions, we chat rapidly and uninhibitedly about our lives and whatever big questions either of us has been mulling over since our last chat.

Over the years there were times when I was forbidden to write or to visit anyone in the prison.[5] For example, on one occasion I wrote a letter to Leslie and enclosed an article I'd authored, in which I mentioned the Venceremos Brigade, referring to groups of young people from the States who, despite the U.S. ban on travel to Cuba, went there every year to help with the sugarcane harvest. The problem was that the word *venceremos*, a call to overcome obstacles to freedom, was also the name of a political group that had freed a prisoner from Chino (a neighboring male prison) at the expense of a guard's life. So, understandably, the authorities weren't taking any chances when they read that word in my article. Some months later, after more intensive background and security checks than those to which I'd already been subjected, I was able to resume my visits and our correspondence.

Writing about Leslie

For three decades the dominant media images of the Manson "family" have neglected to convey the continued bewilderment of those directly involved in the infamous crimes. As a former Manson disciple, Leslie is troubled by young people who romanticize the mythic Charles Manson. Thirty years ago Leslie's devotion to him exceeded her survival instincts, and so she is in prison, but now she is speaking. She speaks out to demystify a seasoned deceiver who tricked and trapped young people—and to not let her own life be ruled by fear of him.

Overcoming fear of any kind is a challenge to anyone in prison. A life sentence can be more frightening than execution. Leslie tries to transform that fear. She says, "I accept that society rejects me and that this is my world. I don't feel compelled to connect with society. I am a banished person. What I do is educate, when possible, those who cross my path, and help young women find a different way. I care about those in my world, and try to help them reclaim their lives."[6]

My formal research on women and criminal justice has involved participant observation in the prison; court-watching; interviewing over one hundred women in prison and gathering data from institutional records and from answered questionnaires, from library searches, and from document analyses. Leslie's story, as I tell it, unfolds from and is illuminated by these sources, but my primary research on Leslie is personal and is based on our communications over many years, in various locations, and from our changing perspectives. For reasons of critical method and of basic integrity, I cannot feign detachment.

The day will come when Leslie will be able to tell her own story in her own words. I offer this book as an introduction to Leslie from the perspective of our friendship buttressed by research. The bulk of this book is not Leslie's story so much as it is the story of my perception of how she got to where I see her now. This story of Leslie is based on my observations, records, and memory of events at which I was present; interview transcripts and audio- and videotapes; notes from court and from taped parole hearings; miscellaneous documents; secondary sources; and twenty-five years of correspondence. I have quoted from the dialogue with Anne Near. And I have quoted from Leslie's letters and audio- and videotaped interviews and conversations—within the prison, and on the outside, during Leslie's six months of freedom in 1978 when she was out on bail following a second trial—all with Leslie's permission. As I wrote, I tried to keep Leslie's voice at the center of my mind, no matter who is speaking in the text, in order to avoid misrepresenting her. Part 2 consists almost entirely of excerpts from Leslie's letters to me between 1972 and 1998.

Leslie is not looking for anyone to serve as her apologist. In her interactions with others she is humble, never forgetting her part in a crime she remembers all too well—viscerally with all her senses, rubbed raw on a regular basis by the repetition of details in legal rituals. When Barbara Walters interviewed Leslie for ABC television in January 1977 (seven and a half years after the crime), she asked Leslie to explain how she copes with the nightmare of the crime. "Is it something that you think of [as having] happened to somebody else?" Walters asked. Leslie replied, "No, it's very real to me. It's very real to me at night when I'm alone in my cell with my thoughts. It's at that point that I—I don't try to block it out. That's part of the hell that I'll have to live with forever."

Part 1: The Journey

One

GETTING ACQUAINTED

WHEN THE MANSON MURDERS broke in the press in late summer 1969, my children and I were in Jamaica, where I was doing research with the Rastafarians. The press there didn't dwell on the murders, but when we returned to California we encountered the U.S. media's onslaught that lasted for over a year. Following sentencing in 1971, Leslie Van Houten, Pat Krenwinkel, and Susan Atkins were sent to the California Institution for Women (CIW), to await execution.

As a History of Consciousness graduate student at the University of California at Santa Cruz, I was then teaching in Soledad, a men's state prison, and preparing to go to CIW the following spring to do research and teach. This would be where my life converged with Leslie's.

The California Institution for Women is situated about sixty miles east of Los Angeles, in "Corrections Valley." Three other prisons (Chino adult men's prison, a youth prison, and a prison for narcotics offenders) dot this stretch of flatlands in the midst of pastures and orchards. For much of the year the heat is exacerbated by the heavy smog that blows in from L.A. and settles over the valley. The stench of manure hangs in the thick, deadly-still prison air. It was on such a day, in late spring of 1972, that the warden called me in to ask if I'd be willing to tutor the three women who would be held indefinitely in her prison.

The California State Supreme Court had abolished the death penalty in February 1972. That decision was confirmed in June by a U.S. Supreme Court decision that outlawed capital punishment as cruel and unusual. (Capital punishment was not revived in the United States for another four years.) This decision meant that the "Manson girls" were now condemned to life in prison. Since there was not yet legislation allowing for life imprisonment without the possibility of parole, this meant they also had the possibility of eventual release.

My first visit to the old death row at CIW in 1972 was a top-security operation, a long escorted walk ending at a small brick structure located in an isolated corner of the grounds, across a grassy yard from the psychiatric unit. The strict surveillance procedures surrounding this visit surprised me, because I'd been doing research and volunteering as a tutor/adviser at the prison for months, with independent, unobstructed easy access to every other part of the prison. Moreover, I was going to the unit at the direct request of the warden. On this occasion, two security people, a man and a woman, gave me a body search before I was escorted from the administration building by a uniformed, armed guard and the associate warden (both men). We stopped at locked gates and fences en route, and at the guard tower, for identity checks. Women I worked with who had heard I was going "over there" were watching the maneuvers through the shrubbery at the perimeter of the main prison grounds.

The Special Security Unit (SSU) staff members were expecting me, having received relayed radio reports as we crossed the grounds. They were friendly, a man and a woman, as they unlocked the outer door after we rang. As soon as I was safely deposited in the tiny entryway of the maximum of maximum-security segregation units, and despite the presence of the somber associate warden, who stayed, I felt the atmosphere suddenly change to sweetness and light.

The five women in SSU had their own guards, who did their jobs efficiently and cheerfully. On this first visit, the guards chatted with me pleasantly, welcoming me. They explained the security system and the women's restrictions, such as the rule that all the women could not be out of their cells at once (a rule they soon changed for our "school"). They processed my paperwork without a fuss, while I listened to the women's voices from the cell unit beyond the entranceway—youthful, softly cheerful, not at all the voices of brutal murderers. My first impression was how relaxed it felt to me, even though it was a spartan, dreary little jail.

The associate warden kept a tactful distance while the male SSU guard took me to meet the women individually, through the bars of their cells, each of which was six feet by nine. Each woman had a metal-framed single bed attached to the floor, an open toilet, and a miniature sink; their few possessions were in cardboard boxes. I was impressed at how the guard treated the prisoners with the same respect they showed me, the visitor.

After meeting each woman, I was positioned on a folding chair in front of the cells where they could all see me. On this exceedingly hot and humid day, over 110 degrees Fahrenheit, everyone's eyes were red and smarting from the toxins in the polluted air. In a chorus from their cells, the three "Manson girls" offered me a glass of cold grape Tang, a powdered drink popular at the time. When I said, "Yes, thanks," one of the guards went immediately to a tiny refrigerator in the entryway and got it for me. I was in their home.

I found the three "Manson girls" to be instantly engaging, a blur of human vitality behind the steel bars, which separated me from them and all of them from each other. The faces, mannerisms, voices, and remarks all blended together as if they were one person—Pat-Leslie-Susan. The two other women, Jean and Linda, had also been convicted of murdering women, statistically the rarest crime for a woman to commit.

All five women were friendly, relaxed, and hospitable. They couldn't see each other, but they kept up a lively conversation that included everyone. The congenial and peaceful atmosphere disarmed me. It was a welcome contrast to the negative tensions and punitive attitudes that circulated in the main prison, where there were always a few troublemaking guards or prisoners.

The warden had asked me to focus my SSU tutorial program on the "Manson girls," because she was sure that the other two women would soon be leaving death row. Because of the public's fear of Manson and her concern about his continued control over them, it was not clear that the "Manson girls" would ever leave this segregated unit. When I met them, they had been incarcerated for almost a year at CIW, after spending the previous year and a half at the Sybil Brand Institute, a women's jail in Los Angeles.

On our first visit I told the women that their crimes weren't on my agenda. I explained that I was a graduate student researching and tutoring in the main prison, and that I was prepared to set up classes for them if any of them were interested. All three expressed enthusiasm.

In the preceding two years I'd gone out of my way to minimize my reading or hearing the details of the Manson "family" crimes, but there was no escaping the steady barrage of headlines or the continual discussion on city buses and everywhere. I couldn't reconcile the media's images with the women I faced through the bars to their cells. It was hard to believe that women of their demeanor and apparent disposition could have been involved in the crimes associated with Charles Manson.

Although at first reluctant, after a few weeks Jean and Linda joined our tutorials. For a short time they remained on death row and, like the "Manson girls," they produced excellent essays. Within months they were transferred to the main prison, and I lost contact with them.

Our sessions were held as a group. We sat on the floor of a cell we called the schoolroom. Over the following months, I began to see the women as individuals. Leslie later spoke to me about Jean, who, though more than twenty years older than she, had become a trusted friend. Leslie said that Jean taught her how to survive prison life with her spirit intact. "I'd be talking to her, and she would say, 'That doesn't make any sense. Explain yourself.' And I knew I couldn't." Ultimately, Jean inspired Leslie to hope that one day she could do something "to bring to light some of the things that can happen to young people."[1]

On numerous occasions over time, the "girls" did tell me and others of the murders in elaborate detail. Even when hearing about the crimes directly from them, I could not reconcile my sense of who they were with the crimes that they said they committed and for which they were imprisoned.

Facing Violence

For the LaBianca family and for Leslie's family and friends, the crime is painful history; a man and a woman were killed and that is the reason

Leslie is still in prison. In a later chapter I discuss the violence because that is where the public interest in Leslie's story begins. But seldom does brutal crime receive the kind of media coverage—and the resulting merciless sentence—that the Manson "family" crimes received.

Imagine the following fictional, but in some respects not unusual, brutal double homicide:

A middle-aged couple has just arrived home from a party in their unlit, low-income, inner-city neighborhood. Before they can close the door behind them, a neighborhood leather-clad bully bursts into their apartment, followed by his tough-looking but submissive girlfriend. The two men recognize each other from the street. The bully demands money, grabs the woman's purse, and kicks the man to the floor to take his wallet. When the victims put up a brave fight, the bully pulls a knife and instantly kills the man with several stabs in the chest. Then he thrusts the knife toward his girlfriend and orders her to kill the woman, not wanting to be alone with a murder rap. The girlfriend balks, horrified at the first death, paralyzed at the prospect of herself killing someone. The enraged bully plunges the blade into the screaming woman's heart; she dies. Now, putting the knife firmly in his girlfriend's hand, the bully screams at her, "You do it—you . . . do it now—do it!" until she too stabs the already dead woman; in hysterics, the girlfriend stabs and stabs—fourteen times.

Several days later, the newspapers simply report that two people were found in their apartment stabbed to death with multiple wounds; no known witnesses; assailants unknown; police do not as yet have any suspects.

In real cases similar to this fictional example we seldom hear another word about the crime. Unlike the sensationalized Tate and LaBianca murders, these victims would be unimportant in terms of newsworthiness, in accordance with the marketing values of commercial media. Given the dynamics of class structures and racism, the mainstream media treat people in low-income ghettos as disposable; they rarely make the news even when they're murdered. Since there is no singular intriguing detail about this (fictional) crime, it would be written off by reporters as a straightforward robbery-murder, probably for drug money.

Unlike most crimes, murders reported to the police are generally solved. This is partially because police give more attention to this most serious of crimes, and partially because killers and victims usually know one another—as acquaintances, friends, or family—which makes it easier to trace suspects.

Being killed by a stranger in one's home is a commonly feared but highly unusual way to die. Whatever the location, stranger homicides are the least common type of murder, and generally the most difficult to investigate. They are especially hard to solve when they occur in a home without witnesses. All but 10 to 15 percent of murders in most Western nations are male-on-male or male-on-female. Women rarely kill; when they do, their victim is often an abusive spouse.

Whatever the victim-killer relationship, investigations and media attention are motivated in significant part by the social status of the murder victim(s) or of the accused. Attention by the media is fueled by the pressures of advertising sponsors to accommodate "public interest"—a public interest that is generated by the media itself. The dominant, commercial media generate lowest-common-denominator definitions of what constitutes the news that is fit to print or air. Famous and/or rich victims or offenders in major crimes will generate attention and guarantee corporate media profits.

The hypothetical crime described above is basically the same crime that Leslie Van Houten and members of her "family" committed in 1969 against Leno and Rosemary LaBianca. Except that LaBianca was a wealthy, white owner of a grocery chain, and his wife was the co-owner of a boutique. They were killed in their comfortable home in the elite Los Angeles neighborhood called Los Feliz. Three of the four accused (and then convicted) "killers" were clean-cut all-American kids—a Texas farm boy and two girls from California suburbs. The highly sensationalized "Tate murders" had been committed the previous night, and the newspapers linked the two crimes immediately. Because of the failure of the Greater L.A. sheriff and police departments to communicate, however, it was months before police finally linked the crimes, identified suspects, and laid charges.

Sensationalistic details and dark inferences dominated reportage. The word *pig*—a common epithet of the day for police and for anyone in power—was written in blood at both the Tate and LaBianca murder sites. Another coded reference—to "Helter Skelter," a Beatles song on their White Album—was left at the LaBianca home. In England, a helter-skelter is a spiral slide on a playground. Manson used the phrase to describe the chaos of the times, a precursor to a race war. The murders were committed just before the Woodstock rock festival, just after the landing on the moon by three astronauts, and amid sustained national protests against the Vietnam war. The Black Panthers were gaining national influence in African-American communities and among leftists. Against this backdrop of heightened social tension and landmark events, the Manson murders dominated the California media for over a year. When the accused were found to have come out of a hippie commune, the attention intensified. The media latched on to people's worst fears about hippies and the antiwar movement. By the end of the trial, Manson's murders were touted as a singular milestone in the annals of homicide.

After successfully prosecuting four of the accused, Los Angeles District Attorney Vincent Bugliosi wrote a mass-market novel-like book (*Helter Skelter*) about the murders. At the time, its cover made the promise, "No matter how much you think you know about the Manson case, this incredible book will shock you." It was a best-seller, and is still in print today, replete with inaccuracies due to the defendants' false testimony in court and their own propagation of sensationalized myths. One reviewer describes this book as "a morality play of the highest order, with the crusading prosecutor battling a demonic Manson on one hand and the bumbling of the Los Angeles Police Department (LAPD) on the other."[2] One of Manson's messages, like St. Augustine's, was that he (and everyone) represented the perfect dialectic of God and the Devil, life and death, good and evil, sacred and profane. The symbolism was perfectly geared to a Hollywood sensibility. Through the lenses of the prosecutor, a woefully tragic set of murders became mythic owing to their perversely formulaic entertainment value. Bugliosi went on to oversee the 1976 CBS-TV version of his story, and to make $2,500 per speech (a large sum at that time) on the lecture circuit. The case brought him a celebrity career, but in the process he compromised his reputation as a serious attorney, and he lost a political bid for public office.

The Players

The media were unrelenting in the attention they gave Charles Manson, Charles "Tex" Watson, Susan Atkins, Patricia Krenwinkel, Leslie Van

Houten, and also Linda Kasabian. Linda was present at the Tate murder site, but she didn't participate in the killings, and she received immunity on murder and conspiracy charges in exchange for her testimony. The media also focused on Lynette "Squeaky" Fromme, Sandra Good, Catherine "Gypsy" Share, and other girls who lived on the sidewalk outside the court during the trial.

When I met Pat, Susan, and Leslie in 1972, they had been incarcerated for almost a year at CIW, after a year and a half at the Sybil Brand jail in Los Angeles. Knowing now that they weren't going to die, they pinned their hopes on soon being able to mix with the other women and to work in the main prison. Their hope grew when Jean and Linda, the two other death row women, were transferred to the main prison a few months after we met. From the three remaining women's point of view, the prison across the yard represented a world of freedom and of opportunity to be useful.

Like the three "Manson girls," Jean and Linda had been sentenced to death, and their sentences, too, were commuted to life in prison with the temporary abolition of capital punishment in the United States in 1972. Their crimes were serious: Jean killed an elderly woman in her home during a robbery; Linda killed her lover's wife. Like the crimes in which the "Manson girls" were involved, women were Jean's and Linda's victims, which is unusual when women are the offenders. Both Jean and Linda were paroled a few years later, after having served approximately eight and nine years respectively. Even though they were "death-penalty overturns," their release on parole was consistent with that of most individuals convicted of first-degree murder in the 1970s, a crime for which the rate of recidivism is extremely low for both men and women, no matter how many years are served. That Jean and Linda could achieve parole, and receive the same treatment from the board as had prisoners who had not received the death penalty, set a significant precedent—from which, however, none of the "Manson girls" benefited. (In Leslie's case, it's a moot point, as I discuss in chapters ahead.)

Reality set in when the women were informed that they would *not* be moved to the general prison population, that until further notice they would live out their years in the same isolated death row cells where they had waited to be transferred to San Quentin to die in the gas chamber. Virginia Carlson, the warden, came in to explain this to them.

They had a right to meals, a shower, and an hour outside each day, she told them. "Anything else is a privilege."[3]

The three women shaved their heads in protest, to no avail. They remained in SSU for four more years. Then, one by one over the course of a few years, they each finally entered the main population, though under tight security for a time.

When they were left behind in SSU, the "girls" came to appreciate what they did still have. Some of their guards had become friends to them. The women managed to use their time constructively. But they were sociable, active young women who enjoyed people, and the isolation and inaction were painful—as intended.

What Susan, Pat, and Leslie missed the most at the Special Security Unit, they told me, was contact with other prisoners and access to the admittedly minimal resources and work available in the main prison. They took little comfort in the fact that they were being spared oppressive prison jobs and hassles with abusive guards or prison mates.

For other prisoners, SSU might not have been so serene, but these three women had been well trained by Manson to "follow the program." They were nonconfrontational, cooperative, and submissive to authority. As Leslie later said to me, "We got along easily with our keepers because we did not challenge or make trouble."

The Warden

It was Virginia Carlson who asked me to meet with the women in SSU in the spring of 1972. Officially called the Superintendent, she was good-natured in an officious kind of way. Women in the main prison treated her as if she were a kindly but stern housemother in a boarding school. Sometimes they made fun of how prim, proper, and earnest she was; they complained about not getting in to talk with her, her unavailability to them. But they generally expressed more trust in her than in her associate wardens or most of the guards. The warden was running a little town, with everyone doing his or her part most of the time, and more or less getting along superficially, within the parameters of hierarchical, punitive power.

Carlson earned respect during a legendary summer talent show on the prison lawn. No one recognized her when she came out on the makeshift stage as a glittery Arabian Nights dancing girl, her blond hair in a fancy up-do, her face covered by a veil. The mystery lady, whom everyone assumed to be a prisoner, was a total success with the women. They roared their approval as she danced in a somewhat silly, parodic way, but sexy nevertheless. As the dancing girl lifted her hip in farewell, she took off her veil and put on her glasses. There stood Miss Carlson, smiling broadly. The prisoners went wild. Even though she reverted to her no-nonsense, conservative manner of dress after the show—pumps, a pastel suit, and a quiet hairdo—she won over many women on that day. Carlson proved to have genuine interest in the welfare of the more than six hundred women in her care at CIW.

As women, Carlson and I had found common ground. It was clear that she viewed the prisoners sympathetically, whatever the nature of their crimes, even if they were obnoxious to her. Long employed by Corrections, she was a line staffer who had worked her way up in a system that pits "us" (the good guys) against "them" (the bad guys). Despite this, she did not reduce the women to "criminal types." She tried to understand the circumstances that resulted in women's incarcerations. She voiced the whole spectrum of inequalities that justify prison sentences for victims. She supported the high court's abolition of capital punishment (which punishment would again be reinstated in 1976). And she cautiously identified with the goals of women's movements, which were just entering the mainstream culture in 1972.

No bleeding heart, Virginia Carlson was a pragmatist. She believed that any woman, however she had broken the law, was sufficiently punished by losing years of her life in prison. Many lost their intimate relationships and families—even children—in the process. She saw no benefit in exacerbating the fundamental pain of imprisonment with debilitating or deadly disciplinary practices; to do so, she felt, was inhumane, and ineffective in keeping order. She tried to keep order in more constructive ways: by providing the women with a variety of programs that could ease the strain of incarceration, by offering each woman some sense of choice and a feeling of usefulness in her day-to-day prison life. This would not describe her prison as I found it, and prisoners' versions did not match her rosy picture. Her job removed Carlson from day-to-day contact with the women, except for periodic visits to various cell units or self-help group meetings. But she worked at improving the situation at the policy level.

She wanted the women's years in prison, however few or many, to reeducate, not damage. She wanted the women in CIW to leave stronger than when they arrived, which would be the antithesis of the effects of prison on most people. Only exceptional people successfully, consciously resist the self-destroying pitfalls of imprisonment.

With the 1972 suspension of the death penalty, the warden was particularly concerned about how to work with the "Manson girls," and she called me to her office to discuss it. Now that they were not headed for the gas chamber, her responsibility for them had been extended. She couldn't just ignore them for the duration of her tenure at the prison. She had to ensure that their mental and physical health would not be destroyed by the sterile, isolated conditions of their confinement, year after year. She said they were model prisoners, and hoped I would help them use their time constructively.

Already she had given them permission to plant a little garden in a narrow, double-fenced strip of dirt alongside their small brick building, technically the "yard," to which they were released for an hour each day for "exercise." She had also discovered that Susan, Leslie, and Pat all had exceptional needlework skills, and had encouraged this activity by having Mrs. Smith, the prison occupational therapist, come to SSU every week with supplies. Smith reported enthusiastically about the women's creative talents, and became one of their valued friends, a comfort to them.

Carlson had tried installing a television set in each of their SSU cells, assuming it would help pass the time peaceably, but the women had asked that they be removed. Anne Near observed, when I spoke of their rejection of the TVs, "This shows an astonishing centeredness in such a barren environment!"[4] I agreed. Their lives were intentionally monkish and meditative. During their years in the Special Security Unit they didn't want the distraction of TV noise and pushy advertising invading their cell space.

Prior to meeting the women, while listening to Carlson discuss them, I found my curiosity piqued, but I was also resistant. I was concerned that getting involved with "the girls over there" would be too much of a diversion from my work in the main prison, where I was doing life history interviews as well as teaching women's studies. Carlson and I had bantered several times in the privacy of her office about various socialist and radical feminist issues hitting the news, and about the liberal-professional offshoots of the pioneering second-wave women's liberation movements. Virginia Carlson may have been the only feminist prison warden in the USA at the time (1972), although "feminist warden" may be an oxymoron. She did not identify with what she called feminist "extremists," but she had worked her way up to a radical feminist analysis of the girls in SSU.

On that day in her office, Carlson spoke of how disarmed she was by the girls' likeability, talents, candor, and charm. Whether or not being a victim while committing a crime absolves one of guilt was moot, from Carlson's perspective. The women had been judged by the California state court to be legally sane and guilty, and so they were in her care, but in her view they were still "good girls." She spoke of their innocence—which she said they had never lost. The warden attributed this seeming contradiction to Manson's control over their minds. She could see how, in their own perception, they were innocent of wrongdoing.

Carlson was the first person to suggest to me one of the themes of this book: that Leslie, Pat, Susan, and virtually all the young men and women who were involved with Manson were in some ways innocent victims of a dangerous cult leader. She spoke with disgust of how he'd taken control of their minds and bodies. She saw that "the girls" had lost their own identities in Manson in a much deeper way than that of sexual attraction. They needed him in the way of ultimate submergence, as a savior. She wanted programs that would divert their attention from him.

Despite her progressive attitudes, Carlson lasted several years as warden at CIW, far exceeding the average of less than a year for the five or six wardens who followed her into the 1980s, most of whom took a hard-line, unabashedly punitive approach. As my friend Anne Near commented, "From such a high turnover [of wardens] it would seem that many people go into the job thinking that a change of personnel, rather than of the system, will make a difference."

In the end, it was Carlson's insistent concern for these women that persuaded me to meet them.

Cult Behavior

What Virginia Carlson was saying in 1972 was that Manson had effectively brainwashed his followers. At that time, cults like Manson's "family" were not yet well understood. Today we are more aware of how common—and dangerous—brainwashing in cults can be.

The concept of brainwashing entered popular vernacular after the war against Korea in the 1950s, when captive U.S. soldiers switched loyalties, in part because of the constant barrage of "political education" to which they were subjected. They began speaking against the United States as if they were reading from a script.

Not long afterward, the CIA funded brainwashing (or "depatterning") LSD experiments at the Allan Memorial Institute in Montreal. Dr. Ewan Cameron, the experimenter, was known as one of the world's leading physicians for his "psychic-driving" electroshock treatments to depattern subjects. He would wipe the slate clean, then program new messages while the patient was immobilized by drugs.

He selected subjects from among regular patients seeking medical attention for all manner of health disorders. He never informed them of the reason he was treating them. Many were seriously damaged; most suffered loss of memory of anything in their lives prior to meeting Dr. Cameron. With extensive publicity, nine of his experiment's subjects, all Canadians, sued the CIA, and in 1997 they were collectively awarded a mere $750,000 as reparation for harm committed on them without their knowledge or consent.

One gentleman spoke on CBC-TV news (May 17, 1998) of how, along with being given LSD every other day as well as other drugs, they were all wired to a tape machine that played the same individualized message over and over again. His message was "You killed your mother," which played into his ears every two minutes night and day for many weeks. He came to believe it, and was shocked to find his mother alive when he was finally released. During the same period, LSD experiments were conducted on women in the Canadian federal prison.

Brainwashing is also the modus operandi of cults. There is a subtle difference between committing a crime and blaming it on another person, and claiming to have been the victim of brainwashing. Not one of the women involved with Manson has ever denied responsibility for the crimes in which she participated; indeed, until they came to their senses, all took credit for crimes they *hadn't* committed. Manson has taken responsibility for nothing. He persists in doubletalk and continues to seek attention. The courts and parole boards, holding each of the codefendants equally responsible, collude with Manson's failure to acknowledge his control over the women and their male companion before, during, and after the murders. Leslie said, "I resent that he mocks what happened . . . that he makes light of it."

One of Manson's admonitions to his followers was "Don't ask why"— a totalitarian imperative. One of the psychiatrists who testified at Leslie's second trial (see Chapter Five) defined brainwashing as "coercive persuasion," following Edgar Schein, the social psychologist who institutionalized the term in 1961. Brainwashing occurs when someone purposefully confounds targeted subjects and intentionally restructures their thought patterns—their beliefs, opinions, priorities, habits, values, and attitudes. This can be done by repeating something again and again until it is believed (which is also the basic principle of commercial advertising, the most pervasive form of brainwashing in capitalist cultures). The subject learns to comply with the wishes of the omnipresent "authority" without thinking for himself or herself at all.

Brainwashing can also be accomplished with the 1950s operant conditioning techniques developed by Harvard psychologist B. F. Skinner, who, in Pavlov's tradition, worked with reward and punishment to attain desired behaviors from animal subjects. His goal was to develop techniques for systematic controls over human behavior, in order to reach a better society. Ostensibly like Skinner, Manson was working toward a utopian society where the group could live in love and harmony. This society could be achieved by rewarding compliance with group needs rather than gratifying the individualistic ego. Utopian communities were common in the late 1960s, but Manson's power became abusive. He wanted to kill every ego except his own.

Cults accomplish brainwashing in several ways. Initially, fasting, meditation, and any form of sensory deprivation result in physiological changes that affect perception. These changes may have positive spiritual effects but they may negatively affect the individual's practical judgment. Certain neurological brain patterns commonly occur among those converted to cults, and these changes are attributed in part to the physical stress due to changes in sleep patterns and diet.[5]

The diet of the "family" often depended on scavenging, and although the girls prepared nutritious meals when they had the ingredients, they didn't always have them. When the police came in and scoured the Spahn Ranch, a Western movie set where the group was staying, in search of stolen cars (prior to naming Manson and his associates as suspects in the murders), they found infants who appeared to be suffering from malnutrition. I believe many of the "family" were suffering from hypoglycemia. I base this on some of the women's accounts of how they ate an abundance of candy bars, apparently to compensate for low blood sugar. Another clue to their ill health came from Charles "Tex" Watson, who recalled that many members of Manson's group suffered from various skin diseases while living together.[6] Poor diet, erratic sleep patterns, giving sex on demand, coping with sexually transmitted diseases, physical stresses, drugs, and isolation from the world coupled with nonstop Manson influence would certainly have weakened their judgment.[7]

In the late 1960s, for many people, no institution or tradition was sacred. The call for social change was profound; dozens of single-interest movements formed, coalitions came and went that hoped to join those of different color and class. In this era, women throughout the United States were organizing to bring about independence from male domination. The young women involved with Manson, however, were absorbing very different values through the misogynist lenses of his "truths," as detailed later in this book. Alternating between a rat-a-tat-tat, imperious delivery of clichéd speech and a tender demeanor, Manson was heard by his disciples as a genius with a master plan. It didn't matter how benign or banal his remarks might be; those who stayed heard them as prophecies, even when they couldn't understand everything he said and had to take his words on faith. Quoting from the Bible and from Beatles songs—which he played to them over and over—Manson relied on metaphor to instruct his charges. If he had been more crudely literal, explicit, honest about his intentions—saying, for example, "I'm going to send you fool kids out to carve up some rich white folks"—he might have found himself short of troops. Instead he quoted the book of Revelation. He presented himself as exalted, and his followers believed he was divine. It was this continuing faith on the part of Leslie and Susan and Pat that concerned Virginia Carlson in 1972.

The Warden's Plan

When Carlson first asked me if I would set up tutorials for the women, she said she wanted the program to help them benefit from some of the insights of women's liberation movements. She saw the girls as victims of their cultivated femininity, sweetly submissive to and being used by Manson, the self-appointed avenging knight in hippie armor. Carlson was disgusted by his prostituting his girls to the bikers, the pretty boys, and the so-called businessmen he attracted. He had expected the girls to be domestic and sexual goddesses, and to do the chores. Yet, in his view, women were so contaminated that, though they cared for the children, they were not allowed to speak anything other than gibberish to them—in case they gave the children bad ideas. Carlson's contempt for Manson was undisguised.

She asked me to get acquainted with the three young women and find out whether they'd be interested in studying something, and if so, what. If any of them showed any interest, I'd go in twice a week to work with them, which is what happened. Later, when things went well, we expanded the work to include Jeanne Gallick, my teaching partner in the main prison, and began recruiting others from universities and grassroots communities throughout California. Carlson wanted to engage the women's attention with books, ideas, creative activities, and opportunities to meet young scholars, artists, and community activists with whom the women might identify in some life-affirming way.

The warden wanted to raise the women's consciousness to a point where they would be able to think clearly for themselves, and recognize how deeply their subordination and rote obedience to Manson had degraded their humanity. She was confident that, if they could see this, they would reject his psychological power over them, build new self-identities, and thus reclaim their lives, though still residing within the confines of prison.

Reeducation

What Virginia Carlson was requesting was a program of reeducation. In considering the variety of stories of women who have been sent to prison, Anne Near observed that "many of the crimes would have been avoided had the women been in touch with ideas of feminism, through the women's movement or women's neighborhood groups, consciousness-raising, and support groups. A large part of the problem derived from an immense loneliness they felt in trying to depend wholly on men."

Few women who are in prison have grown up with parents whose marriages were intact. Most prisoners' own marriages are not intact, but many still hope to find a strong man to lean on when they get out. Few have (legal) marketable skills with which to support themselves. Anne identified this dependency among the majority of imprisoned women (and many women in society at large). They are oversocialized to be dependent—on men, on drugs, on social service agencies. They are, in this sense, obedient to their gender assignment within a class-stratified political economy.

By the early 1970s, feminist analyses had begun to enter popular culture. I heard both male and female guards remark that if the women in the prison would think for themselves, they wouldn't get involved with destructive men. Virginia Carlson took this further when she gave explicit instructions that the women in the Special Security Unit be introduced to the ideas of women's liberation as a way of gaining self-sufficiency. In this view she was in sync with the ideas of radical feminists. Anne Near agrees, saying, "It would be hard for me to see how someone inspired by a sense of women's bonding could have found herself where Leslie was."

Together with their families, friends, and other outsiders who worked with the women and came to know them, we who had been working in the main prison were involved in reeducation. We did not discourage free thought, as was practiced in the Chinese Cultural Revolution,[8] but rather we encouraged it.

At the same time that I was getting acquainted with the women in the Special Security Unit, Jeanne Gallick and I, and soon other coordinators, were organizing the Santa Cruz Women's Prison Project with a large statewide network of volunteers. In the main prison we began offering regular courses, workshops, and performances sponsored by the University of California, with about a hundred prisoner-students voluntarily attending on alternate weekends in the main prison's school building, and hundreds coming to the nightfall concerts and dances in the gymnasium. Over four years, many of these volunteer teachers and performers also paid visits to the Special Security Unit, presenting the three (sometimes five) women there with a steady barrage of new (and often conflicting) information, images, and ideas.[9] Along with these numerous positive influences in their lives, the women had time and memory. The university program's teachers offered the women pedagogical tools to question everything, to become independent thinkers with choices as to how to use their minds. The kind of education we offered to the California prisoners both in SSU and in the main prison was imbued with a range of liberating values taken for granted in the "free world." Unlike other aspects of their lives in prison, there would have been no dire consequences to the students if they rejected all or any part of our offerings. That never occurred, however.

Working in SSU

We, the university and community volunteers who worked with Pat, Susan, and Leslie, were not generally judgmental. We were repelled by what we thought we knew about the crimes, but we didn't presume to know or judge the criminals. We were reluctant to leap to conclusions about why people do the things they do—knowing there are always reasons, justifiable or not. The point wasn't to excuse people their grievous crimes any more than it was to add to their punishment. Nor were we there to dissect or analyze these famous criminals. We were there to teach, to facilitate the women's learning, to help them embark on a life of the mind as a way to live in prison.

Because they each had such an open personality, and because the environment where we met was so intimate, we all got acquainted very rapidly. Some of the outsiders—men and women—nurtured the women as well as taught them. This strengthened the positive qualities of the interactions, and in many cases friendships formed.

I always looked forward to my visits at SSU. It was sublimely peaceful and cheerful there, in contrast to the noise, harshness, suspicions, tensions, and crowdedness of the main prison. Both staff and prisoners at SSU did their best to keep things positive and constructive. There was an atmosphere of trust and an absence of fear. No one raised a voice or spoke with sarcasm. This small building, the most highly secured and guarded cellblock in the entire prison compound, was the only place at CIW where I could just relax.

Through their indoctrination by Manson, the girls had let go of their attachment to the material world. When they began their studies, just after being condemned to life instead of to death, they began to take a serious interest in the society that they had rejected. It may have banished them, but it had also restored their right to life.

The Beginning of the End of the Manson "Family"

When I started teaching in SSU I was filled with feminist intention. The women cracked women's lib jokes and teased me mercilessly about being a women's libber. Robin Morgan's *Sisterhood Is Powerful*, a compilation of writings from the women's liberation movement, was a breakthrough feminist book very popular around the time we met. It had become a big hit with women in the main prison. When I brought a copy to SSU, they each found it "interesting," but they were noncommittal about it. Only much later, when they told me they had passed it along to a young prison psychologist because they thought she might benefit from it, did I realize that they had paid it some mind. At that time, however, they didn't recognize feminism as having any direct relevance to their own lives.

When sentenced to death after the original trial, all three of the women were judged to be sufficiently sane in legal terms to recognize the state's right to put them to death—which they had all anticipated with outward equanimity. They spoke blissfully of life and death flowing together, like one big river. Otherwise, despite an air of youthfulness and innocence belying their years (they were in their early twenties in 1972) or circumstance, they seemed perfectly in command of their mental faculties.

At the same time, they seemed to be operating on more than one wavelength in the beginning, as if always tuned in to Manson. His name came up frequently, and they would refer everything we talked about back to him in some way. When speaking of life with Manson, they spoke as if of one voice. And just as they were not afraid to die, neither were they afraid to live and to take chances.

In our first meeting we talked about what they could read, to prepare for a focused academic program. They asked for books about pioneer women and Native American women, with whom they had identified when they lived with Manson as "earth mothers." In this respect they were not unlike tens of thousands of other young women in rural communes throughout the USA. They were seeking ways to collectively live off the land and share what little they had, away from the crass materialism of conventional society.

For almost four years, numerous instructors had frequent contact with these women in SSU, and sporadic contact with them after their transfers to the main prison. In some cases, friendships were sustained over time.

I met members of Leslie's family, a few of the women's old (pre-Manson) friends, and four other women who had been involved with the "family." Most of the women had rejected Manson by the mid-1970s, when they were in their early twenties, and by casting him off they lost their connection to one another as well. By 1974, Leslie virtually never mentioned Manson. She later attributed her shift back to herself partly to her work with the prison psychiatrist. By day she was busy with her school assignments, artistic projects, the mail, tending the garden, meditation, her contacts with family and other visitors. By night she suffered her nightmares in private.

When our program was accredited by the University of California at Santa Cruz, the three SSU women signed up for official college credit. In time, Catherine Cusic, Debra Miller, and Nancy Stoller, new coordinators, brought in men and women of diverse cultural backgrounds, ages, academic disciplines, artistic genres, and communities. They were presenting new perspectives on politics, culture, history, the arts, philosophy, economics, human relations, and gender issues.

Some engaged the women in debates that shed critical light on some of the errors in Manson's thinking. For example, Manson believed that killing white people and blaming the deaths on black people would cause an uprising in which blacks would gain dominion over whites. Their teacher pointed out the likely futility of a race war in the USA, given the numerical disadvantage of blacks against whites, and given the military force at the white government's disposal. More complicated was reckoning with the racism inherent in the idea of white people starting a race war on behalf of African Americans, the flaws in strategies based on the means justifying the end, and the sexism inherent to Manson's methods. Politically minded tutors placed Manson's thinking in context, bringing it from the realm of the remote revolution to the immediate challenges facing people in their day-to-day lives. Some volunteers didn't attempt to change the women's thinking; they just listened closely in an effort to understand their devotion to him.

The women's contact with their instructors, who didn't always agree with each other but who all sounded logical, forced the women to start thinking for themselves. One by one, they began articulating points of view that diverged from one another. This took courage because it also meant breaking away from their blind faith in Manson, who still kept tabs on them through the prison-to-prison grapevine.

Leslie was branded by him as a traitor when moral values with which she'd been raised began to resurface into her adult consciousness, speech, and habits. By the end of the decade most of Manson's "girls" had betrayed him.

Conversing with Anne Near

As I explained in the Introduction, much of my thinking about the Manson case was formed in a series of taped conversations with my friend Anne Near during 1980 and 1981. Although I was initially reluctant to quote myself in this book, the excerpts from those discussions, in which I was putting some of the pieces together and articulating my impressions, serve to document our mutual process of coming to some understanding. In that vein, I tried to describe Leslie, as follows:

> KF: *When I first met the women I don't think any of them knew, consciously, that what they'd done was something terrible. Leslie came through it with a startling innocence that only a person who meets her can quite grasp. It's an ineffable, not easily described innocence. You see it on her face. It's not just that she looks people right in the eye with a just-awakened expression.*

It's as if she had passed through a horror show without participating in it. It was so terrible and yet had nothing to do with her even though she was in the middle of it. The core of this person neither participated in nor was touched by this thing—that happened, that was done—by her friends, in her presence, with her participation. In the first few years after the crimes, Leslie and the others lacked signs of suffering from a seriously injured conscience. They were relaxed, soft-voiced, considerate. They laughed a lot, with healthy, easy humor.

ANNE NEAR: *But surely they were aware of how it had affected other people, and saw the attention it had brought them . . . ?*

KF: *Yes, they could see they were actors in a drama that involved all of Los Angeles County, for starters, and much of the world took notice. When they went to court, they were scrutinized in fine detail. But it was Charlie's drama. The women were incidental players, decorative and in service to Charlie.*

Among the troubling depictions by the press of the women involved with Manson was the idea that they were somehow witches. In Europe and Great Britain during the Age of Reason, women were often convicted as witches on the evidence of what were seen as witches' marks. These were identified first by midwives and then, when professional men usurped their authority, by the physicians, the so-called experts, who identified birthmarks, scars, or changes in pigmentation or indentation to be proof of a woman having copulated with the devil.[10] The women themselves didn't always dispute the "scientific" veracity of the judgment: they commonly did, however, claim not to know that they had had sex with Satan. They believed they must have been violated by the Devil— the "proof" was stated in court—but they had no physical memory of the event. Any knowledge they possessed was relegated to unconscious states, the very idea of which was itself suggestive of witchcraft. In some jurisdictions, if a woman could successfully plead that she committed her actions while in a trance, she could not be held culpable even though she would be feared. Since she didn't know what she was doing, she couldn't be held responsible and found guilty. It was understood that when out of the trance she was utterly innocent.

Having been exploited by Manson, who used the women in whatever ways suited his fancy, upon separation from him, the women were targeted for exploitation by the press and television. In the media blowout following the crimes, it became a cliché to connect the "Manson girls" with witchery, given Manson's vague identification with Satan (as well as Christ) and given their own appearance and behaviors during the trial. The differences were that the accused witches of yore had not actually had sex with the Devil, they only assumed or imagined that they must have done so. "Manson's women" had actually become "Satan's" servants, through believing him to be sacred, akin to Christ. Historically, accused witches had their heads shaven forcibly, as Joan of Arc did, to ensure they were not hiding amulets, anesthetizing herbs, or other tools of witchcraft. The "Manson girls" shaved their own heads on instruction from Manson. Leslie, exasperated with the analogy, said with twenty-nine years of hindsight, "I didn't sleep with the Devil. I slept with an ex-con who had an extensive record of pimping and abusing women. But I didn't know that."[11] Like most cult gurus, he relied on the appeal of the supernatural to buttress his authority with his followers. The rational world could not understand why anyone would believe that Charles Manson was the reincarnated Jesus Christ, but that same rational world was easily persuaded that he was the Devil incarnate.

Anne Near questioned whether Manson actually identified himself as satanic, in light of the media's attention to this theme:

> *KF: Manson's own view, as I understand it, expands on the basic idea that we all contain the potential for all good and all evil, and that he himself maximizes the human possibilities, whatever they are. He both transcends and incorporates this good and evil in his being, not as dichotomy but as integrated whole of universal experience.*
>
> *ANNE: Was this a delusion of grandeur or a bona fide vision?*
>
> *KF: Aren't people who suffer delusions of grandeur usually alone in their delusions? But what Manson would say about himself was consistent with his followers' perceptions of him. He readily persuaded people close to him. They could entertain his self-image. They encouraged his egomania.*

In demonizing the accused murderers, the media overlooked the apparent ordinariness of these young people. As Anne Near summarized it, "The Manson crimes were remarkable; the people involved in them were not."

Leslie's remarkable post-crime strengths have come in part from decades of avoiding any destructive association, staying on course. She has coped remarkably well within the walls of her interminable punishment. She knows she is guilty of something terrible made more terrible by the stories about it, including those told by herself when she was thirty years younger. Today she lives with her sorrow over the crimes and their effects, and like all the other imprisoned women, she suffers from the daily deprivations and indignities of prison. But she also shows composure and humility in a negative environment, suggesting that she might well have lived an extraordinary life on the outside.

Two

LIFE BEFORE THE CRIME

LESLIE'S FAMILY'S EARLY LIFE reads like a post–World War II working-class success story. She was born on August 23, 1949, in a modern southern California hospital. It was the era when the greater Los Angeles area was rapidly changing from a lightly populated agricultural paradise to a string of technology- and tourist-dependent boomtowns. Her handsome father, Paul, was an automobile auctioneer; her mother, Jane, was strongly beautiful; they both had great love for Leslie and her older brother. Later the Van Houtens adopted a younger boy and girl who had been orphaned in Korea. Honest, hardworking, churchgoing people, the Van Houtens were devoted to their four children. By 1960 they were a clean-cut, loving family living in a comfortable middle-class house with a pool, in a southern California suburb. But trouble was brewing; major change was in the offing.

Leslie's parents divorced in 1963, when she was thirteen. Jane Van Houten, now a single mom with four kids, went back to school to renew her teaching credentials. Paul, who moved to a city nearby when he left the family home, continued to give his children attention and financial support.

Jane went on to develop a successful career in special education, but according to Leslie, her mother "loved being an at-home mom and would have loved to stay one."[1] It seemed clear that, however well Leslie's mother succeeded in sustaining a good life for herself, her first priorities were always the welfare of her four children.

Entering her third year of high school, Leslie appeared to be without problems. She had a boyfriend, and for the second time she was elected homecoming princess. But she was coming into womanhood at a time of cultural upheaval, when girls were paying heavily for "free love," and she, like other teenagers, discovered marijuana and hallucinogens. At age sixteen she took LSD for the first time, unbeknownst to her parents, and continued to use it with her boyfriend on weekends. Meanwhile, she became pregnant and secured an abortion, a trauma to herself and to her family.

As she gravitated toward the counterculture, Leslie reduced her participation in most school activities and became more esoteric in her interests. She read Timothy Leary, a proponent of the consciousness-raising benefits of LSD, and P. D. Ouspensky, an evolutionary cosmologist. She began studying with a spiritually oriented group called the Self-Realization Fellowship. Soon her grades were declining, and her teachers were talking to her about the importance of fulfilling her academic potential. Though she no longer identified with her classmates, she remained on good terms with them, continuing to be reliable, trustworthy, and likable.

After graduation in 1967, Leslie lived with her father and attended a business college where she trained to be a legal secretary. She was not planning a career. Rather, she was preparing to be useful to a yogic spiritual community, where she intended to reside upon completion of her studies. The confounding life questions that had been looming over the culture at large were taking shape in her personal life. By the time she finished her course, she, like many, was restless. Instead of joining the yogic community she went on the road.

In the 1960s the USA was swooning with the weight of challenges to every traditional value, every hypocritical practice, every war and injustice. White middle-class kids like Leslie were bursting out of cultural constraints all over North America. They were listening to folk music's strummed messages, the groove of rhythm and blues, and the beat of rock 'n' roll. They were elevating their spirits, not with alcohol, but with marijuana and other recreational drugs. Young people were constructing a vibrant counterculture to their liking. Rebellions were generated by protests against civil rights violations and the Vietnam war, or were reflective of new contact with Eastern religions.

With tens of thousands of apolitical others, Leslie—a California girl in search of meaning—wandered in search of someone or something to show her the way. There were many spiritual movements with charismatic leaders to choose from. Their activities were not always solely of a spiritual nature, however. In particular, the very popular Moonies (named after the founder of their Unification Church, Sun Myung Moon) were investing heavily in ethically dubious enterprises, such as munitions. In the mid-1970s, the word *cult* began to be used by the public when speaking of these groups. Their methods of keeping members increasingly came under attack. Some cults were successful in acquiring large membership, wealth, and legal standing as alternative religions in the States—the highly disparate International Society for Krishna Consciousness, the Divine Light Mission, and the Church of Scientology.

The late 1970s saw the beginning of the deprogramming industry, whose services could have benefited Leslie and her codefendants a decade earlier. Deprogrammers themselves were arrested on charges of kidnapping and conspiracy. Young people prosecuted parents who interfered with their right to religious freedom.[2] Deprogrammers, notably Ted Patrick, who coined the term, argued that cult techniques were "robbing people of their natural capacity to think and choose."[3]

In late summer 1968, Leslie was staying with friends in San Francisco's Haight-Ashbury district, the counterculture's Mecca. One day her roommate brought home a group of young people with whom Leslie felt instant kinship. The group included Gypsy, a raven-haired, free-spirited, vivacious young woman. Gypsy told Leslie that she and her friends lived in the here and now. She invited Leslie to drop out totally and join their pilgrimage with a guru of love and peace, a man named Charles Manson. Leslie went off with them that day. In this easy-come, easy-go psychedelic counterculture, it was not unusual to pick up and move on with strangers.

In September, her new friends, Bobby Beausoleil, Gypsy, and another girl named Gail, took her for a one-night visit to Spahn Ranch, the movie set the transient group had made its home. Three weeks later Leslie returned to stay, to be with this man who gently admonished her to give up her personal identity, to let her ego die, to become, as she put it, "like a finger on a hand."[4] Manson would watch her and mirror her moods with his own expressions, which reassured her that he saw her and understood her feelings. He would hold up his open palms, facing her, and she would do the same. She would then try to mirror his changing hand movements and facial expressions, to anticipate and be in sync with his moves and impulses. On one occasion he told the whole group, gathered for the evening, to "Baa-aa like sheep," and, as Leslie said in her interview with Diane Sawyer aired in 1994, "every single one of us did it, exactly at the moment that he said it."[5]

Those who were with Manson at that time have attested to how gentle and mystical he was then, inspiring them with tender, insightful utterances and gestures. He found them wherever he wandered, these young people ready to follow him. For a short time before Leslie knew him, he called himself "the Gardener," because "I tend to all the flower children."[6] One of his trust games was to have one of the girls stand against a tree, and he would then throw knives in her direction, never hurting her. As he gained power over more young people—and more women in particular—he became more obsessed with death and violence, asking if they were willing to die for him. By then they trusted him so thoroughly they accepted his negative turns as necessary to their humility and enlightenment. Once enlightened, they could start saving the earth, or black people, or whoever needed help according to Manson.

He may not have set out to gather a family of runaways; he may not have consciously used deliberate mind-control techniques. But accounts of his 1967 and 1968 initial meetings with a number of the women have a similar tone. His first follower was Mary Brunner, a twenty-three-year-old librarian at the University of California at Berkeley. He was playing his guitar on the street outside the university gates, and she was walking her dog. He started talking with her and he affected her deeply. Since he didn't have a home, she offered him her couch. This openness was not unusual for young people then. Manson confirmed for her how alienated she felt from the rigid inhibitions of the life she lived, and he offered a much more honest and loving way of being in the world. Before long Mary had left her job, cashed in money from her retirement benefits, and gone off with him.[7]

Restless, Manson migrated between northern and southern California. One day in Los Angeles, he was walking along the Venice Beach boardwalk and came upon Lynette Fromme, age eighteen, sitting on a bench looking dejected. Lynette was in college and living with her parents, to their mutual distaste. In particular, she did not get along with her father; she wanted to leave, but couldn't afford to. Manson approached her with, "What's the problem?" From her biographer's account, she was instantly entranced by him. She thought he looked like an elf, or a "hobo with a touch of class." He explained to her that he was "the Gardener." She told him her problems and he responded like a comforting, "warm father figure." He talked in riddles that made sense to her: "The way out of a room is not through the door. Just don't want out, and you're free"; "Am I right or left of anything . . . or is it all relative?" Manson was heading back up north to the San Francisco Bay Area, and he said she was welcome to go along with him. When he started to leave, Lynette grabbed her schoolbooks, ran to catch up with him ("I didn't know why—I didn't care"), and was thereafter devoted to him.[8]

Patricia Krenwinkel, whose similar story is told in a chapter ahead, was the third girl to join up with him at that time (in 1967–68); Susan Atkins was the fourth.

Susan met Manson in the Haight-Ashbury district of San Francisco, where they were both "crashing" in other people's "pads." She entered the communal house where he was staying, and she writes, "My eyes landed instantly on a little man sitting on the wide couch in front of the bay windows. . . . Without moving his head, he opened his eyes and stared directly into my face. I stared back." He was playing his guitar, surrounded by young women. Susan thought he looked like an angel. He read her mind when she thought to herself that she'd like to play his guitar, and he handed it to her. "It was as though our minds were speaking." She put on a record, the Doors, and began to dance. Soon he was dancing with her. "Suddenly, something happened that has no explanation. I experienced a moment unlike any other. This stranger and I, dancing, passed through one another. It was as though my body moved closer and closer to him and actually passed through him. . . . We mirrored each other perfectly. . . . 'You are beautiful,' he said. 'You are perfect.' " As Jesus had done with his chosen disciples, he washed her feet. He told her to love herself. She believed he was a saint disguised as an ordinary man.[9]

Two days later he said, "Come on, we're going to L.A.," and she went with him and Mary and Lynette and Pat, in an old school bus he'd acquired. She said of him, "Charlie had instantly seemed more of a father to me than my own father."[10] Soon, though, not unlike a father, he was criticizing her for being disobedient. "He played me like a yo-yo, first hugging and praising me, then demeaning me in some way."[11] But she and all of them stayed, spellbound.

Mary and Lynette were alone when they first encountered Manson, and Susan was among strangers. Pat and Leslie—and all seven of the young women I met who were devoted to him—have spoken in various ways of how he presented himself to them as a wise man with uncanny, intimate insight, a powerful protector. All seven of those I met reported that he spoke their thoughts. Each of them, from the first moment, trusted him utterly. A number of them said that with him they felt truly beautiful, perfect, for the first time in their lives. Each instantly made a radical change in her life to be with him.

He was about fifteen years their senior—a semiliterate, mystical, bright, self-styled social critic, a musician, songwriter, and clown—irresistible to them and to many other young people. All raised as Christians, when they learned that he was an ex-prisoner (without knowing the details of his crimes), they were more than ever convinced that he was a savior, persecuted by the state just as Christ had been persecuted by the Roman state.

According to his own telling (in 1978), Charles "Tex" Watson struck the final death blows of all seven of the murder victims, contrary to the press's and D. A. Vincent Bugliosi's renditions, and contrary to the women's own testimony in their trial. As enthralled with Manson on their first meeting as the women had been, Watson met him at the home of Dennis Wilson, a member of the popular golden-imaged rock band, the Beach Boys. Dennis had given shelter to a number of the girls in Manson's rapidly expanding "family." Watson said of their first meeting in late spring 1968, "There he was—surrounded by five or six girls—on the floor . . . with a guitar in his hands. He looked up, and the first thing I felt was a sort of gentleness, an embracing kind of acceptance and love."[12] A year later, with his followers gathered around a campfire, Manson would be holding a knife, turning it slowly to catch the light of the fire and asking each person, in turn, if he or she was ready to die for him. Watson later described his response, while Manson turned the knife slowly, menacingly, "I didn't even have to think about it: 'Sure, Charlie, you can kill me.' I meant it. Like some mystic, so filled with the love of God that nothing is too great to ask, I was filled with Charlie. He *was* God to me."[13]

While growing up in a rural Texas community, Watson had been very involved in the Methodist church his parents attended. "[I] even led devotions for the youth group and gave talks for Sunday-night evangelistic services."[14] He was also an all-around athlete, a record-breaking track star, an honor student, and he raised a prizewinning calf. In a phone call from California to his mother in Texas, after having become an instant Manson convert, Watson told her:

> "You've always wanted me to be religious. . . . Well, I've met that Jesus you preach about all the time. I've met him and he's here right now with me in the desert." Charlie was Jesus. He was my messiah, my savior, my soul. . . . He could ask anything, even my life, and it was his. . . . My ego was dead; anything that asserted I, me, or mine was dead. . . . "Sure, Charlie, you can kill me." As I said it, I knew that Charles Denton Watson—all-American boy, letterman, Scout, Future Farmer of America, twice voted "Campus Kid" at Farmersville High School—that Charles Watson was totally dead.[15]

Manson and his growing entourage claimed a special spot on the barren desert near Death Valley as their own wilderness retreat. It was here that Leslie (renamed LuLu or Lu) first met Pat (then known as Katie). Manson called Pat "my complete reflection," and Pat became Leslie's close friend and mentor. After Leslie's arrest, still very much under Manson's control, she said, "Katie was my best friend. She was strong enough [to kill]. So I would too. I wanted to be just like her."[16]

When they were at Spahn Ranch in the carefree pre-crime days, they would all dress up in costumes and play out fantasy theatricals. These were the halcyon days of the Beatles' *Magical Mystery Tour* and Ken Kesey's hippie clan, the Merry Pranksters. The women were in the majority at the ranch, and when successful at scavenging they prepared beautiful meals, not only for Manson's sake but also out of love for each other. After dinner they would gather, and sing his rock and folk songs with social messages. The women cared for the babies and shared in all the chores. They were sensuous, imaginative, childlike creatures who fantasized imps, gnomes, gremlins, fairies, and other mythical creatures, and incorporated those fantasies into their day-to-day interactions. They lived with the faith that life could be joyful if people loved each other. They worked at being free in their sexuality. They dropped LSD once or twice a week to more fully experience their senses, to see reality in a new light, and to kill their egos. Propounding on the necessity of killing egos was Manson's first step in conditioning his acolytes to accept physical death as no big deal, since the body is just a transient vehicle for the spirit—a common view among established world religions as well as passing cults.

During one of his sojourns in the Haight-Ashbury district of San Francisco, Manson (and those who started joining up with him) got acquainted with some of the staff at the Free Clinic there. A number of his followers needed treatment for venereal diseases, a result of frequent unprotected sex with whoever drifted in and wanted it. When they were living at Spahn Ranch the clinic administrator, Al Rose, made a visit to them with David Smith, physician and clinic director. They later published an article in a 1970 issue of the *Journal of Psychedelic Drugs,* in which they described the "family." They identified Manson as a "spiritual leader" and a "father figure." They observed that he expressed a philosophy of nonviolence. Significantly, they saw him as a "persuasive individual who served as absolute ruler of this group-marriage commune." They also took note that he referred to himself as "God and the Devil."[17]

Charles "Tex" Watson later described Manson as a chameleon. His lengthy description, in his now out-of-print book, is given here because it echoes everything I heard from the women themselves.

> *He was, as some of the girls put it, always changing . . . and with each change he could be born anew—Hollywood slicker, jail tough, rock star, guru, child, tramp, angel, devil, son of God. He was a magician; he charmed—in the original sense of the word—and he had an uncanny ability to meet a person and immediately psyche him out, understand his deepest fears and hang-ups,*

his vulnerabilities. It was as though he could see through you with the all-encompassing eye of God.

Like a cat with one ear cocked even in sleep, Charlie was always aware, tensed even in stillness, always picking up the smallest details in any situation. He told us it came from being in prison so long—you never knew where a knife might be coming from. His awareness seemed not only intensive—able to look inside you and know all that you were—but comprehensive: holding all the elements of a situation in his consciousness at once.

His eyes were hypnotic; they could wash you in love and gentleness or they could terrorize you, like the face of hell itself. He knew the tricks he could play with his face and he used the force of his undivided attention consciously. . . .

As for the magical powers with animals which some of the Family later claimed for him, I only know that I once saw him walk through a gully full of rattlesnakes, gliding among them and touching them gently on the tails. None of them struck. I think this had less to do with magic than with the fact that animals of all kinds can pick up on the fear in a person. Charlie had no fear left in him and somehow that was calming to other creatures. . . .

And it was a curious deity we were serving. While it meant nothing [to him] for a human being to die, Charlie would fly into a rage if we killed an insect. While there was supposedly no right or wrong, only what was, Charlie was a fanatical vegetarian because, he said, killing an animal or eating a dead animal was a crime. While love was supposed to be the meaning of everything, the source of our oneness together, Charlie spent a lot of his time talking about fear.

Fear. To Charlie it was the source of awareness, of connection, of clarity. Wild animals live in a constant state of fear, he told us, and they don't miss anything in their environment; they achieve total awareness of what is around them and in the process are totally lacking in self-consciousness. That was how we should be.

Yet we should overcome our fear as well, push ourselves to its limits until nothing frightened us anymore.[18]

As far as the women knew, Manson did not identify with or take part in any satanic secret rites and rituals, but he had had at least fleeting contact with self-styled Satanists in prison. However secondhand his influences, they surely could have subliminally supported his impulses to exercise mind control, and to act violently without conscience when he saw evidence that the Armageddon he called Helter Skelter was coming down. As he interpreted this expression from the Beatles, Helter Skelter was the impending chaos of a society that was unraveling, and he wanted to speed the process. Some of his girls on the street during the 1970–71 trial adopted witchy robes and symbols associated with cults, but none of them had been in any way exposed to or indoctrinated in anything satanic or occult. As a sixties commune, the "family" was much less structured, routinized, and ritualized than most cults,[19] but Manson was typical of cult leaders in that he was totalitarian, at first in a soft voice, later aggressively. What Manson seemed to be saying, with a mishmash of creeds, was that all is all, everything is everything, everything and everyone are connected, and all humans contain within themselves both God and the Devil.

It was not the dark, death-driven Manson to whom Leslie or the other women were attracted. When she entered his circle in September 1968, the "family" was about peace, love, and harmony, and Manson exemplified those virtues. Less than a year later she and the others were ready to help him initiate a race war. In the year she was with him, the group grew into a troop of loyal disciples who migrated between camps—the Spahn Ranch, their special places out on the Mojave Desert near Death Valley (for which trips they used stolen cars and dune buggies), and some rented or borrowed suburban houses. They listened incessantly to the Beatles' White Album, which Manson was convinced prophesied his promised Helter Skelter. Manson correlated songs like "Helter Skelter" and "Piggies" with the apocalyptic messages in the ninth chapter of the book of Revelation, of which the first verse reads: "And the fifth angel sounded, and I saw a star fall from heaven unto the earth: and to him was given the key of the bottomless pit." In Manson's interpretation, the Beatles represented the first four angels and Manson himself was the fifth. He also claimed that a bottomless pit had been prepared for them in the desert. He knew just where it was, and that's where they would go after they started Helter Skelter; there they would be safe while cities burned. Verse eleven reads: "And they had a king over them, which is the angel of the bottomless pit, whose name in the Hebrew tongue is Abaddon, but in the Greek tongue hath his name Apollyon." Appropriately, "Abaddon/Apollyon" is translated as "Destroyer." Apparently Manson didn't identify the sixth angel, referred to in verse thirteen: "And the sixth angel sounded, and I heard a voice from the four horns of the golden altar which is before God." He presented his eclectic views as if they were supported by biblical authority.

With the combined effects of LSD, Manson's theatrical preachings, and their belief that he personified Jesus Christ, Savior and Lord, his followers heard what he heard. When he reenacted the crucifixion, they believed they saw wounds on his hands. Leslie (and perhaps others) imagined her own body being crucified. They accepted Manson's delusions of grandeur for himself and for themselves. They believed.

When Charles Manson said that a race war was the greedy, arrogant white man's karma, they believed it, and believed in their role in it. He persuaded them that Helter Skelter was necessary, and all for the good, with "good" defined by Manson. They didn't know any details of what Helter Skelter would entail until the time came. He was never explicit.

He was typical of cult leaders, though he didn't proclaim himself as one. Cult researchers point out that "the cult process is one we call *covert induction*—driven almost entirely by suggestions, code words and other indirect commands." As Leslie explained it, "He'd say 'The question is in the answer,' and 'No sense makes sense'—things that would make your mind stop functioning."[20] Once Manson had confounded his followers, he could place in their minds whatever belief—however irrational—he wanted them to share with him. The more pervasive and consistent his control over them, the more entrenched the new beliefs became.

When the "family" returned from the city to Spahn Ranch early in 1969, they began to practice survival techniques under Manson's tutelage. They learned to walk on their heels so they wouldn't leave footprints, to cover their tracks, and to go without water. Each had an individual knife for self-protection. As exercises in both experiencing and going beyond fear, Manson had the men drive dune buggies at dangerous speeds on hazardous roads. They traversed the desert in search of the hole where they would find safety during the conflict. He sent both men and women on what he called creepy-crawls, where they would break into homes in the night, while the occupants were asleep, and rearrange household belongings, usually without taking anything. They all believed

Helter Skelter was coming, that it was already happening. Only Manson and a few of his male followers, who did not participate in the murders but who listened to him in private, had heard his meandering plans, with their ever changing details, for the start of the final race war. Yet, when the time came, they all knew they were on a mission for the "Son of Man, Man's Son." The details didn't matter. There was room for only one voice of authority, a decidedly male voice: Manson's voice.

Man's Son was one of the most consistent names Manson gave himself in 1969. He would say, then deny, that he was God, Christ, the Devil, Lucifer, or the son of any of them, for everyone is everything. But always he was the Son of Man. On the street, "the Man" is the tyrant, the landlord, the authority, the boss, the cop, the one with rules, regulations, and punishments. The Man is to the street person what he was to Bambi. The Man is the one who points his gun at you, who has the power to do it, who poses danger to you and to your mother. That's what prison is about. The Man. And indeed, Charlie was the child of that man.

Three

THE CRIME AND FIRST TRIAL

THE CRIME FOR WHICH Leslie and her codefendants were convicted has been already subject to media overkill. Anyone who is old enough to have paid attention to the news in 1969 through 1971, or who has seen the commercialized, sensationalistic accounts that have been recycled in print and on TV periodically ever since, is already aware of the brutality that was inflicted. Manson himself manipulated the media, enjoying the publicity. He used the women to contrive images that have been indelibly inscribed in the collective memory of North American culture. The parole board panels that have had the power to keep Leslie and the other women in prison indefinitely have shown a clear unwillingness, or political inability, to move beyond the crimes and their publicity in evaluating the women's suitability for release. Rather than considering who they are today, who they have been for decades, or questions of proportional justice, the board continues in 2001 to punish them for what they did in 1969.

As Leslie's friend, I would rather not participate in her punishment by subjecting her to the pain of rehashing the details. None of us would want to be perpetually, publicly identified with culpable behaviors of which we're most ashamed, however minor or major the consequences and however long ago. On the one hand, then, to recount the crime once again seems redundant and exploitive. On the other hand, without acknowledging the crime that brought Leslie into public light, there would be no basis for a book that seeks in part to publicly reveal her humanity. Further, there is a need to contextualize the events that Manson orchestrated, to clarify what happened at the LaBianca residence, and to demystify the young people who were doing his bidding.

The Reports

On Saturday afternoon, August 9, 1969, the population of Los Angeles County, one of the U.S. crime capitals, learned that five adults had been murdered the night before at the Benedict Canyon rented estate of film director Roman Polanski, who was away. The victims included the young actress Sharon Tate, Polanski's wife, who was in the final stage of pregnancy. Susan Atkins's later testimony as to the ways she killed and grossly mutilated her victim(s) was false (see, for example, Watson's account of the murders), but the truth was nevertheless horrible. The word PIG was written in blood on the front door. The media didn't spare readers any of the graphic details, accurate or otherwise.

Monday morning, the news headlined a similar set of murders that had taken place early Sunday morning in another affluent L.A. neighborhood. The victims were the wealthy owner of a chain of grocery stores, Leno LaBianca, age forty-four, and his thirty-eight-year-old wife, Rosemary, a boutique owner. The killers had again stabbed their victims and left catchwords written in blood on the walls and on the refrigerator door. A fork and a knife were left protruding from Mr. LaBianca's mutilated body.

The media reports of the LaBianca murders hit like an aftershock to the massive wave of publicity that had followed the Tate murders. There was no obvious motive for the crimes. Valuable belongings had been left in place at both sites.

Fear was rampant. People wondered: if the rich—who don't take a bus or walk home from work in the dark, who have reliable cars, police protection for their neighborhoods, and expensive electronic security systems—weren't safe in their homes, who was? According to Vincent Bugliosi,[1] who investigated and prosecuted the case, gun sales skyrocketed in Los Angeles over the next year or so. Guard dogs, security alarm systems, private locked gates, security cameras, and human guards also became commonplace.

The Killings

The girls were not privy to all of Manson's activities; they saw him only when he wanted to see them, in contexts he chose. Leslie herself didn't learn until long after the fact that, in late July 1969, Manson had instigated the murder of Gary Hinman, a gentle neighbor friend who taught music. For a time, Hinman had shared his humble home with Bobby Beausoleil, and it was Beausoleil who now kept Hinman captive for two or three days, hoping to talk him out of money Manson wanted. (It is unlikely that Hinman had any money to give.) The day before Beausoleil killed Hinman, Manson came by, sliced Gary's ear, and left Hinman bound in rope and bleeding.[2] Both Susan Atkins and Mary Brunner had been sent by Manson to the house to help Bobby, but neither assisted with the actual murder. After the killing, Susan, on Manson's instruction, left the words POLITICAL PIGGY written in blood on the wall. This was the apparent beginning of Helter Skelter, Manson's mission.

Beausoleil was picked up and jailed on suspicion of the murder. It is theorized that Manson decided to stage a copycat crime while Beausoleil was in custody, to vindicate Beausoleil as a suspect. According to Bugliosi's account of events, however, this motive for the Tate murders, like that of the murder of Hinman, was not known by most members of the "family." It was certainly incidental to Manson's plan.[3] Bugliosi's view is confirmed by Charles "Tex" Watson, who was present at both the August murders.[4]

Following the Tate and LaBianca murders, but months before any arrests for those murders, Susan Atkins, Charles Manson, and Bruce Davis (another follower) were also arrested on suspicion of involvement in the earlier murder of Gary Hinman. Susan was held in the L.A. county jail, having "confessed" to stabbing him in the legs; it was later revealed that he had not been stabbed in the legs. Few of the "family" knew of this murder until much later. Months after the Tate and LaBianca murders, tips from Susan's cellmates began a chain of investigations by the Los Angeles Police Department and Sheriff's Office, but it was not until December that the California Highway Patrol picked up some of the suspects. Leslie, meanwhile, had been arrested on October 10, 1969, on charges related to Manson's stolen parts for dune buggies. She was first jailed in Inyo County, and was then transferred to the Sybil Brand jail, where she remained upon police discovery of her presence at the LaBianca murders. Tex, who had fled home to Texas, was picked up there on November 30, in Copeville, where he was held while he fought extradition.

Ultimately, it was judged that Manson conspired the murders and was guilty according to the "vicarious liability" rule. None of the young people who killed or attempted to kill for him knew in advance whether or how they would do Helter Skelter. They never gathered together in a family circle to plan who among them would go out to kill people, or when they would do it, or whom they would kill, or whether they would actually kill anyone. It was all up to Manson. After the Tate murders, Manson was unhappy because the young people he sent out the night before had done a "messy" job. On this second night he resolved to make sure the killings were done properly. He handpicked a six-member potential crew, Tex, Linda Kasabian, Pat, Leslie, Susan—and Clem. (Young Clem, who was heavily drug-damaged, helped Manson and other male followers kill Donald Shea, a Spahn Ranch horse wrangler, two weeks after the Tate-LaBianca murders. Apparently, Manson believed Shea knew too much. It's clear to me that the women didn't know about Shea's murder until much later. Clem was later tried and incarcerated.)

Late Saturday night, Manson drove them all to the Los Feliz district, planning to select the residence at random. En route, he rejected one house because, through the front picture window, he could see photos of children on the walls. He stopped in front of a church, but it appeared no one was there. Finally he settled on a house next door to a home where he had, at least once, attended a party. Leaving the others in the car, Manson and Tex broke into and entered the LaBianca home and tied up the victims. After exiting the home, Manson sent Pat and Leslie back inside with Tex, with the admonition not to cause fear and panic, and not to let the victims know they would be killed. Now it was spoken. He told Pat and Leslie to follow Tex's instructions. He then drove off with Susan, Clem, and Linda, leaving Tex, Pat, and Leslie to do the killings and then hitchhike home.

When Manson drove away, Pat and Leslie led Rosemary LaBianca from the living room, where she and her husband were tied up at the wrists and ankles, to the bedroom. There they stripped the pillows of their cases. In the prosecutor's version of the story, after Mrs. LaBianca attempted to ward them off by swinging a lamp at them, Leslie put a pillowcase over Mrs. LaBianca's head and secured it with the lamp cord. Leslie herself is confounded by her inability to remember doing this; she wonders if she really did it, or whether she has incorporated the images of the prosecutor and others into her own conflicting memories of what happened in the LaBianca house. According to Charles Watson, however, it was he who performed that action. He says in his account of the crime, "Following Charlie's instructions . . . I went into the living room, put a pillowcase over Leno LaBianca's head and tied a lamp cord around his skull. . . . Then I went back into the bedroom and did the same with Mrs. LaBianca, telling her not to make a sound."[5]

Everyone agrees that Leslie then held on to Rosemary until Mrs. LaBianca reacted to the sounds of her husband dying in the living room. She cried out, "What are you doing to my husband?" and Leslie reflexively let go, backed away, and fled from the room to the hallway, to another bedroom, and then back to the hall. Her conscience was exposed in that first instant when her instincts recoiled against the actual deed of killing.

Despite her furious attempts to stab Mrs. LaBianca while holding on to her, Pat was not efficient with the knife, and she summoned Tex. He ended Mrs. LaBianca's life hurriedly, with a bayonet. He then demanded that Leslie, now standing back and looking on in terror, also stab the woman, "even though it was obvious that Rosemary LaBianca was already dead."[6] He wanted to ensure that all three of them would have done their part as one entity, to please Charlie.

Mortally frightened by the scene, Leslie obeyed, stabbing once, then quickly again, fourteen to sixteen times, into Rosemary LaBianca's lower back and buttocks. She later described her feeling of stabbing Mrs. LaBianca in various ways: Leslie felt like "a shark with its prey," "a primitive animal," "a wildcat who had just caught a deer." To a parole board, she said she felt at the time as if she were at war with herself—fighting her desire to be a good soldier for Charlie against her horror at the killings.

The entire double murder, from beginning to end, took just a few minutes. The testimony is conflicting as to whether it was Pat or Tex who went to the living room and, with kitchen utensils (left protruding from the victim's body), further mutilated Mr. LaBianca, now dead. It is clear, though, that with his blood, Pat wrote references to Beatles songs on the living room wall and on the refrigerator door, including RISE and HEALTER SKELTER. Bugliosi and the press made a lot of this misspelling but I know that Pat is not a poor speller. I suspect that she was as fully "out of her mind" as were Leslie and Tex, and she probably hadn't seen the words *Helter Skelter* in writing; she had learned the expression not from print but from Manson's harpings.

Meanwhile, Leslie, on Tex's instruction (and on Manson's directive to her to obey Tex), thoroughly removed fingerprints from everywhere in the house.[7] This action was later interpreted by the prosecutor as evidence that she knew that what she was doing was wrong. In fact, she did know that the killings were wrong according to society's values and laws; that was never a question. Like the others, she simply believed that Manson's laws were of higher authority than those of the state.

Just under twenty years old that night, Leslie chose to obey as well as she could. She was disappointed in her failure to kill as instructed. She didn't want to fail also at the fingerprint job. It was important to her that the "family" remain free, intact, and effective as a group, to carry out Charlie's mission. She removed the fingerprints to avoid any of the "family" getting caught, not for self-preservation but for the good of the collective. This reasoning of Leslie's was backed up by psychiatric examinations done on her for her second trial in 1977. (See chapter 5.) If more knowledge of cult behavior had been available in the first trial in 1970–71, and if she had agreed to a separate trial for herself (which was in her own interest, and which she refused to do), she may not have been convicted of murder and sentenced to death.

After cleaning themselves up (Tex took a shower), having a snack, and pocketing some collector coins, the team hitchhiked home. They bought their driver breakfast at a café along the way.

Reflections

The Manson murder cases garnered intensive judicial, media, and public scrutiny because they didn't fit any formula. Everything about the murders—the plot, settings, characters, motives—in no way resembled conventional murder. And certainly none of the participants considered themselves to be "ordinary criminals." Leslie did not ever aspire to kill anyone; she wanted only to be a good soldier in the revolution planned by Manson. Reacting to descriptions of the murders as "senseless," she said later, "The killings were not for killing's sake. It was to start a revolution. Whether it made sense or not wasn't the issue. Even though in reality the deaths were for nothing, in our minds it was necessary and important."[8] In the end, it was their adulation of Charlie more than their belief in his Helter Skelter race war that motivated the women to follow him into battle. They trusted his prophecy, whatever it was.

In an academic typology of women who have killed,[9] a female "disciple killer" is one who kills (or attempts to do so) under the influence of her charismatic male leader, whose personal acceptance she seeks at the cost of forfeiting her own identity. He is her idol, obeyed without question. He decides on the crime and the weapon(s), selects the victims, and dictates who among his followers will participate. Such women would never be involved in murder on their own initiative; under their leader's influence they abdicate their will.[10]

When I first spoke with the women in CIW's Special Security Unit in 1972, it became clear to me that they were as taken as Manson himself with the age-old Western view of the dualism of good and evil. That dualism can produce a conflict within one's own soul. For Manson, as with counterculture philosophers who were influenced by Buddhism, the duality was not a conflict but rather a unity. Even in Christian mythology, Lucifer, the angel of darkness, was also the bearer of light.

In one of his poems, Manson, the so-called Son of Man, said something like, "When a mother sends her son to war, who kills? The government, or his mother? Mother, behold your son. When will woman get behind man and die for him?" It's an enraging question when you consider the women who do die for or at the hands of men, and because it assumes somebody has to die. But mothers do send their sons to war, usually with the complicity of silence, and among many Christians war is conducted in the name of the Father, Son, and Holy Spirit, just as others go to war in the names of their gods. One of the incidental ironies of Leslie's story is that her brother served time in a military brig for refusing to bear arms.

Life does not easily tolerate death. I wrote these words in my journal after a day in which Leslie's prison companions began talking about their states of mind during their crimes. From their perspective at that time, the person perpetrating the deed identified with the victim to whom the deed was being done. There was no death and no life; all were part of a river flowing on and on. Long before her rebirth as an evangelical Christian, Susan Atkins described to me the dance of life and death, when the killer and the killed became one in the sphere of universal energy. It was, she said, the quintessential unfolding of good unto evil. This was before she separated herself from Manson. It was still Manson talking through her.

As a species, we strive for life. I thought it a hideous rationalization for the "Manson girls" to identify with those they claimed to have killed. I wanted them to recognize the death in what they had done, now that they were condemned to live. They lived on what was once death row, but now they were no longer going to die. This was their problem. They were retroactively injecting their experience of death—in a cosmic sense—with life.

The girls didn't blame the victims, as do many people convicted of murder. They explained the act of killing (or attempting to kill) as a variation on spiritual communion with the fish before sinking your hook into it, or with the deer before you release the arrow, and making communion with the grain, leaf, fruit, or vegetable before eating it. It was Manson's philosophy that in killing a person they would be killing a part of themselves, because all of life is connected.

The women's after-the-fact philosophy about killing, for as long as they were devoted to Manson, was a perversion of aboriginal religions around the world that believe that the hunter and the prey are forever bonded. For the first few years of their imprisonment, neither Leslie, Pat, nor Susan repented because their intentions, from their Manson-defined worldview, were so honorable.

In later years they did repent, and since then they have continued to repent without rest because they are so ashamed of those same intentions. Most of us judge ourselves by our intentions, whereas others judge us by our actions (or inactions) and effects (or lack thereof). Like cult terrorists everywhere, in their hearts the women's *intentions* were pure. As good had been redefined for them, they really believed their actions were all for the good.

Before starting the dialogues about Leslie, Anne Near and I had been editing stories of other women I'd interviewed in the state prison, and Anne recognized that all those other stories could serve as parables. Details of the real-life characters and events resonated with the life experiences of so many women inside and out, the ordinary struggles of women to survive in California's inner cities. The moral truths that emerged from those struggles highlighted the ordinary valor, and sometimes heroic feats of courage, in various situations in which women found themselves. Apart from their crimes and punishments, the problems of women in prison taken together represent the extreme problems of women in society at large: sexism; racism; difficult relationships; violence at home; undereducation; humiliations because of poverty and welfare; unemployment or underpaid labor; medical crises; untreated illnesses; difficulties in mothering; and dependency on men, drugs, social services. One can readily generalize women in prison in terms of discriminatory social patterns and policies, and specific stories illuminate the collective experiences. As Anne put it, their stories brought to light "the incarcerated woman-soul for whom there had been no advocate, the hidden silences."

With parables, the recognition factor is important, the element of familiarity. Most imprisoned women are otherwise ordinary women who have been convicted of some of the most common of women's crimes: chronic but relatively minor thefts, drug offenses, welfare fraud. These are offenders who do not frighten; when considering their stories, their reasons, many women can identify with them in some way. Women who kill an abusive spouse are women with whom others can identify.

By contrast, nothing about the Manson murders, as presented by the media, signified the familiar. Anne asked, "Are there lessons to be drawn from the Manson case that will be clear? Do the Manson crimes have something to teach us? Is there anything our society can learn from what happened to Leslie and the others?"

Just as Leslie's background was uncommon among imprisoned women, so her crime had little in common with those of anonymous but more representative women in terms of degree of seriousness and harm to others. The warnings to young people to avoid following gurus, and to avoid indiscriminate drug use and sex, were the most obvious moral lessons to be drawn from the story of Leslie's association with a dramatic crime, a crime that has no redeeming value. But consider that the Manson murders were emblematic of the ending of the late 1960s' idealism, the closing of a historical era. In the end, Leslie's story, a 1960s search for enlightenment gone bad, resonates because on some level, like other crimes, it could have happened to anyone in her situation in those times.

Manson's followers had certain things in common with each other: they were idealists and social rebels and spiritual seekers in the 1960s. So were millions of other young people who shared their values and visions, and who might as easily have been caught in Manson's lair.

Women aren't usually conditioned for physical violence. In mainstream cultures women get approval for being the weaker sex. If women were not trained for physical weakness, why would women need protection? It's basic to the social and legal traditions of all Western nations that men are supposed to protect women from other men. Certified men (and now some women) are authorized to use force and state-legitimized violence to conquer myriad enemies locally, nationally, internationally, and these enemies are usually men. People—generally, but not only, men—kill from patriotism, anger, fear, territorial defense, nationalistic, ideological, or religious duty, regular pay or promises of big money, pride, jealousy, self-defense, orders from official "superiors," conscience, greed, control, and vengeance.

Many years ago, my then-teenage son Todd observed that every case of unprovoked violence is simply misplaced, delayed self-defense. From then on I saw bullies as avenging some harm done to themselves, often long ago, when they were defenseless. When they eventually lash out, it's usually against the wrong target.

But for the women in the Manson case, none of these manly reasons for violence can be readily applied. It wasn't about the girls whose attempts to kill weren't successful. They weren't filled with that kind of rage. It was about Manson, who was. He had a will and they had given their wills to him. They tried to kill for a particular man—all of them, the same man—for a shared set of beliefs with which he had indoctrinated them in his own special way of communicating, which only they understood or which they accepted even when they didn't understand. This is cult behavior.

Manson's Girls on Trial

When Leslie was in jail in Los Angeles, undergoing questioning, the police offered her immunity, protection, and "maybe money," if she would testify against everyone else. She refused. She said later that it would have been like playing the role of Judas.

The trial, which lasted almost eleven months and ended in the spring of 1971, was like a circus, with Manson and Bugliosi as co-ringmasters vying for attention. None of the defendants—Leslie Van Houten, Patricia Krenwinkel, Susan Atkins, or Charles Manson—appeared to take it at all seriously. Nor did they show fear or remorse when they were convicted of first-degree murder and conspiracy, and sentenced to die in the gas chamber.

Charles "Tex" Watson, who had escaped to Texas, where he was apprehended, was jailed there for nine months. His lawyer fought extradition on the grounds that, given the publicity in California (which equaled that of John F. Kennedy's assassination), a fair trial wasn't feasible in that state. Watson was finally returned to California and tried and convicted in a separate trial. Like the women, as of early 2001 he continues to serve a California life sentence with the possibility of parole.[11]

During both the pretrial hearings and the trial, other "Manson girls" who hadn't been involved in the crimes kept vigil on the sidewalk in front of the courthouse. For almost two years they lived in sleeping bags, with little cooking pots and everything they needed to survive on the street. They helped transport messages from Manson, whom they visited at the jail, to the girls, who were jailed in Sybil Brand. It was through them that Manson managed to orchestrate his codefendants' testimony and the hiring and firing of attorneys. (Lawyers who did what Manson wanted kept their jobs.)

Leslie's first lawyer was Marvin Part, whose taped, private interview with her was later offered to the court. Ira Reiner, her second lawyer, was later elected L.A. County district attorney; like her other lawyers, he had been keen to separate her case from the others, but Manson wouldn't allow it. Lawyer number three was Ronald Hughes, who died by accidental drowning while on a camping trip, just prior to the close of the trial in 1971. He was replaced by Maxwell Keith, who continued to represent Leslie through an appeal and two retrials seven years after her original conviction.

The women associated with Charles Manson collectively followed his ever-changing agenda and persona. They served him cheerfully, with synchronicity, singing in harmony in the face of their own execution. Taking their cues from Manson and from each other, they yelled in unison at the judge, vilified him, turned their backs on him, chanted. As Susan put it, she, Pat, and Leslie were "three young women clearly not in their right minds who were in slavish obedience to a madman. . . ."[12]

Bugliosi observed that Manson's signal to someone to change lawyers consistently occurred when the lawyer attempted to separate his client from the group. This is a divide-and-conquer tactic all lawyers employ when defending one member of a group crime, just as prosecutors offer reduced sentences to one or more individuals accused of a group crime in exchange for information against other members of the group.

In Leslie's case, her first (pretrial) lawyer recommended that she receive a psychiatric evaluation. Manson was opposed and instructed her to fire him. She did, and she refused to see the psychiatrist. The scenario was repeated with her second lawyer. Both of them believed that she shouldn't be tried for first-degree murder when she had neither planned nor technically committed a murder: the coroner confirmed that Mrs. LaBianca was killed by the bayonet stabbing, before Leslie began her frenzied assault on a lifeless body.[13] Each of her subsequent lawyers likewise tried to separate her case from that of her codefendants. Given her continued submission to Manson, and her determination to accept responsibility even though she faced the death penalty, the lawyers believed she could not possibly be in her right mind. Eventually, however, court-appointed psychiatrists did determine that, legally, she was sane.

Vincent Bugliosi readily acknowledged Manson's hypnotic power over the women, but he nevertheless insisted that they had followed him through their own free will, invoking the classical eighteenth-century view of crime as a matter of "rational" choice, therefore deserving retribution. Both Bugliosi and Stephen Kay—Kay later prosecuted her in her two retrials—opposed psychiatric treatment for lawbreakers and sought straightforward punishment. Attention is seldom given to the reasons an individual commits a crime, because "few judges or juries are willing to take into account a potential causal factor which is perceived rightly or wrongly to emanate from volitional behavior."[14]

Max Keith entered the picture as Leslie's final lawyer and was clear, during his closing argument in 1971 and later, that he recognized that she was the victim of a cult. As Keith summarized, "The record discloses over and over again that all of these girls at the ranch believed Manson was God—really believed it. The record discloses that the girls obeyed his commands without any conscious questioning at all. . . . If you believe that they were mindless robots, they cannot be guilty of premeditated murder."[15]

In 1972, psychologist Rollo May made reference to Manson's "cult"; to him the evidence was plentiful that Manson's followers were victims of mind control. Had the courts given attention to these interpretations, the first trial might have been conducted from different premises and might have had a different outcome in establishing the defendants' degree of responsibility.

Vincent Bugliosi, however, was determined to get first-degree convictions for each of the brainwashed women whom he was so keen to prosecute as an individual with free will, even though he promoted the opposite appraisal. In his opening statement in the 1970–71 trial, he said, "Charles Manson was in fact the dictatorial leader of the Family; . . . everyone in the Family was slavishly obedient to him; . . . he always had the other members of the Family do his bidding for him; and . . . eventually they committed the seven Tate-LaBianca murders at his command."[16] He claims that Manson studied mind-control techniques in prison, "which he later put to use in programming his followers." In his closing argument he called Manson "the dictatorial master of a tribe of bootlicking slaves," and the girls were "a closely knit band of mindless robots."[17] In 1974 he wrote that Manson's domination over his codefendants was "so total, so complete, that they would do anything he told them to do. Including murder." He also said, describing "Manson's girls," "They all have the same thought; they use the same language; each one was a carbon copy of the other. They are all still totally subservient and subject to Charles Manson. They are his X'd-out slaves."[18]

And yet, to the jury, even while acknowledging Manson's domination, Bugliosi pleaded that the girls knowingly, willingly placed themselves in that position. He thought they were "human monsters, human mutations,"[19] and he held each of them liable for the crimes—whether or not they were present and no matter how much, by Bugliosi's own account, they were not thinking for themselves. No excuses. They deserved to die. As journalist Paul Krassner observed, given that Manson wasn't present at the murders, "the jury had to be convinced that Charlie's girls were zombies who followed his orders without question."[20] The jury accepted Bugliosi's conclusion that, brainwashing aside, they followed his orders willingly, with awareness. Given their displays in the courtroom, the women gave the jury ample evidence of Manson's power over them, but in order to gain a conviction, the D.A. had to try the women as individuals who exercised free, premeditated will. The contradiction presented by the prosecutor did not dissuade the jury from a guilty verdict.

Manson's control cost the "Manson girls" dearly. During the trial, when he told them to shave their heads, they did, as a protest against the legal proceedings, as an affirmation of their solidarity, and as a symbol of their separation from the world. They believed in him enough to refrain from defending themselves, enough to try to keep evidence of his guilt out of court records, enough to carve X's on their foreheads with a smuggled razor blade and darken the wound with heated bobby pins. (The girls on the street followed suit.)

On the same day as their sentencing, April 19, 1971, Lieutenant William L. Calley was sentenced to life for killing twenty-two Vietnamese civilians in the My Lai massacre. His sentence was later commuted.[21] His defense was that he was "just obeying orders."

During the sentencing phase of their trial in 1971, Leslie and Pat and

Susan, unwavering in their fidelity, tried to take full responsibility, with Tex, for the murders. They were still trying to fully exonerate Manson. When they were sentenced to die in the gas chamber, they showed no fear. They believed only in Charles Manson. Society's judgments and plans for ending their lives were, in their minds, society's judgment of itself. With their heads shaven and their foreheads scarred, they walked down the courthouse hallways, escorted by their guards, smiling and singing.

Effects on Popular Culture

In addition to Leslie, Susan, and Pat, in the course of a few years I also had contact with Mary Brunner and Catherine "Gypsy" Share, when they were imprisoned at the California Institution for Women in the mid-1970s (as I discuss later), and with Sandra Good and Lynette "Squeaky" Fromme, when they visited my home soon after I first met the girls at the prison. All seven were pretty, talented, sensitive, and intelligent. Just out of their teens, they and others like them had entered Manson's world long before he displayed his penchant for violence. Four of these now aging women—Pat, Susan, Leslie, and also Lynette Fromme, who was convicted of attempting to assassinate President Gerald Ford in 1975—are still, in 2001, serving prison sentences as a direct result of their association with him. (Sandra was in prison for many years for what were interpreted as death threats against a number of corporate executives; she and Lynette sent them letters telling them that if they didn't stop polluting the environment they would die.)

Despite his horrific effect on the lives of so many young people, and his responsibility for many murders, in 1976 Charles Manson was voted among the top fifty individuals most admired by schoolchildren and teenagers in the United States—along with then-President Ford, O. J. Simpson, and Chris Evert.[22] (Twenty years later, the murder trial of O. J. Simpson was the first to match the Manson trial for intensity and duration of media attention.) Despite and because of his unadulterated contempt for other human beings, Manson has been mythologized by marginalized youth as a romantic rogue hero. In 2001 there are dozens of Manson-related Web sites. His earliest and most devoted followers were primarily gentle young women who thought he personified peace and love. Now it is primarily wannabe tough boys on the street and in youth prisons who look up to Manson.

The story of Charles Manson is shrouded with a dark mystique transmitted through popular song, comic books, airport book displays, talk shows, "cult" movies, and souvenirs. Even opera got in on it, with John Moran's free-form *The Manson Family: An Opera,* commissioned in 1990 by Lincoln Center and recorded for a CD release in 1992. John Waters, film director, dedicated his quirky 1972 film *Pink Flamingos* to the "Manson Family" as a flippant, punk gesture. Later, having gained more serious awareness of the players in the Manson drama, Waters became a public advocate for Leslie's release.

Interestingly, Waters's friend Patty Hearst has played convincing minor characters in his offbeat films. The daughter of a wealthy California newspaper magnate, she was kidnapped in the mid-1970s, abused, and indoctrinated with antiestablishment fervor. Her experience of being brainwashed by the Symbionese Liberation Army was not unlike Leslie's brainwashing by Manson; both believed themselves to be soldiers in a liberation army. Hearst didn't kill anyone or attempt to do so, but she participated in armed robbery, publicly chastised her parents for their wealth, and otherwise acted entirely out of character while with the SLA and under the influence of Cinque, her charismatic leader. After a brief period of confinement, she was released by President Carter. Hearst was a straightforward victim. She didn't enter into a cult voluntarily as Leslie had done, and she claims, reasonably, to have acted from fear rather than conviction, although they are not mutually exclusive: inducing fear in the subject significantly facilitates the process of brainwashing.

Within his prison cells, for years before the murders, Manson constructively translated alienation into song. When released on parole in 1967, he found a burgeoning counterculture whose musical sounds and poetry expressed his own agonies and longings, but which also, like Eastern religions, encouraged kindness, compassion, and positive attitudes. As a colorful outlaw, he attracted rock 'n' rollers, notably Dennis Wilson of the Beach Boys. As a hopeful songwriter and musician, he sought connections with show business circles; eventually some bands did record some of his tunes. For example, the Beach Boys recorded his song "Cease to Exist," but because they were uneasy about that message, they changed the title to "Never Learn Not to Love," and gave writing credits to Dennis Wilson.[23]

Manson released albums recorded in prison (with very poor equipment), such as *Manson Live at San Quentin,* and *Lie,* which in the 1980s was being sold as a collector's item for $500 despite the severely poor sound quality. In the 1990s, the Lemonheads recorded his "(Your) Home Is Where You're Happy." When his song "Look at Your Game, Girl" was recorded by Guns N' Roses (1993), he achieved fleeting commercial success. In the video for that song, Axl Rose wears a T-shirt with Manson's image. As a prisoner, Manson could not receive royalties. According to *People* magazine,[24] any royalties were diverted by law to the (now adult) orphaned son of one of the victims at the Tate residence.

The Manson murders caused great distrust of hippies. Symbolically, it also didn't help the counterculture when, the following December, a man was killed by Hell's Angels bodyguards at a Rolling Stones concert at the Altamont, California, racetrack, just after Mick Jagger sang "Sympathy for the Devil." It seemed a strange coincidence that one of the world's most successful rock bands was chummy with the Hell's Angels, just as Manson had tried to be with the Straight Satans and Satan's Slaves. Manson too seemed to have sympathy for the Devil; moreover, as the flip side of his Christ-like persona (which only his followers seemed able to recognize), he identified with him.

In Indonesia, in 1981, a man with fifteen wives proclaimed that he was the "spiritual heir of American mass murderer Charles Manson."[25] One of the most popular of raunchy performers of the late 1990s was Marilyn Manson, who fashioned his performance persona as a synthesis of Marilyn Monroe and Charles Manson. With a remarkable flair for orchestrating chaos, he created himself as a legend, fueled by the media and consumed by the public. His imagery is permanently inscribed on contemporary culture and history. Respected author Anne Lamott, criticizing her own early writing as a food reviewer, wrote of her "black-humored friends" who accompanied her to restaurants as sounding "more like the Manson girls than food lovers."[26] She didn't feel the need to explain what she meant by that.

Fascination with the Manson case has been similar to the popular fascination with horror shows: the worst imaginable terrors and deaths supply entertainment for people. They gladly pay for the adrenaline rush from heightened fear and suspense, or from identification with the hero or antihero. They find vicarious satisfaction in watching macho fictional characters act out dark, violent fantasies, after which they, the spectators, can walk back into the real world intact, perversely empowered. Such fascination is a matter of taste, but understandable.

It is, however, difficult to digest the glorification by the young of someone who inflicted permanent damage on real people in the real world, and who, as he enters old age, gives no public sign of remorse or accountability.

Twenty-three years after Bugliosi won the death penalty for Leslie and her codefendants, he showed a new regard for her. In a live interview broadcast in August 1994 (following Larry King's taped interview with Leslie), King asked the former D.A., "Were you impressed with her tonight [on video]?" Bugliosi replied, "I was impressed by her. In defense of her, I can say this: she seems to be a model prisoner, and everyone seems to say that she is very remorseful for these murders."[27]

Four

REMINISCENCES AND TRANSITIONS

When I first met the women in 1972, over two years after the crime, there was a vague incongruity. The Special Security Unit, by whatever name, still felt like death row, even though the prisoners had been reprieved. I enjoyed the women from the start; I became friends with them as weeks and months passed. But I was bewildered at their nonchalant acceptance of their imprisonment. In the beginning the women didn't speak of the murders, but the murders were the reason we were all there together in that cage.

When I started working with the women at SSU, the rule of their being allowed out of their cells only one at a time was relaxed. One of the empty cells became our schoolroom. I arrived twice a week laden with books and academic exercises—to which they were always responsive. Every session lasted three to five hours, everyone contributing to discussions of the readings. They all had quick minds and they had plenty of time to study every day, so they invariably met deadlines and produced good work. During breaks we drank grape Tang and shared personal memories. They liked to hear about my children. They wanted to know about the main area of the prison and what was going on with the women (then six hundred) "out there."

Every day I spent in the main prison produced some new revelation about the workings of power and resistance in a closed environment—some of it, thankfully, comical. I shared my amazement at the resourcefulness of so many women crammed together, denied almost all basic amenities—such as tampons. One of the male prison administrators told me in earnest that he thought the women might be tempted to use the packaging as dildos! I confided my heartbreak at watching an elderly friend from the main prison, who had every reason to expect parole, stagger out of the boardroom after her hearing, slump to the floor, and break into gut-wrenching wails. I told them about the night that a woman played a guitar in the hallway a few minutes past curfew, and how a guard punished her by hauling her off to "rack" (solitary confinement).

They were all empathetic. Leslie, who at the time had not had a parole hearing but who, in the years ahead, would go through many such denials, said, "I'd have felt just as you did, that terrible helplessness when you know there isn't anything you can do."

And I told them how inspired I was by some of the characters I encountered in my day-to-day work over there—mostly prisoners but staff as well—people whose positive energy countered the negative environment. One such individual I told them about was the psychologist in the main prison, Vera Dreiser, who was near retirement. She had a quirky, compassionate personality and wonderful stories about her immigrant heritage. I loved learning that, in 1900, it was her uncle Theodore who published *Sister Carrie,* a great novel depicting the kind of urban street life that still opens doors into prison.

The women often talked about their problems with the male psychiatrist who saw each of them regularly, or as often as met his fancy. They described his sexy, gleaming bald head, the way his glasses glistened in the sunlight, and his attachment to his huge, glittering diamond ring. They stared at it while he questioned them.

His method was to challenge them in a loud voice, trying to provoke them to express anger, trying to get them to yell back at him. The more excited he got, the more he would agitatedly twist his ring back and forth on his finger. But they responded in their calm, undefensive way, not liking it that he was after them to reveal "the monster inside." His sessions seemed to be reinforcing their loyalty to Manson.

From their stories and others I'd heard, I didn't think he sounded entirely competent. My opinion was reinforced a few years later, when I heard him, at an investigative state senate hearing on his practices, reiterate the age-old patriarchal perception that "females have more mental problems than males."[1] Eventually, however, he was helpful to the women in certain respects, especially Leslie.

The vast majority of the prisoners who sought psychiatric counseling were given medication, with no personal attention at all. To him, medication *was* therapy for all but a select few.[2] He expressed his pride in how attentive he was in responding to women's requests for pills. "You cannot find a person in here who said that they were actually mentally ill that I didn't see [and put on pills]."[3] To me, his attitudes seemed counterproductive to a therapeutic environment. He was committed to the custodial management of potentially unruly caged human beings, whom he generalized as "sociopathic." Leslie, Pat, and Susan were spared his condescension and his assembly-line pill treatment because he thought they had something he wanted—the keys to the mysteries of what had turned them into "monsters." For this reason they were given what few others were granted—individual therapy sessions. Eventually, his approach did help Leslie to get focused, and he made a significant difference in her transition away from Manson.

The "Family" B.C.

For at least six months from the time I first met Leslie, Susan, and Pat, the main topic of informal conversation was "The Family B.C.—Before the Crimes." They had many happy memories of the harmony they had experienced with Manson in the beginning. They expressed nostalgia for the days when, out on Spahn Ranch (the decaying, but then still active, Western movie set on the desert near Los Angeles), they had enjoyed a communal life with one another, isolated from mainstream society.

The "family" had been made up of beautiful people, a collective perception enhanced by Manson's frequent dispensation of the sixties' route to awareness, LSD. Since Manson was a prolific songwriter, everything they experienced with him became a song. The women knew all his songs, and within our schoolroom cell they often sang them in sweet harmony. To them life was beautiful. This included scavenging for food by rescuing still-edible cast-out bread, cheese, canned goods, fruits, and vegetables from grocery store Dumpsters, and writing a song about it.

Market Basket, A&P:
I don't care if the box-boy stares at me.
I don't even care who wins the war.
I'll be in them cans behind my favorite store.

If you're livin' on the road
And you think you're starvin',
Get off of that, my friend,
Just get in them cans and start carvin'.

Oh garbage dump, my garbage dump—
That sums it up in one big lump.
We are the garbage pickers of America:
Hup 2, 3, 4. Hup 2, 3, 4.[4]

The song sounds macabre, given the events that followed their garbage frolics. At the time, their approach to gathering edible food was tribal, it was harmless fun, and it was ecologically prescient—they recycled, and cut down on waste. The women had fond memories of how (between periods of malnourishment) they had prepared sumptuous meals from the garbage they collected.

As in many communes all over the land, Manson's "family" milked the warmth of mutual kindness through every sun-kissed day in their southern California hideaways. They talked about how, for a while, their "family" seemed ideal to them. When Susan gave birth to her baby (not fathered by Manson), everyone gathered to celebrate the cosmic miracle. The women cared for the children collectively; at one point there were four infants, one of whom, I surmise, was sired by Manson. During those early months, the women all described him as having evoked feelings of pure love. They said he had a calm, saintly demeanor during the "gentler days."

Being Brainwashed

When arrested in 1969, Manson was booked by police as "Manson, Charles M., aka Jesus Christ, God." Usually he didn't directly introduce himself as Jesus. But he made blatant implications in his speech and in his gestures, which everyone in the group heard and saw together in the same way. If he *was* Jesus Christ reincarnated, as he sometimes seemed to be, how could his followers deny him anything?

The women's descriptions of their feelings toward Manson when they first met him resemble the testimony of other ex-cult members. An ex-member of the Hare Krishna cult described how temple leaders talked in soft voices, always slightly smiling mysteriously, and how hypnotizing it was. The ex–Hare Krishna said, "I completely forgot about everything. I got the feeling I couldn't leave, like there was no way I could get out. I don't know what that was. I had the feeling that it was God calling me, and that the whole outside world had sort of vaporized."[5]

Similarly, an ex-follower of Jim Jones, leader of the 1970s People's Temple cult, described her experience of losing her will. "You voluntarily choose not to question. You voluntarily choose to allow someone else to make your decisions. Then you kind of turned off this logical portion of your mind which people use to make everyday decisions. You stopped using it. And eventually you lost the capability of making decisions."

Leslie describes how she felt in the early 1970s, when she became aware that her thoughts weren't her own. "When I'd be questioned and not have any answers, I'd go blank and become frustrated, like when a machine jams and just sits there making noise. In my head, nothing was functioning. I was trying to understand, breaking down stiff little slogans that had been drilled into me."[6] Leslie's experience, and that of Manson's other young women, bear similarities to the experiences of women suffering from battered woman syndrome; their spouses abuse them but they are brainwashed by the batterers to blame themselves. They lose (or have never had) their personal agency, and without intervention they won't leave, even if they know they can.

Descriptions of the women attached to Manson also resemble those of newly born-again Christians, or anyone in the first blush of having been converted to a doctrine that purports to have all the answers and relies on faith. Bugliosi described Sandra Good and Lynette Fromme, who were the first Manson associates he met, as follows. "I was immediately struck by their expressions. They seemed to radiate inner contentment. . . . They smiled almost continuously, no matter what was said. For them all the questions had been answered. There was no need to search any more, because they had found the truth. And their truth was 'Charlie is Love.' " When Bugliosi met other women involved with Manson, he observed, "Same expressions, same patterned responses, same tone of voice, same lack of distinct personality. . . . Their answers were as if rehearsed; often they gave identical responses." Bugliosi's impressions were not unlike my own when I first met the women in 1972. Of Manson, he says, "he was not only capable of committing murder himself, he also possessed the incredible power to command others to kill for him."[7] And yet Bugliosi professed to believe that the women were sufficiently self-directed and sane to be prosecuted for first-degree murder!

The flip side of the happy commune story, which turns Manson's utopian messiah hype on its head, is that he exercised overt and covert control over everyone in his fluctuating "family." He was served by the young women in all domestic matters, sending them out hunting and gathering, using them to lure businessmen, bikers, drug dealers, pretty young men, and the eighty-one-year-old landlord, George Spahn, into his fold. At Manson's discretion, the women who served him by day might be expected to sleep with the visitors by night, as gifts from himself, in the ancient tradition of men who held property in common. Manson was the head man deciding how, when, for what purposes and by whom the property would be used.

The men who came to Manson appreciated his generosity with the women. He was not at all like the Freudian father who keeps the women for himself (which is why the sons have to kill him). He charmed the women into feeling important in his presence, even though he was pimping them and treating them as dispensable. As Pat recalled in a 1994 interview with Diane Sawyer, "Sex was a means of control. When he had different men that he was trying to initiate into the 'family' . . . he would offer them whatever women he had." Leslie adds, "When a man wanted you, you went with him. You couldn't resist." Sawyer also interviewed Manson, and interjected clips from that interview in her edited tape of the interview with Pat and Leslie. She confronts him with the women's charge of sexually exploiting them. He replies, "Isn't that what women do? Isn't that what women's for? Women receive men and reflect men. Man holds dominion up over women. It's been that way since [he grunts] . . . since we grunted and we came out of caves."[8]

Given what he did to so many young women, it is appropriate that he later lived many years of his life in the Vacaville maximum-security medical facility, which primarily houses sex offenders. He was also housed in Folsom, and in San Quentin, where, in the 1970s, the adjoining cell was occupied for several days by Timothy Leary, the ex-Harvard guru of psychedelics who told youth to "turn on, tune in, drop out." Manson had once told his tribe that Leary was the father of them all, but in San Quentin he treated Leary paternalistically. Leary was convinced that the authorities had put him next to Manson as a provocation, a test, a game. Leary said, "He was talking to me all the time, giving me advice on what to do or where I made mistakes."[9]

Having been abandoned as a child, and perpetually incarcerated by the state most of his life, Manson could read and prey on people's weaknesses. The young women were affected by the intense accuracy with which he perceived their feelings of estrangement from their former lives. He loudly disparaged the consumptive, punitive, bigoted, competitive, greedy values dominating his country. With the same fierce passion he idealized nature, creativity, music, children, sex, and the freedom to make choices—everything that prison denied him. When he saw an injustice against an underdog it made him furious, but he didn't recognize or acknowledge his own abuses of women and young people. He had lived much of thirty or so years in segregation cells or with other convicted boys and men. When on the streets (for short periods) he had been a pimp, among other street occupations. He had a short-term marriage, during much of which he was incarcerated, and another brief relationship, and incidental encounters while on parole. But for the most part he could only fantasize about women; they were rarely part of his day-to-day adult world in any significant way until March 21, 1967, when, newly paroled, he discovered the Age of Aquarius.

Paroled into the era of the hippie movement, he found young, free-spirited women, attracted to his outlaw ways, mindlessly responding to his fantasies of what they should be as women—sex goddesses and domestic slaves. Margaret Singer,[10] who has interviewed thousands of former cult members, defines a cult as a group with a charismatic leader who is worshipped by followers and who subjects them to coercive manipulation. She considers the process of recruitment to be an essential feature of cults.

Certainly many of the young people who joined up with Manson were recruited by those already attached to him. But my sense is that, in the beginning, he wasn't seeking disciples. The girls he approached virtually gave themselves to him. Later, young men lured vulnerable girls into Manson's fold. New devotees, women and men, brought in yet more candidates for their growing "family."

This was an age of rapidly proliferating pseudogurus. A few people who associated with the "family" did not worship Manson. They were men and they dropped away before the violence began. Like any wannabe dude, Manson appeared to want other men to respect him for his toughness. Also for his sense of manhood, he wanted the attentions of beautiful, young, compliant women who would take care of him in every way. This included helping him get even with his adversaries. On his own in the mainstream world, in the absence of the girls' adulation and that of attractive young men, he would have seemed an unlikely candidate for the position of guru. But they willingly gave him their power; he took their trust, and he used it against them. One can readily surmise that Manson's own power as a human being to think, choose, and act rationally had been cruelly destroyed by a retributive justice system. Whether or not brainwashing the middle-class young white girls who came to him was his conscious intent, it was misplaced vengeance.

Payback Justice

Manson acted out payback justice, whereby if one white man oppressed him he could kill any other white man (and his women) as revenge. He saw anyone with any privilege as fair game, since all were representative of a power system that kept him from his life and didn't appreciate his brilliance. With the murders, he acted from a primitive impulse to destroy the enemy, the rich piggies, rather than from a coherent class or race analysis. The prison experience generally teaches about death, not life, which is why prisoners who resist, and who remain or become life affirming and energized, are so remarkable. I believe that if Manson had internalized the power of positive thinking, he would have been positively remarkable instead of frighteningly pathetic.

Another aspect of payback justice is that it knows no statute of limitations. The time never runs out when it is legitimate to gain revenge against those who have oppressed us and/or our ancestors. We can live with these obsessions all our lives, and for generations. Manson gained new "justification" for revenge with each insult he had to endure as a less than favored prisoner for most of his life. He exulted in the infamy that came with the two publicized nights of murder. He apparently felt no sorrow for his victims or their survivors, issuing dangerously mystifying mishmash karma talk about life and death flowing together. I recall that in a televised review hearing in the mid-1990s, he was mockingly acting as if—or perhaps revealing that—he didn't know the names of the people who had been killed at his instruction. He continues, three decades later, to behave as if he feels nothing for them or for the victims of his clean-up murders.

Acts of predatory violence are often, as with my son's theory of "delayed self-defense," expressions of a need to defend one's self that was thwarted at the time of one's own victimization. Frantz Fanon, a revolutionary North African psychiatrist, vividly described Algerian men's compelling need to physically fight against their French oppressors so that they could directly express justified anger and regain their manly dignity.[11] Richard Wright powerfully illustrated those principles with his fictional renderings of African-American men's rage. For all his peace-and-love talk, Manson couldn't absolve his dominant need for violent revenge for all the wrongs that had been done to him as a vulnerable child and lifelong prisoner. He was still trying to find a way to defend himself, especially with women. Pimp that he was, he sent Tex and the women into the field to mow down the enemy while he, the general, conducted the war from headquarters.

With his tribe of disciples, Manson got a taste of power. He had a ready audience for his songs, ramblings, and riddles—for example, "If you're looking you'll never find; don't try to keep up or you'll be left behind." Over time his devotees became prepared to live for him, to die for him, and if the cosmic forces required it of them, to kill for him, trusting that it would be for the good of humanity just as any good soldier must trust. Manson wrote in a song:

Thou shalt not kill, said my daddy
Mother agreed, as she served a meat patty

The Indian said, Kill only what you need
But the Whiteman likes to see things bleed

Look at the Big Man passing to others his fear
Look to the children. Judgment day is near.[12]

Charles Milles Manson had been shifted from one home to another soon after his birth in Cincinnati to a sixteen-year-old on November 12, 1934. He got his last name from a short-lived stepfather before the "parents" ran off separately to break the law in various ways. By 1967 he had been incarcerated much of his life, in virtually every kind of institution. As a young kid he'd already done time in several other reformatories before, as a preadolescent, he escaped from Boys Town in Nebraska, after a few days; later, at age fifteen, he pulled a supermarket robbery with an escapee chum. Charlie graduated to more secure jails for youth and, soon, to hardcore prisons for adult male felons. Prison, by definition, is abusive. He learned about fear, how to control his own and exploit others'. For example, while on parole, he was walking with a friend and both of them were carrying drugs. They recognized a narc up ahead, and Manson's friend wanted to run the other way. Manson, however, approached the man and made small talk until the narc brushed him off. He advised his friend, "Don't let him put any of his fear in you."[13]

During pre-1967 parole breaks from adult prisons he formed at least two serious, if short-lived, relationships with women (including one marriage), both of which produced a child, but apparently he had no ongoing family ties. He worked as a burglar, car thief, forger, and pimp. He achieved his popularity with youth in the late 1960s surge of rock 'n' roll, to which he was fanatically devoted. His followers disregarded the adage of the era (coined during Berkeley's 1964 free speech movement), "Don't trust anybody over thirty." Ultimately, his dogma was an inventory of the flaws of the society that rejected him and infantilized him as a prisoner without choice or responsibility. As a leader he exhibited a frenzied hunger for control. As a kid he had been excluded and locked up. As a prisoner, in 1985, he said with wistful sadness, "I've lived in your tomb . . . wishing I could go to high school and to proms."[14]

When Manson selected a specific residence for the first night of murders he was not operating at random. Apparently he did not know that the house was leased to Roman Polanski; whether that is true is not crucial. Because Manson *did* know that the house had formerly been the home of rock producer Terry Melcher, who had befriended Manson but who had aroused Manson's ire by not turning him into an overnight success. Manson and Tex Watson had both been to the house on several occasions. According to one journalist, the murders were justified by Manson owing to his "failure to find a market for his songs," and he projects what he saw in Manson's media images at the time of the murders: "If they won't hear me [through the music], let them *feel* me [through violent deeds]."[15]

Taking Power

Manson targeted his followers' emotional vulnerabilities to both exalt and demolish them. He became a tyrant because so many people, especially beautiful young women, were willing to do his bidding. Into the ears of impressionable idealists he articulated the hypocrisies of the establishment with the eloquence of street poetry, and he offered a vision of a counterculture that was irresistible to those in his inner circle. He initiated them into open sexual practices, playing on their physical insecurities. His furious insights brought to him a devoted, if small, band of followers: over time about twenty-five girls and young women from age thirteen to early twenties, and ten young men; in his inner circle were three men and ten women, most in their late teens and early twenties.

At the time of the crimes in 1969, when Leslie was still nineteen, Manson was approaching age thirty-five. He had kept his "family" in isolation, in their own little world, which is how cult leaders operate. They didn't read newspapers. They didn't have clocks. To them there was no time. He effectively separated his young followers from their families and the world; he gave them new names and they gave up their birthdays, starting life anew. He acted from a sense of biblical destiny but he tore away at the conventional religious, white, middle-class values with which most of his followers were raised. He raged at what he wrongly presumed to be their own parents' moral hypocrisies. He extended this judgment to all middle-class people who enjoyed their comforts at the expense of the world's depleting natural resources. His followers' task was to lose themselves, to eliminate their pasts, to become as one, one with the Son of Man. He used endless repetition of platitudes to indoctrinate them—to "take on his will," as his followers expressed it.

As an older man with street smarts, Manson played on the fears and uncertainties of young people trying to find their way in the world, independent of their families. It was a time of dynamic social change when many people were questioning traditional values, yet he offered himself as a surrogate patriarch. Under his protective wing, they would change society. Jeanne Gallick, my co-teacher in SSU and the women's friend, described the "family" as "the shadow and logical extension of the nuclear family."[16] Like the old patriarchs, he demanded obedience from every member of his "family," but unlike most fathers, he used drugs, music, role playing, and sex as tools of manipulation. He intimidated those under his spell, determined to kill their egos by telling them they were stupid or were missing some personal quality necessary to enlightenment, which made them even more submissive in their efforts to gain his approval. Leslie came to him as an extroverted young woman, but the eventual effect of Manson's beratings was that she crawled into a shell when she was around him.

Although part of his inner circle, Leslie was never in Manson's inner, *inner* circle. She would lapse into thinking for herself, which made her a less than perfect devotee. This problem took on profound significance when, at the murders of the LaBiancas, she was unable to follow orders. Some element of conscience was at work on her mind, breaking against will through the layers of prophecy and apocalyptic images inscribed on her brain by the Son of Man. He *saw* the apocalypse happening, as did they: the 1960s California droughts, floods, fires, and earthquakes; shootings in the streets and poisons in the air. None of them challenged Manson's view that 1969 was the time for the world to undergo a major rupture and change, the ultimate revolution, which would empower African Americans.

Several years after the crimes, in 1972, with five or six of us in a circle on the floor of our tiny schoolroom cell—with the guards watching from the doorway—Susan, Pat, and Leslie sang Manson's songs a cappella with clear, harmonious voices. When the sunlight streamed into the cell through the small, barred window, it would strike against Pat's hair, gleaming gold and red, this laughing woman who wrote poetry and music and played her guitar. Susan, also very musical, was always intensely focused when engaged in conversation. Leslie was sensitive to any movement by the guards, or sounds of birds outside, the wind in the trees, approaching sirens—alert to any change in the environment. Leslie and Pat did the most bantering. All three expressed very similar attitudes and opinions based on their guru's reasoning. It wasn't until each fully separated from Manson that I recognized them as truly distinct individuals.

While still beholden to Manson, and with pleasure in the remembering, they ingenuously, nonjudgmentally cited examples of how he had manipulated their thinking. He gave everyone LSD systematically and frequently. For weeks, in a rented house in an L.A. suburb, when they were all under the effects of large doses of the hallucinogen, he played and replayed the Beatles' White Album, demanding their full attention to the lyrics. He made inferences concerning the song "Revolution 9," and ranted to his hypnotized disciples about the Bible's book of Revelation and the apocalyptic race war that was inevitable, that needed to be started in order to shift power from the white man to the black man. He claimed with outsiders that it was other people who saw Jesus in him, but to his followers he posed himself as Christ on the cross. He later wrote a song about the power of music that said, "How did you think I could talk to you, except through the music? How else did you think I could stop the confusion in your mind?" (It is sadly ironic that Beatle John Lennon, Manson's hero, was later assassinated by a rabid fan who envied Lennon's fame and who, as a counterpoint to Lennon's pacifist music, like Manson, could imagine having power only through use of a deadly weapon.)

Manson, the Racist and Misogynist Guru

Manson has never accepted the idea that he was a cult leader, and I am persuaded he never systematically planned to be one. But his exploitation of young people looking for answers, especially charming, pliable, feminine young women with wanderlust, and his gradual accumulation of purposeful and incidental controls over them, resulted in a classic cult group with Manson as the singular patriarch. Others, like Bobby Beausoleil, had their own charisma and followings of young women; a guitarist, Bobby sometimes jammed with Frank Zappa and the Mothers of Invention, which gave him status with young people.[17] Manson favored Bobby, and expected Leslie in particular to serve Bobby's needs.

But within Manson's circle it was on Manson's head that the light shone. It was his wisdom that inspired his followers and guided their actions. His word was the first and last word, and although he assigned specific women to the men who came to him, he didn't intend that these "couples" would form a commitment to one another. As explained by Charles "Tex" Watson in his discussion of group sex at the ranch, "As long as we loved any one person more than the others, we weren't truly dead and the Family wasn't one."[18] Watson goes on to marvel at how all the girls clearly preferred Manson to any of the other men who joined up with him, even though, apparently, he was not a particularly skillful lover. "Charlie did not provide the ultimate in the physical side of sex. The attraction must have been psychological and emotional, perhaps even spiritual."[19]

Although he was himself completely devoted to Manson, and served as his henchman in the murders, Watson was mystified by Manson's ability to control so many beautiful women, given Manson's negative attitudes toward the female sex. As Watson described Manson's views and practices, "Women were the primary source of ego programming; thus no mother in the Family was allowed to take care of her own child and the women were always supposed to talk to the babies in nonsense syllables to avoid contaminating them. Women built the prisons; women caused the wars; women upset the natural order by refusing to keep to their intended place—slaves to men. Charlie seemed to have a special hatred for women as mothers, even though he taught that childbearing was one of their major purposes in life."[20]

According to Charles Watson, Manson was also aggressively racist, and "insisted that blacks were less evolved than whites and therefore only fit to be their slaves." Nevertheless, Manson believed that "now all the centuries of oppression and exploitation for blackie were over, his karma had turned, and it was time for him to rise and to win."[21] In Manson's convoluted theory, if rich white people were killed in their homes, the crime would be blamed on poor black people, which would start the race war that was Manson's self-styled Armageddon, which he called

Helter Skelter. White people would assume that blacks were embarking on revenge for the centuries of damage done them by whites. The whites, in response, would seek out and punish blacks for the murders. The blacks would retaliate and they would be the underdogs who survived, arose, and conquered their oppressors. During the race war the "family" would live safely in a hole in the desert, an underground paradise on the edge of Death Valley, until the turbulence settled. They would live in this bottomless pit for years, and because of their transcendent powers they would never age—forever the beautiful people with the energy of youth. In Manson's fantasy, they would save people from burning cities, especially the children. When the troubles were over and they returned to the earth's surface to stay, the black people would welcome them as allies in the task of reorganizing the planet. Charles Manson's divinity would be recognized.

The Gender Factor

It's common for people who have been involved in murder to report that they felt as if they were watching themselves, as if they were out of their own bodies. The effect of LSD is likewise an out-of-body experience, and a vivid short-term memory of the LSD trip—a flashback—causes a person to recall that nonphysical state. On the perceptual level, not all the women were in their bodies at the times of the murders. From their perspectives, as instructed by Manson, their own as well as other peoples' bodies were insignificant to life, an obstacle to perfect understanding. Freed from the body as an obstacle to flight, under the illusion that the body has been transcended, the spirit becomes one with the universe, to the point of infinity. When the time came for the countdown to the gas chamber, the "Manson women" had been ready to depart their bodies for a long time, so taken were they with Manson's "truths."

Gender, age, race, and class all loom large in the Manson scenario. He attracted both women and men, but women were much more numerous among his followers and it was not a coincidence that it was primarily women whom he chose to do his killings. Some of the men, such as Tex Watson, who had a strong Christian background but who experienced his devotion to Manson as a religious conversion, were as submissive to him as the girls were. Generally the men who came to him seemed to identify with his outlaw persona, even when their own backgrounds were conventionally middle-class. Most obviously, his power over men seemed related to his ability to attract women, and his generosity with the women's bodies, offering the girls to whoever wanted them for a night, was certainly a draw. He presented himself as a mystic, and he was convincing to men and women alike. But clearly the women were his trophies, symbolic of his masculine power; they gave him status with other men, including those seeking spiritual enlightenment.

Of the many young women and men who came, some stayed a short while, others permanently. Many of the girls who came were below the age of consent. The fourteen-year-old daughter of a Methodist minister, Ruth Moorehouse, came to visit and later returned, convinced like the others that Manson was the reincarnated Jesus Christ. The girl's father came to retrieve her, but he was himself converted, and for a time remained there under Manson's spell, one of the few older people in his tribe.

Manson sexually exploited young women with their tacit permission because they believed in his authority. Each of them, all white girls, had been successfully socialized to be attractive to men—soft and feminine in appearance and demeanor—and they honored men's hierarchical privilege in the social order. They excelled in submissiveness. He used their dependency to coerce them to stay, if that was his desire. He excluded doubters. He attracted teenagers and young adults from every background, but especially from the middle class. When he'd used up someone's trust fund, he'd send them packing if they were not otherwise attractive or useful to him.

His selection of victims was reflective of straightforward class antagonism against materialist consumer "piggies," and his plan to start a race war was patronizingly racist. He controlled group gatherings, flattering or intimidating individuals in one-on-one encounters. He demanded exclusive loyalty from those closest to him and he was not always kind. As Leslie says, "It was an honor to be that close to a chosen person of God, but he made me feel stupid, and it was clear by his behavior that I had a lot of 'giving up' to do, to be worthy of my position and closeness to him."[22]

My impression is that any one of his female disciples would have gotten involved in the murders if he had asked them, as verified by Ruth Moorehouse, a former follower who testified in Leslie's second trial. She described how they were true believers and sexually passive, which suited Manson's purposes. He had favorites, whom he protected, in a manner of speaking. In his inimitable style of leadership, he decided who would stay home and who would go to war. It was a privilege to be chosen. It was speculated that Lynette Fromme did not intend to kill President Ford in 1975, that she staged the attempt to impress Charles Manson (whom she hadn't seen for the six years he'd been back in prison), to make up for having been excluded from the Helter Skelter of 1969.[23]

From the women's cheerful recollections of their life on the edge with Manson, it seemed to me that his madness was unequivocal, but his brainwashed "family"—certainly the seven women I met—had been actively receptive to his "revolutionary" intentions. Manson could seem saintly, his eyes glowing with cosmic insight, and he could be demonically cruel, his cruelty interpreted as teaching them yet another important lesson. He obscenely berated the young women who came to him, and treated them as disposable when not treating them as desirable, a classic double bind. Because, as he told them, everyone is perfect as they are, he didn't permit anyone to wear eyeglasses. He broke at least one woman's glasses to make his point. He violently struck at least one young woman on more than one occasion, to "discipline" her. As they obediently strove to be who Manson wanted them to be, they lost themselves in his energy, absolving themselves of personal responsibility or agency. One by one they gave him their power, the power to build them up and to knock them down. He was writing the script, and they were playing their parts in this fantastical world Manson was inventing for them.

The Santa Cruz university tutors who worked with Pat, Susan, and Leslie over the course of several years came to know the women well. They marveled at how such bright, rational women could have ever been attached to the twists of logic that had come from Manson. They thought it remarkable that the courts had found the girls to be sane. According to the judgment, the girls not only did the deed, they did it with conscious, deliberate intent. Certainly Manson and his tribe weren't the only people to believe in the inevitability of a race war in the USA. Manson was ridiculed in the press as a dangerous fool, but the Ku Klux

Klan, the Aryan Brotherhood, and other white supremacist organizations (which draw men and their families from every social status), have also predicted, for over a hundred years, that a race war is coming, and continue to do everything they can to accelerate its arrival.

Spahn Ranch has been mythologized as a sinister place by definition. Yet, until the paranoia and violence surfaced, the Manson "family" appears to have been in many ways a haven for good kids needing a safe place. In an interview, Manson said of Leslie, clearly wanting her trust, "I ain't never lied to her. She knows it. I've never told her a lie—none of those kids." He talked about his "family" as a "soul movement. This person had no place to stay and this person was lost and had no place to stay, and I didn't have no place to stay. They were nobody and I was nobody."[24]

Only in retrospect is it easy to recognize the pathological level of Manson's push to power over the young women, and men as well, and their eager acquiescence. In a 1969 interview with her lawyer Marvin Part, following her arrest but prior to the first trial, Leslie expressed Manson's hybrid spiritualism: "The trial is pre-ordained. Everything that happens is perfect. Sounds far out but it's true. *Sometimes I doubt it and get shaky*. . . . I hope I can walk out. I want to be free. But I'm not afraid to die. I think I'm an angel. Not with wings. But I believe I am one of the disciples. I can't talk the reality of it. But I can feel it."[25] At the time, Leslie may have been alone among the disciples in her fleeting acknowledgment of sometimes suffering doubt.

All of the girls who came to Manson were well prepared to serve him; before they ever met Manson they had already accrued years of practical training in the arts of femininity and service. They all had healthy figures and faces, and personalities to attract a wide choice of partners. To superficially stereotype Leslie, Pat, and Susan as I saw them on the surface some months after we first met, I would write: Leslie is the classic beauty—poised, elegant, well spoken, and vivacious; Pat is the girl-next-door beauty—natural, healthy, cheerful; Susan is the exotic beauty—soulful, sensual, a risk taker. All three, and the other "Manson girls" as well, had been successful *as girls* before they met Manson, pretty victims of (over)socialization to feminine gender scripts. Pat, Leslie, and Susan are all skilled in the domestic arts, including needlework. They, like all his women, were talented in all the skills that go into the making of a beautiful home and taking care of a man's needs.

The most conspicuous quality the women shared with one another in abundance was that they all aimed to please, which Manson exploited. To that end they maintained positive frames of mind and agreeable attitudes no matter what transpired in their lives. I was impressed that none of the women ever spoke against their prosecutor, Vincent Bugliosi (or his then-assistant, Stephen Kay), who had mythicized them as monsters with his book, TV movie, and speaking tours. They took a long view of things. They were initially distressed at Bugliosi's sensational and frequently false portrayals of them, but emerged undismayed because they had faith that, in the end, karma would balance everything out.

Facing the Truth

To separate from Manson, the women would have to separate from every reason they were in prison. They would have to admit to an unspeakably huge mistake, a grievous error committed utterly in vain, shameful beyond expression, destructive to its core. There is no language that doesn't somehow trivialize the somber enormity of the murders, and what it has been for their own and especially the victims' families, and for themselves. Had they been executed as expected, they would have gone back to dust with their beliefs intact. As they saw it for the first several years of their incarceration, if they hadn't been caught they would have triggered the race war that guaranteed justice to black people. Early in our association I sensed that they were consoled with the belief that they were right for having at least tried.

With the enemy of unrelenting time in which to face their memories, to run them and rerun them again and again in their minds, to be forced into reflection, to be faced by those who love the sinner and hate the sin, each of the women had to live, year after year, through a terrifying awakening—from believing that Manson was a god and that they'd done the right thing, to recognizing the profound wrongness of their actions and, therefore, the emptiness of Manson's authority and the magnitude of their guilt. Their acceptance of their crimes was finally transformed into immense regret as their perspectives on life gradually normalized.

With more teachers and other visitors coming to their unit over the years, they met a wide range of people who challenged different facets of Manson's beliefs and methods. The violence was de facto condemned. Some of their tutors were feminists who challenged their obeisance to a male guru. Another was an African-American scholar who protested the racist flaws in Manson's thinking about race wars. In the absence of Manson's authoritarian voice, each woman in her own time and way, under influences of her own choosing to a certain extent, and independent of everyone, began to reveal ambivalence. After a few years when they had drifted even from one another, they were united in their rejection of Manson's omniscient power over them. Their rational minds and consciences came to the fore, which brought grief to them and relief to others.

The media were extraordinarily aggressive in the Manson case. Early on, Susan's first lawyer wrote a book over a weekend, based on his initial interview with her. It was inappropriately published before the first trial started, and contained her false confession.[26] Only much later did it come to light that she was, at that time, taking responsibility for crimes she didn't commit. Some speculated that she told fictions to cellmates, correspondents, lawyers, and jury because she was subconsciously eager to be convicted, to do penance. The book threatened the trial even before Susan had testified before the grand jury. After months in jail, away from Charlie, she had agreed to testify because, in exchange, she was promised a life sentence instead of the death penalty. She was as truthful as she knew how to be in her testimony before the grand jury. In the trial, however, she was in Manson's presence and once again under his spell. No longer afraid of the gas chamber, she repudiated her grand jury testimony. Again she attempted to exonerate Manson with false boasts; her grand jury testimony was voided, and nothing would save her (or Pat or Leslie) from a death sentence.

In the trial, Susan claimed to be the one to have killed Sharon Tate and her almost-born child, and to have felt a mystical connection to her victims. In fact, as he later confessed (though he had gone along with Susan's story in his trial), it was Charles "Tex" Watson who killed Tate, and all the others: "I was the one who'd stabbed that beautiful blond (pregnant) actress, stabbed her again and again, over and over, stabbed her because Charlie told me to."[27] Susan had also claimed to have been involved in both nights of murder, even though she was not present for the LaBianca killings.

To my knowledge, Susan was the only one of the women who had a police record prior to meeting Manson, and as a young rebel she enjoyed being a fledgling outlaw. As a teenager she'd lost her mother to cancer. She'd been a Girl Scout and had sung with the church choir, but she'd also shoplifted as a kid, worked as a topless dancer, and done some teenage robbing and car thievery, for which she had served brief jail time.[28] Not until she met Manson was she in touch with murder, first at Gary Hinman's, and then at the Tate house. She was perceived by other followers as most wanting to be seen as the female Manson, his mirror—a desire many of them shared.

Susan had abandoned her Manson-devotee posture entirely by the time, in the late 1970s, that she was transferred to the main prison, where she became an active member of the church. For years she has been clear that she did not in fact engage in killing rituals of the kind she described in her testimony. The lore notwithstanding, not one of the women was successful as a killer. In every case Charles Watson, the clean-cut college kid from Texas, had come to their aid in brutally ending others' lives. Despite their commitment to Manson, they were incompetent and apparently terrified at the scenes of the crimes, as any "good girl" would have been in such a situation.

Doing School

In the presence of outsiders who came to see them when they were still on the old death row, none of the three women was ever disrespectful toward another. Their harmonious rapport was in some ways a façade built on their mutual adherence to Manson, now a tenuous link because he really was not there anymore. While with Manson, the three women and others had, in effect, been a harem, lumped together as his girls. After some time in prison they were no longer the "Manson girls," but three very different young women, each coming to terms with her own distinct self and circumstances apart from their shared experiences, guilt, and interminable incarceration. At the same time, they were mutually interdependent on one another for the company of humans who could truly understand the situation.

The congenial SSU staff was not opposed to our having fun during our schooltime and visits, and music was often a focal point—singing, playing tapes, talking about music. They sang a great close-harmony trio rendition of "Crying Time," and a rousing version of "Big Red Balloon," written by Jean, their friend and prison mate when they first arrived. Occasionally, performers came in to give them private concerts, standing in the passage in front of the solitary cells with open bars. Singer-songwriters, starting with Cris Williamson, Holly Near, and Country Joe McDonald, came in and sang their hearts out. Judy Grahn, a poet of consequence, also inspired and energized them, as did others. These experiences had deep effects on the women, as did lively encounters with tutors such as Paul Krassner, a humorist and author of note with a fascination for the ways that certain historical events are linked. Prior to his work in the prison, he had spent time as a journalist in the company of Lynette Fromme, Sandra Good, and other women involved with Manson, talking about conspiracy theories.

Men like Country Joe, Paul, and others did workshops in the Special Security Unit. Bill Barlow did one on the history of the blues; Bill Moore on African-American history; Rory White on art history; and Michael Rotkin on politics. Other dynamic, nonsexist men introduced the women to relevant new information, literature, music, and political perspectives—introducing them at the same time to new kinds of men. The women who tutored were likewise progressive: Catherine Cusic, Debra Miller, Jeanne Gallick, and Nancy Stoller were program co-coordinators and instructors who arranged workshops in psychology, philosophy, literature, and medical sociology. Candace Falk gave a workshop in economics, Tanya Nieman in law, Cheryl Anderson in midwifery. Pat and Susan and Leslie absorbed new ways of thinking of women's lives in broadened contexts.

The young women in SSU also had the benefit of some enlightened staff, including the young guard John Ellis. One day at the women's request, while we drank our cold grape Tang, he stood in the doorway to our schoolroom and, in his lush, grand tenor voice, sang "Ebb Tide"; there wasn't a dry eye in the cell. The women reported that some days the guards would arrive at their unit in the morning singing or whistling, not typical prison guard behavior. Most of their guards—men and women; black, brown, and white; young and old—enjoyed their work.

It was part of their job to chat with the women about ordinary experience, to help keep them alert to the world beyond their reach, to keep them attuned to the realities of ordinary working-class lives. It was thought that regular interaction would help the women gain and retain their sanity, which proved true. The women knew details of their guards' marriages and kids, their money problems, what they did on vacation. Everyone knew about one another's lives.

When it was just the two of us teaching in SSU, Jeanne and I sought ways to make the hours in school memorable both within and during breaks from academic work. On one hot day, when no one could concentrate on the text, we spent an hour looking through a book of art by Escher. They thought it was spooky and depressing. I expressed surprise that, after what they'd been through, this merely weird art, flat on the page despite illusions otherwise, would repel them or affect them negatively. But they didn't like anything that struck them as "strange." This led to a discussion that revealed some of the psychological complications of their crimes—their denial and detachment at that early stage from the violence itself. None of them seemed to have any taste for bloodshed at all. It was as if they hadn't been there. They could look at it only in metaphorical and metaphysical terms, as the dance of life and death.

After the women had talked a while about how they viewed the crimes, the guard in the doorway asked me nervously, with pointed intent, "Now, are you teaching them, or are they teaching you?" He didn't want them talking about the crimes, certainly not in such eerily detached, mystical ways. I appreciated their talk because I wanted to understand it. I wondered for a time if they had actually been involved in the murders at all, if the whole thing was someone else's doing, and the women were sacrificing themselves as martyrs to their faith in Charles Manson. In effect, that *is* what happened, even though they *were* physically present and tried very hard to be good soldiers.

Our casual conversations were often banal. We talked, for example, about cows, whose nearby presence was known from the ever-present noxious odor in the still, hot air. This led to talk about why prisons are so isolated from other human communities, the "lock 'em up, but not in my backyard" syndrome. (With the 1980s–1990s growth of the prison-industrial complex and privatization of some new prisons, many cities are now putting out the welcome mat.) Like most people, Leslie and the others believed in prisons, that there had to be someplace for people who are known to be dangerous. They knew themselves *not* to be dangerous, but they never expressed the feeling that they shouldn't be in prison. With equanimity they accepted the extraordinary restrictions under which they had to live indefinitely. When we first met, we talked about the ambiguity of their legal status, now that the death penalty was lifted. They didn't know if they'd be returned to court for resentencing, or automatically commuted to life in prison (with the possibility of eventual parole). The latter is what occurred.

Doing Prison Positively

In a typical day, without visitors, the women passed the twenty-three hours in their cells by reading, doing needlework, meditating, thinking, writing, cleaning their six-foot-by-nine-foot spaces, talking with one another, listening to the radio, trading gossip with the guards, and trying to sleep. They longed for diverse human company. As time went on, every six months or so they were escorted from their unit to the dentist's office in the medical building. This was an important event, because it was the only time they got to visit the main prison. Their escorted walks across the prison grounds brought them into fleeting touch with the larger prison society from which they were segregated. Unless they were lucky enough to have a guard who would relax the rules, they couldn't touch hands or communicate verbally with other prisoners who passed by, but they could signal recognition to women they had met in the L.A. jail during their trial. They could make eye contact with other women. They could expand their view of the world in which they were incarcerated. With guard escorts willing to look the other way, they took chances by communicating with women who passed by, with quick whisperings or the brush of fingertips—passing overtures of friendship.

From their cells after dark, Leslie, Pat, and Susan could see through the bars on their windows, beyond the fences that contained their unit, across the yard, and through the barred windows of the Psychiatric Treatment Unit. They gossiped about the PTU women as if they knew them: there was the woman they called the Roadrunner, who furiously paced up and down the hallway every night, and Bald Lady, who always wore a white towel wrapped around her head. On hot nights, when the lights were out but the barred windows were open, they would fall into silence and listen to the PTU voices wafting across the yard. They would match voices with women they'd named from a distance through the windows at night, and would refer to them in friendly terms as if they were pals.

By day they liked to watch out the window for the women from the main prison who were assigned to yard duty near the Special Security Unit. They looked as if they were having a good time riding around on the mower-tractor. To Pat, Leslie, and Susan, the grounds outside their windows looked like the free world. Within a year, two yard women in succession were caught trying to communicate with the "girls" while mowing nearby. As penalty, each was fired from her coveted job and sent to rack.

Like most prisoners, SSU women quickly learned to accept the punitive exigencies of prison life. In my observation, it takes a spiritually evolved or highly self-disciplined person to survive even one year in prison with a positive attitude. In contrast to the frequently negative ambience of the prison at large, Pat, Leslie, and Susan were consistently enthusiastic about life. They were committed vegetarians who obtained permission for a while to order health food through the mail. They grew their own vegetables from mail-order seeds, in the strip of stone-clotted dirt that was their yard. When permitted, one at a time for an hour, they would sit in the sun in the narrow passage between their brick hut and the high, chain-linked double fences, and encourage their plants to grow while reading, doing yoga or needlework, or dreaming—all under the omnipresent eyes of the guards.

Within the main prison were many guards who were antagonistic toward the more than six hundred prisoners, and with the authority of the state to back them they often used cruel methods to control the women. But in the Special Security Unit, with only a few very compliant women to watch over, and having been selected for their post in part for their more humane and mature approach to maintaining order, their guards, as I observed them, were almost invariably kind human beings. The normal problems of prison culture simply didn't exist in their small and very separate space.

Sometimes the women would have gifts for the outsiders, often creative ones: music, art, or embroidery. One of my favorite gifts was an exquisite dried leaf from Leslie, which I used as a bookmark. It had blown into their yard. Sometimes the outsiders would bring treats, such as the time on Leslie's birthday when, having asked her what she most missed from the free world, she laughingly said, as she often did, "A banana split." This was an in-joke: one day during a visit long before, in addition to the usual grape Tang, the women had served pastries and Swiss cheese, which, given normal prison diet, was amazing. "Where did you *get* this food?" I had asked, and they rolled their eyes toward the staff office. I had then asked them, as I always did, if they needed anything, meaning medical or dental attention, or envelopes, or a sweater . . . and they all cried out in unison, *"A banana split!"*

Wishing for a banana split in prison is akin to wishing to win the lottery. But on this day, unbeknownst to Leslie or the other women or the guards, when our time was up and Jeanne and I had said our usual good-byes, we drove immediately to town (twenty miles or so down the road). We got all the ingredients and put the ice cream and Cool Whip on ice in a cooler. It worked just so-so on the long, hot drive back to the prison in heavy traffic. We worried. It was against the rules for us to be taking food into the Special Security Unit. It was also against the rules for us to go (or return) to the unit without an authorization slip. The authorities who could give permission would be gone for the day, and the ice cream would soon be melting. . . . Yet, when we got back, every guard at every stop let us through quickly when we told (and showed) them what we were doing. All were amazed and some were amused at our chutzpah. These men did not normally go out of their way to accommodate prisoners—or outsiders who sought to ease the strain of incarceration. To the contrary. But the attitude toward the women in SSU seemed to be that, given the extraordinary restrictions on their lives, and given their reputations as being unfailingly cheerful and cooperative, it seemed okay to bend the rules in this case. Certainly banana splits weren't a threat to prison security.

The SSU guards knew from relayed reports what we were up to by the time we arrived back at their door. They let us in quietly with conspiratorial grins on their faces. They did not announce us to the women. They agreed that, if they haggled over rules, the ice cream would melt. One guard was particularly helpful. He was an older man with grandchildren, and he said very earnestly that they were good girls and he was happy to bend the rules for them.

The guards helped us slice bananas in half lengthwise and put two halves in each brightly colored plastic boat dish. Then we added three scoops of ice cream (vanilla, chocolate, and strawberry), topped with chocolate, caramel, strawberry, and pineapple sauces. Finally we topped it with coconut, chopped nuts, whipped cream, and maraschino cherries. Banana splits for everyone.

Because Leslie had just turned twenty-two, her banana split held a lit candle. The party got even better when several other staff unexpectedly arrived, with found-object gifts, to wish her a happy birthday. Word had gotten out through the checkpoint guards. The gathering was festive, very high energy (partly from all the sugar), and Leslie, Pat, and Susan were ecstatic. We all were. We gorged on the banana splits, and felt cheerfully ill afterward. I said that I hadn't eaten one since I was a teenager when I had worked at two soda jerk jobs—one at an ice cream–hamburger joint and the other in the drugstore, in our railroad town in the Montana badlands. I'd forgotten how good they were. The guards agreed.

For months after that, whenever I'd ask what anybody needed or wanted, banana splits would still be the reply and we would all laugh. It was their code for every seemingly unfulfillable but irrepressible dream.

On that day I was wearing a green crystal-prism necklace that was given to me by a friend in Eritrea, East Africa, where I'd worked with the Peace Corps and where my fourth child was born. I gave it to Leslie and she cherished the rainbows it brought to her cell when she hung it over her small, barred window, and the way it extended her space. It brought color and motion to a drab, still enclosure. She wore it around her neck intermittently for years. Later, in a box from home, she received another crystal for her window. Like anything sent in or out, including letters, it had to first pass the scrutiny of the prison censors. While she waited for them to give it to her, she wrote a seriocomic plea to the censors to hurry, explaining what a prism can be to someone imprisoned.

Yes, I said Prism in Prison

Prying through my present from home,
you persist on being persnickety.
I suppose that's your prerogative.
After all, that's your position, Dear Censor.

> *But in perspective, prisms in prison are permissible.*
> *No more impractical than pomegranates in Pittsburgh.*
>
> *Hanging amid the steel bars on my cell window*
> *for an hour each day the dingy walls dance*
> *and spin with city lights.*
> *Red, yellow, green, blue, purple, orange*
> *Vivid rare rainbows reminding me*
> *never to forget my pot of gold.*
>
> *Perhaps I'm being presumptuous in*
> *thinking you could appreciate the*
> *small crystal's permeations.*
> *Don't prick me with your procedures.*
> *Please, permit my prism to free me from this prison.*

The three women, all artistically talented, were generous gift givers. For example, Susan hand-sewed an elaborate burgundy velvet riding coat with lavish embroidery for her friend and teacher, Jaki, using fabric remnants supplied by the prison occupational therapist. I was the recipient of beautifully strung beads, books of value to them (notably *Be Here Now*, by Baba Ram Dass), embroidered garments, and the complete collection of Charles Manson's song lyrics. The lyrics were neatly typed, with whimsical colored pencil illustrations by Leslie. They were bound in an exquisite black, burgundy, pink, and white cover, cleverly handmade from cardboard covered with scraps of velvet, taffeta, satin, and lace. My unease at possessing anything so intimately connected to Manson was overcome by the women's pleasure in my response to their handiwork.

Leslie and Pat's final project as "Manson girls" in the early 1970s, was a large, stunning embroidered dragon, a layered, multidimensional riot of bold colors and form in motion, minute stitches of thread and human hair woven into a deeply textured, frighteningly charismatic creature signifying Manson himself. When they passed the dragon along to an outside friend it was a way of parting once and for all with the guru, although loyalties did not dissolve so cleanly, clearly, wholly, or simultaneously.

In the mid- to late 1970s, starting with Leslie, the women were transferred one by one to the psychiatric unit for a brief period and then to the secure main-prison "cottages," where they had many other women to interact with and relatively more choices for how to occupy their time. Finally, each of the women was able to embark on her own path, entering this transition to the real world of the prison after many years in isolation. One of the important reasons they enjoyed our school while they were still in the Special Security Unit was that it got them out of their cells and into their schoolroom cell. Just that much movement, maybe fifteen steps, expanded their horizons. The physical restriction had the inevitable effect of restricting their knowledge of the world. As another prisoner friend once said, "In prison you forget the art of the possible." Conversely, some women can learn a sustained patience unfathomable to the frantic pace of most lives in the "free" world, and often difficult for visitors to comprehend when they witness the stressful conditions of prison. Leslie in particular has demonstrated an ability to remain still within herself, to wait and watch, to avoid conflict or confrontation, to be always ready to be useful without trying to make it happen every moment. The Buddhist influence is pronounced in her practice of patience.

An important part of Leslie's grounding was the loyalty of her mother, Jane, who visited her daughter in jail or prison almost every week for almost three decades. In 1998 Jane's health began deteriorating. Now in her eighties, she has since needed to limit her visits. I met Leslie's mother when she arrived at the Special Security Unit one day in 1972 for a visit with her daughter. She was then in her early fifties; she was (and still is) beautiful, then prematurely white-haired with a young face, strong posture. She exuded warmth. I learned that she'd been studying Spanish in preparation for a trip to Mexico. When Leslie introduced us I wanted to say, "You must be so proud of your daughter!" because I knew Leslie as a talented young woman and a good student, and the staff clearly respected her. I didn't, but as I observed them greet each other, I saw Leslie's mother's respect. Jane was family, the real thing—permanent, stable, and full of heart, no matter what—and she didn't need anyone to tell her all the reasons she could be proud of her daughter.

Leslie's father has also been unconditionally loyal to Leslie, and none of her siblings abandoned her. In 1977, speaking of her parents' unconditional love and loyalty, Leslie voiced concern that they "worried that somehow I ended up here because of something they did or didn't do. None of it is their fault."[29]

More about Susan

For years Susan and I exchanged only occasional holiday greetings and messages via our mutual friend, Rory. Since the mid-1990s we've been corresponding again, and I'm on the mailing list for her ministry newsletter, in which she gives witness to her faith and describes changes in the prison environment and problems the women are suffering.

It was clear to me from the outset that black-haired, sparkling brown-eyed, olive-skinned Susan Atkins, age twenty at the time of the crimes, had served Manson with unconditional devotion. Linda Kasabian, who was with Tex, Pat, and Susan at the Tate murders, testified that the experience was unreal; she couldn't believe it was happening at the time and couldn't believe afterward that it had happened.[30] Linda stated that, before anyone was killed, she had begged Susan to make it stop, perhaps perceiving her to have that power. But Susan said, "No, I can't. It's too late. I've lost my mind." As Susan later put it, "I was brainwashed . . . into believing that death was an illusion. . . . I was deceived. Charlie was deceived, everyone involved with the whole thing was deceived into believing what we were doing was right. . . . Everything I said was so bizarre."[31]

For all her bravado, and although Manson and the media gave her a wild reputation by linking her to the Beatles song "Sexy Sadie," I found her to be a sensitive, mystical woman on a spiritual quest. She had a transparent need to be connected with others. I could imagine her as a wild woman as well, but she tried to please everyone, and she was very pleasing indeed.

Susan reveals a quality of fierce strength behind her gentle demeanor. Susan's friend Rory sculpted a dramatic bust of her as he saw her: young, beautiful, with a strong and noble face that, in the sculpture, is staring in fascination at her own outstretched "hand," which is an eagle's claw. Rory was depicting how she discovered in herself the power for terrible destruction, and was in awe of it. Yet over the years, as the truth came out about the murders, it seemed that Susan had much less talent for destruction than she had wanted us to believe when she was still seeking Manson's approval.

In the early 1970s Susan, as a prison journalist, conducted an interview with me, which was published in *The Clarion,* the prison newspaper. She was asking about alternatives to prisons, which I advocated. She pointedly wanted to know what I would do with perpetrators of violence. I conceded that incarceration of some form was essential for those who could be reasonably assumed to be dangerous to specific individuals or to the public at large. She didn't seem to disagree, but she also didn't identify herself as dangerous. She could have told me then that she wasn't guilty of the crimes for which she'd been sentenced to death, but she didn't say that. And she didn't react when I implicitly held her up as an exception to all those women prisoners—the vast majority—who in my view would be suitable for community-based alternatives to prison. At the time I believed she had committed the crimes of which she was convicted.

In 1977, Susan published an engaging autobiography detailing her experience with Manson, her conversion to Christianity, and her prison experience (*Child of Satan, Child of God*), with proceeds going to support programs for reformed street girls in New Orleans. In this book she described her experience of the university tutorials we brought in, and especially women's studies, which gave her incentive to examine

> . . . the male oppression I had so willingly walked into in my middle teen years and had violently sealed in my relationships with Charlie and others in the family. For the first time, I got a view of my sexual degradation, for example. I began to glimpse how I had allowed myself to be domineered in the most primitive fashion by other people. In my drive for freedom, I had entered into the worst bondage possible.[32]

Susan went her own way until, in her transition away from Manson, she found deliverance in Jesus, in 1974. She began telling me in letters and visits that she was praying for me. I was impatient with her desire for me to get "saved," and we drifted in different directions. At the time, I was concerned that she still wasn't thinking for herself. Her beatific expression as a new Christian was not easily distinguished from the beatific expressions all the girls wore while still devoted to Manson. But decades later, Susan remains a loving, devoted Christian.

It's my impression that Susan made a smooth transition to the main prison, where she developed the art of instrument making, wrote religious songs, and ministered to other women through her music. In 1990 she married a man described to me by mutual friends as a "good man," and "a very regular guy." They met through her religious community and he has become a lawyer since they met. Susan has become in every way a good woman, cloistered within the "stone sanctuary" of the prison. She is watched over by her husband from the outside and all those who welcome her ministry from behind the walls.

About Pat

Patricia Krenwinkel, age twenty-one when she was arrested, was, in some important ways, Manson's most valued soldier. Her parents had divorced when she was seventeen, but before that, like Leslie, Pat had had an apparently all-American upbringing in southern California. Like Susan and Leslie, Pat had sung in the church choir, and as a girl she had belonged to Bluebirds, Camp Fire girls, Job's Daughters, and even the Audubon Society. She liked animals, she received good grades, and was, as her father described her in court, "an exceedingly normal child."[33] Typically, it was normal, idealistic young people, often high achievers, who joined the counterculture. After one semester of college in Alabama she dropped out and returned to California to join the 1960s search for enlightenment. She met Manson five months following his parole in 1967. He was visiting at the home of her half sister, who, like so many, had extended hospitality to the stranger. Pat came upon him playing his guitar and felt instantly drawn to him.

As he had already done with Mary and Lynette, Manson gave Pat the gift of seeing herself in a wholly new and positive light, and for that she was deeply devoted to him. Also with Charles Manson she had experienced her first meaningful sexual intimacy. With Manson she felt beautiful. Like so many of the girls, as soon as she met him, she went off with him. She deserted her car in a parking lot to get on the bus with him. She left her job, her last paycheck, her possessions, her family, her identity—the third of the many young girls who would make similar ruptures. Her father was convinced she was hypnotized.[34]

Pat impressed me as having both a girl-next-door youthful wholesomeness and a worldly-wise toughness. Manson was infatuated with Pat, who was readily persuaded of Manson's godlike powers because he was key to her newfound self-identity. Pat had been perceived by codefendants as brave (though inefficient) in helping to start Helter Skelter, the revolution. She did briefly waver in her belief in the correctness of Manson's strategy; as she said to Leslie when she returned home to the Spahn Ranch following the murders at the Tate residence, "the people seemed very young and it didn't seem right."[35] She was very upset. But her loyalty was unbroken.

Pat continued for several years to keep Manson's photo in her cell. Even after she relinquished her attachment and began re-forming her worldview and sense of self, his image seemed to remind her not of her crimes, but of her strengths.

With time, taking incremental steps, Pat did look far beyond Manson, and confronted what she'd done. In the main prison she enrolled in university courses in earnest, earned a B.A., made herself useful to others, and got a new lease on life. For decades now, that new life has not included Manson. From the posture of post–middle age and the benefit of hindsight, she sees clearly the ways he negatively, fatally manipulated her own and everyone else's feelings and actions.

Her letters to me are those of a poetic, active, smart, nature-conscious, good-hearted woman who suffers the anguished burden of interminable guilt. Like Leslie, she has worked very hard to be of service to the women with whom she is confined, and she is active in numerous organizations. She coordinates the taping of books for the visually impaired.

Until recently Pat had little contact with her mother, who lived far away and was ill for many years. Now in her eighties, Pat's mother recently returned to California, and she and Pat enjoy regular visits.

Through the years Pat has remained close with her father, who worked nearby as an insurance agent. He made regular visits to see his daughter, and did what he could to ease her situation. Soon after I began teaching in SSU, the prison officials agreed that we could conduct our tutorials in a bare, unoccupied cell, six feet by nine. Pat's father arranged for the concrete cell floor to be covered with padding and a carpet. To go with the new shag rug, which was a burnt-sand color, the women made pillows with color-coordinated slipcovers. Now we could all comfortably sit cross-legged in a circle on the floor, with all our books and supplies filling the small circle of space at our center.

Reunions and Separations

In the second year of our work in SSU, Pat, Leslie, and Susan acquired two new prison mates, Catherine "Gypsy" Share and Mary Brunner. Mary had earlier been charged in the Hinman murder, but was given immunity in exchange for her testimony. This time she and Gypsy had been convicted of attempted robbery of a gun store, part of a foiled plan to help Manson escape from prison. The robbery failed and no one was injured. The two women were placed in CIW's SSU with the others because of their shared association with Manson, and a presumed need for extraordinary security.

When Gypsy and Mary joined our little school group, casual conversations returned to Charles Manson, who had been at the center of their shared universe. They now viewed him with radically different degrees of reverence or rejection, but their reunion within the prison had resonance for their memories of times at the ranch on the desert when no one doubted. They had felt themselves among the chosen few, and had kissed Manson's feet. He had taught them to be prepared to die long before they were instructed to kill. Now they just sang his songs, all five harmonizing on melancholy ballads and upbeat tunes. One particularly catchy yet mournful melody with lyrical poignance, given their circumstances, was "(Your) Home Is Where You're Happy."

> *Your home is where you're happy,*
> *It's not where you're not free.*
> *Your home is where you can be what you are*
> *'Cause you were just born to be.*[36]

Psychiatrists like to use the expressions *folie à deux*, *folie à ménage*, or *folie à famille* to identify what's happening when two or more people share the same mad, crazy delusions, or when someone adopts or participates in another's delusion. At Leslie's second trial, psychologists debated as to whether the Manson "family" suffered from this group madness. All five of these women, and many others over a few years, had been taken in by Manson, believing themselves to be among the chosen few. Without realizing it in time to prevent disaster, they had entered into the darkest realms of their own souls when they gave themselves to him. But when I would look at them, within the circle on the floor in our classroom cell, on the surface I saw a sorority scene: five attractive, intelligent young women, loving and kind, conscientiously tending to their homework, sharing a bond that will forever exclude anyone unable to understand Manson's appeal.

I watched their selective retrieval of only the most positive memories, and their celebration of those joyful times before the crimes. I was glad that they could feel, even momentarily, at home with each other within their cold, dreary, sterile prison. But I also knew—as did they—that as individuals they were quietly disintegrating as believers and, therefore, as a "family." Life at Spahn Ranch was tainted now, irrevocably. Their past together would be forever the enemy of their present and future lives. Spahn Ranch itself had burned to the ground in an early 1970s fire caused by a major windstorm, an event everyone noted was laden with symbolism. Leslie, Susan, and Pat were each moving away from a life and a set of beliefs and associations that had provided the highest and lowest moments of their lives.

As Leslie began separating from Manson and the others in the early 1970s, so did she begin to punish herself with severe anorexia. At the time, there was little understanding of this disease. It had not yet been widely recognized as an illness suffered primarily by young women who are oversocialized to be unrealistically thin, or who, as a consequence of abuse, are trying to disappear. Many fashion models, in particular, looked like starving casualties of war, but this was the standard of femininity to which girls aspired, and still do, to the detriment of their health. In Leslie's case, it did not seem that she was striving to be attractive; it appeared that she wanted to fade away, as a self-punishment, rather than have to live with the trauma that came with confronting her guilt.

Within a few years, when she began to heal and was eating again, she engaged in meditation. Leslie's aspirations had never been materialistic, and by the early 1980s she had grown into a spiritually mature person. Her positive spirit has suffered setbacks after parole hearings that have seemed to be designed more to humiliate her than to decide on her suitability for parole. But always she has retrieved herself and gratefully discovered, step by step, that her mind and spirit haven't been forever destroyed by her cult experience.

Gypsy and Mary were released on parole from CIW within a few years of their arrival. Whereas Gypsy was extroverted and vivacious, Mary, who was tall, fair, and quietly attractive, was shy and reflective. She made a sharp break from Manson. She wrote to me, just before her release, of her fantasy of playing a flute again. I was living in Los Angeles at the time, where a helpful radio disc jockey asked on air for a donation of a flute for a woman coming out of prison. Within a day one was delivered to me. When she was released, Mary came to visit me in Echo Park and to pick up her flute. She held it in her hands, studied it, walked around my apartment with it, tears running down her face, and finally started to play. We spent the afternoon playing flute and piano duets. She found a place far away where she could start her life over—working, raising her son, and playing her flute. Last I heard, she had advanced her education and she and her son were doing well.

Gypsy's first years of parole were more eventful, involving continued identification with Manson, clandestine activity, and a husband in prison. Many years later I saw her on television, as a member of a religious choir. She was still strikingly beautiful, her thick black hair no longer cascading but still glistening, her dark eyes flashing. I learned that she eventually settled down, is now using her musical talent to sing gospel music, and has recovered her self and transferred her faith to the Lord, yet another of Manson's ex-followers, after Susan Atkins and Charles "Tex" Watson, to be converted to evangelical Christianity, where their capacity for unquestioning faith found a home.

With Gypsy's and Mary's departures on parole, and Leslie's, Pat's, and Susan's transfers to the main prison—all in the mid- to late 1970s—the era of the "Manson girls" had come to a close. For the three who remained incarcerated in the California prison, memories of bygone days were rapidly superseded by the imperatives of building a life within the prison.

Innocence

A quality of recovered innocence is still very evident in Leslie, now an older woman. It is not the innocence of naïveté or youth, although she appears ten years younger than her age of fifty plus. It's the innocence of someone who has lived, is aware of the baser side of the human species, is compassionate toward suffering, but who has herself never intentionally caused harm. It's a quality of open, fundamental fairness that appears at first gaze to be uncomplicated by regrets. Leslie's face also sometimes shows, however, an expression of deep sorrow—the intimate knowledge of the worst harm one can commit. Convergences of innocence and sorrow surface in her face and in her voice, each informing the other.

With Anne Near, I reflected on the ways Leslie made bad choices as a kid, as so many of us do, though with lesser consequences. The culpability we share as adults relates more generally to our complicity in harmful actions by the state. We collude with our silence.

> *KF: Her life was incredibly corrupted by the poison, by the deed, by the place in which she found herself, and to which she literally took herself. We all have a choice as to whether, or how, we participate in the evil in the world if we recognize it for what it is. We have the right to resist the evil perpetrated by authorities in the guise of goodness and superiority. Everything in "America" has to be the best. When you travel abroad, the "best of America" has been imported there. The USA is the best. But it's an illusion, a very big one.*
>
> *ANNE: One might call this illusion, indulgently, patriotism, until one recognizes that the illusion has a negative side. We are equally sure that we could never do those things we all agree are evil. We could never find ourselves in the position of the German people, doing what they did to an integral part of their own population, and to other peoples in Europe. No. And we certainly do not believe that our Central Intelligence Agency is teaching the techniques of torture and surveillance to certain inimicable forces in other countries.*
>
> *KF: Even though the evidence is out. Published all the time. In the name of the citizenry—in our name—a lot of terrible things are done. Most of us, most of the time, are not recognizing our choices, our rights of refusal to participate. We choose to not know, to not confront our share in the evil by virtue*

of our silences. Most of us most of the time abdicate our right to choose and resist. We give away our right to choose before realizing or becoming informed about our choices, and eventually, periodically, we have to struggle to reclaim that right.

As a teenager Leslie made a conscious decision to go on the road. She and her boyfriend had broken up. She'd completed legal secretarial school. She was ready for a new life, a good life, a life with choices that didn't promise social stability or material security, but something more meaningful. In the course of her travels she made the decision to abdicate the choice of a middle-class life of the kind to which her parents had aspired and had achieved. She abdicated the ability to choose. As it seemed to me in 1981, when she had already served about twelve years:

KF: She gave it away, her brain, her life, and didn't catch herself in time to avert the killings. She let it go as if she had no idea what her mind was worth, how valuable it was. Leslie gave it away, and that was her first sin: needing herself so much and knowing so little of what she was giving away. That is the sin that we all—

ANNE: —participate in. And yet heinous deeds in which we all participate don't have the same sort of presence as Leslie's crime.

KF: Yes. Her burden is so defined, whereas most inflicted harms are more ambiguous and unseen. The things of which we're guilty, by commission or omission, are so ambiguous we don't always have a name for them. We don't often describe our transgressions to one another or engage in self-criticism or shaming ceremonies before our communities. In Western cultures if we're ashamed we put it out of sight.

ANNE: And society has no vested interest in exposing all the shameful deeds of major shares of the citizenry.

KF: Because the deeds are so common and so much a product of what we have been taught to do. There was no perceptible reason why Leslie in particular should have gotten involved with murder, no simple reason, unless we fall back on deterministic bad-seed theories, which still wouldn't account for the anomaly factor: it was her one and only serious offense against law or society.

The crime was utterly out of character for Leslie and the others. There was no predicting that her involvement with Manson and his friends would include destroying lives. Risks of the kind they took—roaming, hitchhiking, dropping acid, having sex, moving in with virtual strangers, finding soul mates out of the blue, seeking gurus—were commonplace in the 1960s. What happened to Leslie, Pat, Susan, Catherine, Mary, Lynette, Sandra, and so many others could have happened to any trusting young woman who was on the road in those times, on a quest for enlightenment and a strong man to lead the way.

School photo of Leslie at age seven.

Leslie as a young adolescent.

Leslie as high school homecoming princess, about sixteen years old.

From Leslie's televised interview with Barbara Walters in 1977, just before her second trial. Photo by Rick Meyer for the Los Angeles Times.

Leslie at the Pacific Ocean while on bail in 1978.

Leslie at Karlene Faith's home while on bail in 1978, age twenty-nine.

Photo taken in prison in 1982.

Leslie in the prison yard in 1997, at age forty-eight.

Five

A NEW TRIAL

AFTER SEVEN YEARS IN PRISON, much of it in segregation, Leslie was granted a retrial by the California Court of Appeals. Because her attorney had disappeared, she should have been granted an immediate mistrial; thus the basis for appeal. In 1976 the court of appeals threw out her first conviction and requested a new trial for Leslie, for early 1977.

This window of hope was the result of the assiduous work of her lawyer Max Keith. Keith first met Leslie at the conclusion of the first trial, when he was brought in at the end without time to prepare; he gave the closing arguments on Leslie's behalf and saw her through the death-penalty phase of the trial. He did as well as anyone could have, but at the time Leslie was not cooperating. Now he was back, well informed, with a commitment to reopen the case; the grounds of her defense would be "diminished capacity." For the first time, she would be tried without her codefendants. In the technical realm of the law she had a clean slate: she was not yet guilty because she had not yet received a proper defense.

In late 1976 Leslie was transferred from CIW, sixty miles east of Los Angeles, to an isolation cell in the Sybil Brand jail in the city, to await and then attend trial, and to await resentencing. I was allowed regular twenty-minute visits with her over the course of many months—seated in tiny facing cubicles, speaking over a phone (with our conversations monitored), with a bulletproof-glass partition separating us. We'd been acquainted for five years. We talked about the upcoming trial, her family, my children, mutual friends from the university tutorial program, books we were reading. The outcome of the trial, a headline story for the press, would radically affect the rest of her life, but she stayed calm.

The Barbara Walters Interview

Women's movements in the 1970s produced many changes, and token females were surfacing in jobs formerly closed to them. One of these changes was that, in late 1976, Barbara Walters moved from NBC to the *ABC Evening News* as the first woman in the USA to anchor a network news program. She also continued to do special programs and personal interviews. Three months after she began her new job, she scored a coup, an interview with Leslie, who, because of the impending retrial, was back in the news.

It was almost midnight in Los Angeles in January 1977, just prior to the beginning of Leslie's second trial. In the company of friends, I flipped the TV switch to ABC just in time to hear Geraldo Rivera announce that the now very famous Barbara Walters would be appearing on the show and would be presenting her recently taped interview with the very infamous Leslie Van Houten.

The show's band played Stevie Wonder's song "Isn't She Lovely" as the camera cut to Walters. Rivera introduced her as someone who had interviewed Leslie. He then summarized the crime, and explained that Leslie's conviction had been overturned and a new trial was pending. Then, with typical Rivera drama, he asked Walters, "Do you think that it's possible that Leslie Van Houten—Manson follower—will be paroled?" Rivera and Walters discussed this possibility. Under California sentencing practices in the 1970s, first-degree murder convictions commonly led to parole after ten to twelve years in prison, unless the person was deemed a clear and present danger to society. Walters pointed out that Leslie could be acquitted. If not, she speculated, her release on parole would depend on her ability to demonstrate that she had been rehabilitated.

Rivera said that it was "a chilling thought" that anyone connected with Manson could be released soon, or ever. He then played excerpts from the taped interview, after indicating that he too would be seeing it for the first time.

This was Leslie's first televised interview. It took place in the lineup room at Sybil Brand. For the first time, the nation had a close look at the woman who had outgrown the Leslie depicted six years earlier. In 1971 she had come down the hall of the court building with Pat and Susan, smiling for the cameras, always smiling and singing, obviously as unconcerned about her own fate as she was about that of her victims. In Walters's 1977 tape, the change in Leslie was striking. Her appearance was wholesome: her dark hair was turned under in a classic bob; her bangs covered the scar of the X she had cut into her forehead during the first trial in obedience to Manson. She had a calm, feminine presence on the TV screen and still looked like the homecoming princess she had been.

BARBARA WALTERS: *Tell us about Charles Manson. Did you think he was Jesus Christ? Was he your lover? Was he your friend? What was the relationship?*

LESLIE VAN HOUTEN: *I think at one point I really believed he was Jesus Christ.*

BW: *Was he a lover to the various girls who lived there?*

LVH: *Yes.*

BW: *Was he yours?*

LVH: *No. We went to bed together a couple of times but I didn't consider him a lover.*

BW: *What do you feel about him today?*

LVH: *I was a pawn in whatever his scheme was—I'm glad that I will never again have to see him.*

BW: *Do you remember the LaBianca murders?*

LVH: *Yes, I remember it. I'm not able to speak of it right now [owing to the impending trial].*

BW: Can you tell us why you think you took part?

LVH: At the time it was supposed to help people.

BW: What was supposed to help people?

LVH: The crime. It was supposed to start a revolution that would clean the souls of everyone.

BW: But murder. At the time, murder . . . Didn't that mean anything to you?

LVH: I had been taught [by Manson] that there was no such thing as death. It's hard for me to speak of it now, because I'm back to my normal way of thinking. Now I can't conceive of it, but back then death wasn't supposed to mean anything.

BW: I'm going to talk to you very straight at this point. There is a possibility that you may be paroled . . . that at the end of your trial you may be freed. There will be a great many people who will look at you and say, "This girl is a murderer. Don't be fooled by that pretty, innocent face. This is a girl who killed. It's seven years later and she wants to be let out, and she shouldn't be. She killed." What do you say to those people?

LVH: I know that there are many who feel that way, and I can understand their feelings. I feel now I will be able to go back and tell the truth, which I didn't [in the first trial] because . . . Charlie was conducting the courtroom.

BW: What do you mean?

LVH: He was telling us what to say, when to stand up, when to carve the X, when to shave our heads—every day it was a new agenda, what we should do for the day.

After playing her clips, Walters continued, speaking with her host, Geraldo Rivera:

BW: There are people who ask, "Why do you put a murderer on the air?" If you are in the news business you try not to have a point of view and try not to give a particularly sympathetic point of view. I don't know what's going to happen to this girl. And it's not up to me or to you or to any of us to make that judgment. [Talking to Leslie] is something many news reporters wanted to do and we were able to [do it] first.

Geraldo had the last word. Clearly taken with Leslie, he changed his tune:

> GR: Let people see what she's about. I mean, she's a flesh-and-blood person. Let them see what she thinks and feels, the things that motivate her. I think it's all educational and informative.

The friends who watched Geraldo with me that night were all hopeful that the interview would help bring Leslie an early release. With her open face and calm, straightforward answers to Walters's questions, she seemed to have defused the high drama associated with the Manson murders. She gave a human face to the very sane young woman she had become, effectively erasing the eerie media images of her days as a teenaged "Manson girl."

It was a turning point. From that night on, the tone of the press seemed more weighted in Leslie's favor.

• • •

During the second trial, Leslie's mother and I took time for visits with each other away from jail and prison, sometimes after one or the other of us had visited Leslie. There would be messages to carry, offering encouragement, and requests from Leslie for books and personal items. Jane prepared delicious meals for her family and friends, and we enjoyed sharing mutual tastes in classical and other music. My son Todd, then sixteen, came along on one occasion and he too was warmed by Jane, by her gentle, calm demeanor, her good food, her concern for everyone. She put us at ease.

A Death at the Jail

Several of Leslie's friends in Los Angeles took turns taking notes at the second trial to circulate among those who couldn't be in court. On some days the courtroom was packed. All of us who arrived early stood in line for hours in any weather. Before entering the courtroom we were all thoroughly searched—family members, friends, students, curiosity seekers, and the press alike.

During the testimony about Helter Skelter and the portended race war, many people of African heritage showed up. Some would wince whenever the prosecutor would use the word *nigger* in reference to Manson's racism.

One day about twenty high school students, with their teacher, entered the courtroom during Leslie's sensitive testimony about the "family's" belief in a bottomless pit. The students were stopped in their tracks, visibly shaken by what they were hearing. Leslie herself found it hard to accept that she could ever have believed anything so strange and awful.

Outside on the courthouse steps during breaks, some of the spectators got acquainted with each other. One teenage girl told me she personally identified with Leslie, and had written an essay analyzing her dreams about her. While this girl talked, radiating enthusiasm, I was reminded of how Leslie could beam with optimism in the gloomiest of situations. This was the quality that the teenager had recognized in Leslie—a deep potential for joy, completely incompatible with the crime for which she was being retried.

. . .

Unlike our hours-long face-to-face visits in the state prison, our visits in the jail were generally limited to twenty minutes. We sat facing each other in a booth with a glass partition, talking by phone, guards posted behind us. We spoke over the voices of other visitors and prisoners, who were trying to hear each other in cubicles to our left and our right—about forty of them. It was common for as many as two hundred people to visit prisoners on a given day. Many visitors were women with children or elderly people. Many came a long distance to visit a family member, and like me, would wait for hours to get in. Many were turned away.

Inside, the visiting room was crowded, hot, and noisy. People spoke tensely over their phones, in several languages, with raised voices. Through this din of voices and of doors clanging, bells ringing, children crying, and guards barking orders, Leslie and I would talk. We talked about how truth is not static, but rather a product of historic process. She would tell me why she liked certain authors, such as Lillian Hellman. She was interested in the work of Albert Camus, who said something about how intelligence in chains gains in intensity what it lacks in lucidity. Leslie herself was certainly lucid.

One evening toward the end of the visiting period a troop of guards came in and took all the visitors except me out of the building. Then they moved all the prisoners except Leslie back to their cells. A crisis had occurred at the outside gate, they explained, and all the guards were needed to respond to it. We just looked at each other, bewildered. It was eerie for the two of us to be suddenly, entirely alone in a deadly quiet room amid the rows of empty cubicles with their phones and glass partitions. Time passed slowly. Tightly locked in, with no way of knowing what was happening, we made small talk, with awareness that the guard in the control room was monitoring our words. Self-consciously, we spoke about whether we were losing or gaining weight, what we thought about the then-new "masculine" fashions (retro 1940s) in women's magazines, and which places we'd like to visit around the globe.

After an hour or so, one guard came for Leslie and another for me. When my escort and I reached the high metal gate at the entrance to the grounds I saw a dead man, an African American, lying in a massive pool of his own blood. It looked as if he had taken bullets from several angles. He appeared to be tall, slender, good-looking, and in his late twenties or early thirties. His blood had run in streams all over the sidewalk, and was already crusting. Only now could the sounds of an approaching ambulance be heard.

I stopped and asked what had happened. The guard steered me around the body and firmly led me to my car. There he answered some of my insistent questions.

He said that the dead man had been waiting a long time in the visitors' line, waiting to see his girlfriend. When they told him the visitors' quota was filled for the night, he had become furious. He refused to leave, made threats, and pulled a gun, the guard said tersely. In the ruckus he had been shot down.

The guard went on to explain why they'd kept Leslie and me in the visiting room alone. They had needed to send the visiting-room guards outside to deal with the chaos. It wasn't hard to herd the others out quickly. But Leslie was a priority (highest security) prisoner who needed a special escort to return her to her solitary basement cell. So it had been best to leave her locked with her visitor, monitored from the control room until the staff returned to their posts.

There were two questions the guard refused to answer: Why had it taken so long to call the ambulance for the man? Had the man been shot before or after the visitors had been evacuated?

No TV station reported the killing that night, and it wasn't in any of the papers the next day. So I made several phone calls to the media to see if they knew about the incident. Most were indifferent. One television station manager said he would have it investigated, but it never came to light. A black guy with a gun in his pocket being shot by jail guards is not newsworthy in a city where hundreds of people are murdered every year.

I did not speak of the incident with Leslie until she was out on bail a year later. She said, "It was barely a tiny bleep in there. The guilty officers are probably still on the streets." One of the paradoxes of jails and prisons is that it is there, in those most rule-ridden institutions of society, where the most lawless activity can take place with impunity. It is the guards who wield the frontline power. They decide if a person has broken a rule, and whether an "incident" constitutes an emergency—in which case, anything goes.

Prosecution and Defense

The trial was heavily weighted on both sides by professional experts who were brought in to testify. The implication was that they could speak better for Leslie than she could speak for herself, that their authority was crucial to finding "the truth." Leslie's family and friends gave her support in the courtroom just by being present, but she was under guard and unable to communicate with anyone directly. Important to the defense was the testimony of former Manson devotees, including Linda Kasabian, who had received immunity in 1970 for testimony that convicted Manson. When first charged with murder and conspiracy, Leslie was also offered immunity in exchange for testimony, but she refused to cooperate. Subsequently, neither the Los Angeles Police Department nor the district attorney's office would acknowledge that they had made the offer.

Leslie had been a true believer who accepted Manson's interpretations of her own experience even in the face of the death penalty. The testimony at her second trial of five other people who had been associated with Manson was consistent: they were all describing a cult, and regarded Manson as someone with exceptional powers to sway people. Kasabian testified that he had programmed them into being "virtual zombies." Leslie was being tried not as a disciple, however, but as an individual who knew right from wrong and who had made the worst possible choices. She was tried not as a victim of a predatory cult leader, but rather as a victim of her own poor judgments, choices, and actions, for which she was to be held responsible and culpable.

In her defense, Max Keith introduced a cassette of Manson's voice in an interview. As the tape played, no one in the packed room made a sound—jurists, press, spectators. The staccato force of his voice got everyone's attention. Of Leslie, Manson said, spitting out the words:

People had Leslie Van Houten long before I had her. Her mother had her first; her dad had her; her parents had her; her school had her; the TV had her; the movies had her. She was in a convent for Buddhists—the Buddhists had her. And you come up and say, "Well, you had influence over her." . . . I showed her the way to herself.[1]

Manson then explained how a woman's aura tells who she is by the color she emits. As he saw her, Leslie's color was green.

Let's look down to the ground and see what we're doing down on the earth. That's where we're at, and I say, "Green . . . I'm going to name you Gentle Tree. And I'm going to plant you here . . . so that you can help fix the earth." . . . And she was planted for peace, and she was planted for the world.[2]

The prosecuting assistant district attorney, Stephen Kay, had helped Vincent Bugliosi prosecute the Manson defendants toward the end of the first trial. In this retrial, he was trying Leslie for conspiracy to murder. This allowed him to introduce evidence of the Tate murders—more sensational than the LaBianca murders she had taken part in—even though she had been at the Spahn Ranch caring for children when the Tate murders occurred. She had no advance knowledge, or any voice in the matter.

Kay's conspiracy theory contended wrongly that, before the Tate murders, Leslie knew that murders were being planned. He treated the two nights of Manson murders as a singular phenomenon, as the signature crime of the twentieth century, a crime that required retelling to bind everyone to the hard truth of it. He put enlarged color photos of the Tate murder victims before the eyes of Leslie's jury. Kay's focus on the violent details of a crime in which Leslie did not participate had the effect of distracting from, rather than emphasizing, the deep tragedy suffered by the LaBianca family.

In 1969 Leslie knew theoretically that Manson wanted his followers to be able to die and to kill in order to bring about Helter Skelter (the race war that would result in a social revolution). She was concentrating on killing her own ego, which meant obeying Manson without question. With the rest of the "family," she had been using drugs and was being brainwashed by Manson's hypnotic biblical exhortations and metaphors gleaned from Beatles songs. She gave herself to Manson to be an instrument of his grand vision.

Testimony

After listening to the recounting of the crimes in Leslie's second trial, a *Los Angeles Times* reporter lamented that this "pathetic and horrible story" made no sense, and concluded, "It seems both impossible and inevitable that it ever happened."[3]

We say that a crime is senseless when the motives aren't evident or don't make sense in our own frame of reference. We especially call crime senseless when the victims are children, the disabled, or the aged, and emphatically innocent of any provocation. A crime is quintessentially senseless when the perpetrator likewise seems unaware of the gravity of the act, as when children commit murder.

When a woman kills an abusive husband, she can now expect a certain level of judicial or community sympathy; the mindset that results from her victimization is often treated as a mitigating circumstance. The Manson murders were a convolution of the victim-oppressor type of murder: instead of killing the man who was oppressing them, the women tried to kill women *for* him. Leslie said she was willing to attempt murder because "[I wanted] to let [Manson] know I was a good soldier and that I was willing to lay my life on the line for him."[4]

Leslie's defense strategy was based on what occurred: brainwashing. Ample evidence was presented about ways that individuals can be seduced, disciplined, and coerced to adopt beliefs antithetical to those previously held, and to follow orders issued by those who do them harm. The brainwashing was compounded by the power dynamics between the older man and the younger women who were sexually exploited.

As Anne Near reflected on it she said, "The aspect of the crime that is hardest for me to comprehend is that of a woman holding a woman to be killed, at the behest of a man responding to a sense of impending chaos. This seems to reveal an extraordinary void in a sense of bonding between women." The sex of the victims, however, wasn't relevant to Manson on those two August nights.

In the course of the second trial, presided over by Superior Court Judge Edward A. Hinz Jr., dozens of witnesses testified to Leslie's good character before she met Manson, including family friends who had known her all her life. Repeatedly they testified to her healthy relationship with her parents, her wholesome childhood and teenage contributions to the community. They also spoke of her diminished judgment after habitually ingesting LSD and submitting to the domination of Manson. They emphasized that more recently, for several years, she had shown clear signs of having been rehabilitated; to friends and family, she showed profound remorse, and had firmly repudiated Manson's authority.

The courtroom was hushed during the tearful, wrenching testimony of Rosemary LaBianca's daughter, who, at age twenty-one, with her boyfriend and her fifteen-year-old brother, had found their parents brutally murdered. Her face showed great pain as she recalled that night, but she did not express anger or share the prosecutor's focus on retribution. She and the defendant did not look at one another—the daughter deep in sorrow, the guilty woman deep in shame.

The testimony of the daughter who lost her mother was followed by the testimony of the mother who almost lost her daughter to the death penalty. Jane Van Houten related details of Leslie's upbringing, her involvement in church choir, social groups, marching band, student government. She told how well Leslie got along with others, how she was elected homecoming princess two years in a row. She spoke of how, when Leslie was sixteen, her abortion was "very sobering" to the family. Jane told how she tried to discourage Leslie from her transient, barefoot, hippie life. When Jane was asked whether she thought Leslie was free of Manson's influence in 1977, Jane replied, "Yes, I certainly do. The change became discernible in 1974 or so."[5] That Leslie had regained her mental health was obvious to all who knew her in 1977, as well as to courtroom spectators.

The prosecutor, Stephen Kay, was very hard on Jane Van Houten in his cross-examination. He said to her, "I take it you don't want your daughter to be in prison." Jane, fighting tears, agreed. "I don't want her to be in prison any longer." Kay then insinuated to the court that Leslie's mother would lie to free her daughter from prison, although there was nothing to lie about because the facts were clear.

Keith returned for one last question. "Have you been telling us anything untrue to help keep Leslie out of prison?" Jane responded with calm dignity, "I have been telling the truth, *and* I don't want her to be in prison anymore."

• • •

During the months of Leslie's retrial, the testimonies of three individuals made a particular impression on me and moved me toward some clearer understandings: Paul Watkins, a former "family" member who left the ranch before the killing began; Dr. Lester Grinspoon, a psychiatrist who testified about the effects of LSD; and Leslie herself.

May 1–3, 1977: Former Cult Member

Paul Watkins, sexy and witty, helped find pretty young women for Manson to invite in. He testified that Manson didn't like being identified with hippies, despite the lifestyle of his "family" and despite the fact that several of his followers were free-spirited adolescent refugees from hippie families. Manson thought of hippies as unproductive people, and he was intent on saving the world. So, as Paul related, "We were 'slippies.' We would slip in and out of society without creating much problem."

Watkins, on the stand for three days, described how Manson supported his claim to be the apparent reincarnation of Jesus Christ by reenacting the crucifixion. Manson became preoccupied with death in those last months before the murders, Watkins said. "He rapped at length on what the metaphysical aspect of death was . . . death is an illusion; there is no death. . . . He talked about being willing to die . . . the next step. 'If you can die so easily, how do you feel about dying for me if I asked you?' " Watkins's testimony clearly supported the view that followers had been systematically brainwashed to be pliable enough to attempt to kill someone on his instruction, or to let themselves be killed.

It occurred to me, as I listened to this testimony, that Manson himself was the victim of a kind of brainwashing from his many years in prison, where violence is glorified and the macho man is pitted against the wimp.

The prosecutor played the Beatles' White Album in the courtroom, music that had been so significant to the "family's" brainwashing. Instructed by Kay, Watkins recited the relevance of each song: "Blackbird" was a call to the black man to rise up; "Sexy Sadie" was about Susan Atkins; "Piggies" was about the gluttons of society who deserved extinction; "Helter Skelter" was their mission; "Revolution 9" was a game plan. Watkins's testimony supported Leslie's defense; he conveyed the enormity of Manson's spell over all of them. Leslie maintained upright posture as she listened with sorrowful poise to his testimony.

Paul Watkins's testimony caused me to reflect on how reverberations from the Manson murders affected the lives of counterculture people throughout California and beyond. Since Manson and his followers were reasonably perceived to be hippies, all hippies became suspect and ready targets for disdain and harassment. After the crime, anyone with long hair driving a Volkswagen bus, the hippie vehicle of choice, stood a good chance of being pulled over by the police.

The "dirty hippie" stigma was radically intensified, as was adult contempt for youthful idealism. I didn't have a VW but I had a great old white Plymouth sedan. I'd painted a sunburst on the hood, an eagle on the rear, and installed colorful patchwork seat covers. To me, my car was a work of art. Before the crime all kinds of people would wave at me with an admiring thumbs-up at my artfully renovated car. After the crime people frowned; my car now represented a defiant gesture against the establishment. Mae Brussells, a popular public radio commentator, decided in all seriousness that it was a conspiracy. "The so-called Manson murders were actually orchestrated by military intelligence in order to destroy the counterculture movement. It's no different from the Special Forces in Vietnam, disguised as Vietcong, killing and slaughtering to make the Vietcong look bad."[106] This was a far-fetched theory, but paranoia was a reasonable response to the systematic harassment of the "flower children."

Aspects of mainstream, middle-class society were implicitly criticized by many of the alternative values espoused by the counterculture of the late 1960s and early 1970s: collectivity, familial fluidity, environmentalism, domestic cooperation, ecumenism, child-centeredness, independence, vegetarianism, emotional and physical intimacy, health consciousness, liberal use of soft drugs, antimaterialism, artistry, economic equity and efficiency, relaxation, pacifism, sexual freedom, and love-based spirituality. The fear and harassment of hippies that occurred after the crimes was as destructive to healthy communes as it was to those already dysfunctional. It was as if the dominant culture, in cahoots with the media, had been waiting for the Manson "family" to happen so that they would have "proof" that the hippie movement was no good. The antagonism between hippies and "straight" society was based on their antithetical values. In the context of social disruptions the Manson murders were a convenient excuse for a backlash. Parents were warning their hippie kids, "See what could happen to you?"

May 23, 1977: The Drug Issue

The fear of drugs accelerated with the Manson crimes, one among many factors leading to a worldwide "war" on illicit drugs led by Presidents Nixon and Reagan, and their successors. The issue of drugs in the second trial was significant because the prosecution's case required that Leslie be perceived as being in her right mind the night of the LaBianca murders. Leslie's lawyer, Max Keith, argued that Leslie "was suffering from a severe and debilitating mental impairment" at the time of the murders. To buttress his point, he brought in Dr. Lester Grinspoon from Harvard. An expert witness on LSD, he was one of five (male) psychiatrists who testified in the second trial that Leslie was incapable of "meaningfully premeditating or deliberating" the murders.

With no nuance of irony, Stephen Kay, who fought so hard against the theory that Leslie had been brainwashed by Manson, objected to the inclusion of this witness. He said he feared the psychiatrist would "brainwash" (his word) the jury. Exposing his lack of knowledge of LSD's prolonged and potentially recurrent effects, Kay emphasized that none of the defendants were on LSD the nights of the murders, to ward off a judgment of diminished responsibility. He lost the argument. Dr. Grinspoon did testify.

I had particular interest in Grinspoon's testimony on LSD because I had, over the course of three years in the late sixties and early seventies, ingested LSD six different times, always with skilled guides in calm, natural environments among a few close friends. Each trip was a joyful, soulful, sensual, energetic, surreal, introspective, meditative, and awakening experience. Acid, as LSD was called, was so powerful that I couldn't imagine regularly or casually consuming it. My experiences had all been totally pleasant, unlike some people's bad trips. My curiosity satisfied, and in some ways my consciousness raised, I stopped. The quantities of LSD ingested by Manson's followers, at his instruction and through his provision, were excessive. They used LSD at least twice a week for many months, which would surely help kill his followers' egos.

One question posed to Dr. Grinspoon was whether LSD induces people to commit murder—or whether the law of averages would produce a few murders committed by people who are on LSD trips. He said that, in fact, close to 100 percent of people who take LSD do not murder and, conversely, a vast majority of persons convicted are not users of LSD. (Alcohol is the drug most commonly associated with homicide and other crimes of violence.) If the murders couldn't be blamed on the drug, the murders were Leslie's responsibility. She couldn't plead that the drug made her do it, which she had never claimed, but it could be a mitigating factor in her sentencing.

The expert discussed how LSD makes people introverted and given to fantasies, visceral feelings, and hallucinatory experience. In his view, when tripping, people are easy to influence, and they have a reduced capacity to "reflect on the gravity of an act, or the consequences." On acid they create their own reality, but are also impressionable. The doctor confirmed that "a person's personality structure and the setting in which the drug is taken is as important as the properties of the drug" in terms of its effects. In Leslie's case, as recounted by the psychiatrist, she first took LSD at age fifteen (Leslie believes she was sixteen), an indulgence associated in her mind with drifting between her father's home and her boyfriend's. When she was with Manson, the doctor said, Leslie surrendered herself to him through sequential processes mediated by LSD.

The doctor testified that when he interviewed Leslie in the jail he found her to be "very forthright," and that he had "more confidence that she is telling me the truth than I usually do after interviewing someone for nine hours." He concluded that she had not been able to "premeditate and deliberate a homicide" in 1969, and was not accountable for her actions. He conceded that she knew, at the time, that killing was against the law, but she believed in a higher law. "Her duty to Charles Manson overwhelmed any other duty. . . . She didn't think of murder in the same way we do." When asked if she might still be under Manson's influence he replied, "Absolutely not." He described her as "her own person, a stable person, emotionally healthy, but not complacent with herself."

Surprisingly, since he gave it no weight, Stephen Kay questioned the psychiatrist as to why Leslie waited "until she thought Mrs. LaBianca was dead before stabbing her," to which the doctor replied that she was "acting on instruction" from her codefendants. Kay countered that she'd taken part in the "robbery" on her own volition, to which the psychiatrist pointed out that they had taken no items of significant value, just food, clothes, and collector coins for their immediate needs. The more serious theft of Mr. LaBianca's wallet was committed by Manson while the women were waiting outside before the murders, for the purpose of planting diversionary evidence in a black neighborhood.

Leslie herself discounts any direct effects of LSD on her participation in the crime. She points out that, like a lot of "family" members, she'd been using LSD before meeting Manson, and had never had violent thoughts or behaved violently in any way. To the contrary, she enjoyed mellow trips. But in Leslie's interview with Barbara Walters prior to her second trial, while she didn't blame the LSD directly for her participation in the crime, she did attribute the effects of the drug to choices she made, which led her to Manson and made her vulnerable to his authority.

> BARBARA WALTERS: *Miss Van Houten, at the time of these murders, there were many people, many parents, who aside from the horror of the murders [asked], "Could this have been my child?" This was the hippie period. This was the period of Haight-Ashbury. You ran away from home at seventeen and got involved in this kind of life. Do you know why?*

LESLIE: *Yes, the main reason for my running away was because of my amount of participation in dropping acid. I started when I was about sixteen. At the beginning I could still live—going to school, and more or less living within the structure of society. But the more I dropped acid the harder it was to relate to different people, other than the people who were dropping acid.*

BW: *Would you take LSD every day?*

LVH: *Not every day, but at least a couple of times a week.*

BW: *Were you almost always in some drug state?*

LVH: *Yes—when you drop acid at first it's a nine-hour experience. At first you can go back to work on Monday, but the more you take it the more you become lost in whatever, while you're on acid, is real, and the less you're able to relate to others. The more isolated I became from people with contrary viewpoints, the more I became totally immersed in acid reality. And it's a fairy-tale world.*

In the courtroom, Dr. Grinspoon pointed out that whereas an acid trip generally lasts for no more than eight to ten hours, the effect of altered awareness, with sharper mental engagement and greater sensitivity to visceral and sensual experience, may stay with the person. Brainwashing activity would be more efficient with subjects under the direct or aftermath influence of hallucinogens; they would be more pliable, more open to suggestion, less resistant.

In my experience, LSD dissolved the mind-spirit-body split. Mental images—such as flying—were experienced physically. Long after the trip ended, my physical memory recalled the mental image as though it had been an actual occurrence, even though I knew rationally that it couldn't have objectively happened in the material world. That which was not real became, in the realm of hallucinatory fantasy, "real" again through memory and was therefore imaginable.

At least intuitively, Manson understood this dynamic. All sources agree that, in the weeks leading to the murders, he repeated to his disciples, again and again, biblical and lyrical images full of fire and brimstone, while ensuring that LSD was consumed frequently.

As for whether LSD causes violence, Grinspoon said, nothing is without exception. The overwhelming evidence, however, suggests that LSD has the opposite effect: it causes people to be passive and receptive. A powerful guru can take hold of the minds of his subjects while they are under the effects of LSD, and reinforce his authority over them in times when they are not under the drug's effects. This was surely the case with Charles Manson.

There is no way of knowing to what extent LSD was a factor in Manson's successful encroachment on his disciples' minds. Other factors like his dramatic rhetoric, riddles, insights, tenderness, and energy added to his power over them. There was also the fact that the youths were alienated from the mainstream prior to their encounter with him. The sociohistoric time in which the crimes were committed was a major factor, a time when dropping acid was common.

To simply blame LSD would be as shortsighted as simply blaming Charles Manson. On an acutely interactional level, the young women's gendered readiness to obey his enigmatic instructions, the drugs' preparedness effects, Manson's charisma and coercion and the disrupted social conditions across color and class that set the context for the crimes all converged. The psychiatrist informed the court that there could be no single, simple explanation for what caused the Manson murders. In his view, anyone who believed fervently in any dogma could have done it if they had unqualified loyalty to their leader. Closed-minded true believers, however they come to their beliefs and whatever those beliefs may be, can be dangerous.

There is another drug-related issue not discussed by Dr. Grinspoon in court that may have been a factor in the murders. Manson's delusional thinking and manipulative orchestration of violence, and his followers' receptivity to him, may have been helped along by other drugs. Marijuana was commonplace. LSD was particularly valued by Manson. But significantly, according to Paul Watkins's testimony in the first trial, Manson himself took smaller LSD doses than he gave to the women.[7] After their association with bikers, who were involved in drug deals and who were more involved in amphetamines than in acid, the use of "speed" became commonplace with some members of the "family"—perhaps especially Charles Watson and Susan Atkins.[8]

Although most of the girls did not use speed, it is the view of Dr. David E. Smith, director of the Haight-Ashbury Free Clinic and an expert toxicologist, that "the turn from psychedelics to amphetamines was critical in changing the nature of the Family's activities." As he stated,

"High doses of amphetamines really do create a paranoid delusional system." (Incidental examples of destructive leaders who favored amphetamines as their drug of choice are Adolf Hitler and Jim Jones.)[9]

Certainly from what I've heard from the women, there was a distinct change in the ambience of the "family" coincident with the release of the White Album and the arrival of Manson's new biker friends early in 1969. Manson was behaving erratically and irrationally, with increased talk about violence and death (the violence necessary, the death inconsequential); he became obsessed with the plan he called Helter Skelter. If Manson was using amphetamines, that would partly explain why he underwent radical changes within months. He became frenetic with negative energy that, for Manson, translated into violence. LSD at the time was a meditative, counterculture drug that evoked the feeling of "peace and love," the hippie mantra. Psychedelic bands, notably the Jefferson Airplane, were in vogue, often with both musicians and the crowd under the effect of hallucinogens, much as Ecstasy became the drug of choice for young people going to all-night rave parties in the 1990s. There was nothing shocking about learning from the press that some of the murder victims at the Tate house had themselves indulged in LSD. But the combination—on the one hand, experiencing sharp increases of awareness (including but beyond the physical world) through LSD, and on the other hand, experiencing the nervous, erratic, aggressive energy of speed—would produce a severe psychological and physical disorientation. Manson's followers were so well programmed to follow him that his new paranoid irrationalities seemed no more outrageous to them than the magical, loving, father-protector ways with which he'd cultivated their devotion to him.

June 8–15, 1977: Leslie Speaks

For almost two months the court heard testimony from former members of the "family" and a variety of experts to the effect that Manson had brainwashed the whole lot of them. He was consistently portrayed by witnesses for the defense as a dangerously powerful madman who preyed on the vulnerability and gullibility of youth to feed his damaged ego. But as Leslie's prosecutor repeatedly reminded the court, Manson was not on trial there. He was already convicted and in a maximum-security prison, most likely for the rest of his life. It was Leslie who needed to account for what she had done, and a transfer of blame would be received cynically for good reason.

The courtroom was packed when it came time for Leslie to speak. Her interrogator, Stephen Kay, had assisted the legendary Vincent Bugliosi six years before. The external contrast between the two men's styles was pronounced: Bugliosi was tailored and entrepreneurial; Kay was earnestly serving the role of avenger, trumpeter of justice. When Stephen Kay cross-examined Leslie, he questioned her about the Self-Realization Fellowship, which she had joined as a teenager, for a time practicing celibacy with thoughts of becoming a yogic renunciate (that is, a Buddhist nun). In her testimony she affirmed that she believed in reincarnation. "Your consciousness has been with you since the beginning of time, and you just keep coming back to work out your karma. Karma is a balancing system within yourself. . . . Whatever you do you'll get back, whether it's in this life or another one."

Kay's intention was to discredit Leslie by showing that she had been deviant even before she met Manson, that she walked into the crime with her eyes wide open. He questioned her about her early drug use. She reiterated that she'd taken acid with her boyfriend and teenage friends. She described finding peace at Spahn Ranch, where the goals were to "give up personal identities so we'd be of one thought. Be humble, sensitive to the earth. . . . It was what I'd been looking for." Leslie described how Manson would mirror her face with his own expression if she was feeling down, and how he would "mill around and make comments about your daily growth." She was a persuasive witness on her own behalf.

Although she had maintained her composure throughout the proceedings, when asked to recall the crime, she became distraught and agitated, gulping for air through tears. When calmed, she testified that, at the time of the crime, she was surprised to find she had "no stomach for what was happening." Her inability to follow instructions at the LaBianca home in 1969 was a matter of shame to her then. "I should have accomplished more than just stab a dead body." In response to her lawyer's question about how she was feeling almost eight years after the crime, Leslie replied, "I'm very ashamed"—this time meaning not for her poor performance, but for having been associated with the brutal murders in any way at all. About Manson, six years after their original sentencing, she said, "I try to not hate him. I feel like that's investing an emotion. I've been able to live the last several years without him being a part of my life."

The defendant appeared to impress the jury, and spectators would talk about her in the hallway or on the L.A. County Courthouse steps. She was seen as honest, sensitive, intelligent, visibly humbled, ashamed, and bearing the bewilderment of years in segregated confinement. Her face wore an uncontrived blend of pain and wonder; it was easy to believe in the innocence of this woman on the stand, who was not the girl who had been present at the LaBianca murders.

In his summary, Stephen Kay, as if the LaBiancas were irrelevant, talked about the Tate murders, displayed the Tate photographs, rehashed the Tate details, and instructed the jurors firmly, "When you go in that jury room, *society* will be watching you."

• • •

The jury could not unanimously agree with Stephen Kay's insistence that Leslie deserved to be reconvicted of first-degree murder. The trial ended in a hung jury after twenty-five days of deliberation: seven voted for conviction on first-degree murder and five voted for manslaughter, which would have meant immediate release on the basis of the time already served. A mistrial was declared, which gave Leslie reason for optimism for a plea-bargain resolution. Normally, in a widely split decision in a first-degree murder case, the defendant would be able to plea-bargain for a second-degree murder conviction. Stephen Kay blamed the deadlock on jury emotionalism, saying that one juror identified Leslie with her daughter, and that she'd had dreams that it was her daughter in jail. He was particularly upset that the deadlock was so significant, with just under half the jurors holding out for a manslaughter conviction. He had not won his case. He still held the trump card, however. He refused to agree to a plea bargain.

This meant that, for the first time in California history, a hung jury in a first-degree murder case led to yet another trial. That third trial was scheduled for March 1978.

Six

Temporary Freedom and a Third Trial

AFTER THE SECOND TRIAL, the court granted Leslie the right to release on bail. Thanks to friends who mortgaged their homes to come up with $20,000, on December 27, 1977, Leslie was freed on a $200,000 bond. She would be free until, and for the duration of, the third trial. She remained out of jail for over six months, until July 1978. During those months, together with her family and other friends, I accompanied Leslie through moments of culture shock and easy homecoming, as she ventured back into the world. We visited each other's family homes. We relaxed with friends. We talked about the future. Where would she go if released? Would she change her name?

Free on Bail

Just before the 1978 New Year holiday, Leslie celebrated her freedom by going to the beach with her mother and friends. Later that week, at the apartment of her friend since high school, Linda Grippi, we chatted late into the night. Leslie was excited about all she had to do and all the possibilities. She had been talking about using an alias, but decided against it. Getting released from the jail had been a whirlwind event and she hadn't yet had time to write in her diary. She needed to get centered. She couldn't sleep. She was suffering anxiety, her mind busy with all the challenges and responsibilities she faced. She was still carrying the feeling of "no way out of my confinement," and yet she *was* out, if only temporarily. As tangible freedom began to sink in, she said, "I'm not full of super dreams. I love ironing, the smell of fresh clothes, walks down a sidewalk."

• • •

Her primary concern was for her mother, who feared for Leslie's safety. She wanted to avoid attracting media attention and was equipped with scarves and dark glasses for anonymity if she felt the need. She was feeling the pressures and said, "It would have been easier to go back to prison—[or] I could just stay in this apartment and hide until court starts—but . . . I need time for myself, and I need time with people I love." She knew it was a major breakthrough for her to be released. It enabled her to test the waters. As she said, "I'm out, the pattern's broken, the big taboo [releasing any former Manson associate]. There hasn't been any big fear [campaign], no threats."

Leslie lived a very "normal" life for over six months. She went to work as a legal secretary or, when court was in session, to trial every day. She visited family and friends on occasional evenings, and took short trips on long weekends. She was never accosted by the media or, to her knowledge, recognized by strangers.

• • •

The week of Leslie's release, a group of her friends, including her lawyer, Max Keith, and those who had helped raise the bail, gathered for low-key Scrabble and pizza. We were all accustomed to seeing her in jail and prison, so were quietly affected by her presence in our midst.

• • •

Temporary Freedom and a Third Trial — 121

I gave Leslie her first scary ride in eight years in L.A. freeway traffic. It was rush hour, there was a driving rainstorm, and I was driving a borrowed sports car. I'm a poor driver. We were both terrified, and Leslie asked me to concentrate on the road, which was barely visible. Suddenly the sun burst through the dark sky, the rain stopped, and everything was crystal clear and glistening, even the buildings. Leslie said quietly in wonder, "I hope I never forget how everything looks to me today."

• • •

A group of my friends in Echo Park organized a discreet party for Leslie, to let her know that women can be there for each other even when someone does something beyond the pale. Her hosts, Sue and Liebe, and many of the guests, had followed her second trial. A few had known her through the Santa Cruz Women's Prison Project in the prison. Others were simply curious about her. Once they met her, everyone engaged her in conversation out of genuine interest in her situation, and she reciprocated. Leslie put everyone at ease, although she was concerned beforehand because, as she put it, "Parties are lonely."

• • •

We went together to a supermarket and Leslie was overwhelmed by the crowds and the noise. When we were in line and the bell rang on the cash register Leslie jumped in fright. To her, for an instant, it was an echo of the beeper in the jail. Later, within the safety of Linda's apartment, with the tape recorder on (January 3, 1978), she talked agitatedly about lockup noises. "I'm used to sleeping through beepers; clanging doors; the sounds of drunks in and out; people yelling, going through DTs; the sounds from the ward, right across from me, of people who have lost their minds; people yelling for cigarettes or coffee; keys going *jingle-jangle* nonstop; doors crashing at every exit from or entry into a cage; the beeper system; the intercom; everything repeated twice, like 'Deputy Jones, 1021; Deputy Jones, 1021' or '3,000, 42, 52, line up and proceed to the dining room; 3,000, 42, 52, line up and proceed to the dining room.' The beeper system reaches everywhere; it sounds like those new cash registers that beep. Sometimes I could block out the constant beeping, but if it was a bad day and I was tuned in to every sound, I would lose my mind. Some officers were always making banging sounds with their sticks to provoke us."

• • •

Talking late another night, Leslie's thoughts were centered on the prison and jail in which she had (by 1978) spent more than eight years. These were the people she knew, the relationships that mattered to her, the routines and constraints that ordered her daily life. From time to time she would stop her train of thought and realize with wonder that she was—at least temporarily—free. In her stream-of-consciousness chatter, she said she looked forward to writing to her friends in prison about having keys both to Linda's apartment and to the borrowed car—two keys! Her mind was racing. She worried about someone breaking into the borrowed car. She expressed concern about her weight, saying "I'm getting that ripply stuff." I commented on how she had touched and brought together people from many different worlds who are interested in her case, and she considered it. "Differences fascinate me. I like to know their reasoning, their thinking. . . ."

• • •

Leslie reflected on how "weird" it was that "a bail bond and set of keys can make such a difference in worlds. Like tonight when we drove past the jail, knowing they're all in there in their little cages. . . . It doesn't seem so far away, that building on a hill by the freeway. But inside the building is a warped world."

• • •

I went with her to her mother's home, and they glowed with each other in open, loving, unconditional acceptance. Later Leslie's younger sister, younger brother, and his wife arrived. They were alternately lively and shyly affectionate, dressed up with respect for the reunion occasion. They showed pride in one another, including Leslie, who, I think, symbolizes courage to them. At the same time they despise what she did and how it directly affected so many lives, including their own. She was at ease. Everyone was disbelieving—that the crime had happened, that Leslie had been in prison for more than eight years, that she was now at home with her mother and her family.

Temporary Freedom and a Third Trial — 123

. . .

We drove north and visited with her older brother and his wife. They all talked a mile a minute about family, jobs, social issues, artistic projects, nutrition, the plants that filled their sunny apartment. They spoke with affection of their father, and of the ways their parents continued to show respect for each other despite the divorce. It was as if Leslie had been away on a long journey. One could see her sadness fleetingly recede in the warmth being tendered by people to whom she belonged.

. . .

In San Francisco, mutual friends—women and men who came to the prison as tutors—had a gathering. Hosted by Bill Moore, a scholar and community activist, and his wife, Andrea, who taught art in the prison, it was a welcoming reunion. Bill had been a major influence on Leslie's study of African-American history. He'd taught her about Malcolm X. He'd helped her recognize the folly of thinking that black people would unequivocally defeat white people in a war. He had educated her—and Pat and Susan—to the racist errors in Manson's illogic. With Bill, Andrea, Catherine Cusic, Debra Miller, and other friends Leslie had made through the Santa Cruz project, we reminisced about our school days. We laughed at our various instances of awkwardness in the beginning, and contemplated some of the lessons we'd learned together.

. . .

Gino was a friend of mine in Sonoma County in northern California, where I relocated from Los Angeles shortly after the end of the second trial. Gino knew Leslie because they had been in prison together at CIW in 1976, before Gino's release and Leslie's transfer to Sybil Brand. The three of us sat together in front of the fire, in the converted water tower where I lived. The two of them got caught up on all the news about old friends from the joint—who got released, who got married, who got busted again, who was strung out. . . . Some make it, some don't. No judgments.

They talked about weight and appearance. Leslie had gained twenty pounds since her anorexia, but was still very slender and well-muscled from working out. Gino, even more muscled, complained about how uncomfortable she felt when someone casually introduced her as someone who had been in prison.

She told Leslie about a Santa Cruz conference on alternatives to prison, with a lot of ex-prisoners in attendance. Leslie laughingly related to Gino her memory of when I first came into the old death row: "Hi! I'm here to teach women's lib!" I feigned a pout; they laughed. Gino and I found ourselves just staring at Leslie, amazed that she was there with us.

• • •

Leslie's first long-distance phone call as a free citizen was to her former job supervisor in the prison. They commiserated about the uncertainty of her future. From what I heard at our end, it seemed her boss was encouraging her positive thinking about her chances in the upcoming third trial. She asked about his wife and new baby. Before hanging up, she said to him, "I don't want to lose your friendship. You're a friend."

• • •

Driving to the beach, Leslie exulted at the sight of sheep and horses in meadows nestled in the green rolling hills. She said people looked tall to her.

We stood together on a low cliff above a tumultuous ocean in a storm, tears rolling down her cheeks, reacting to the power, freedom, and eternity of the sea. Having grown up with it, she'd missed seeing the ocean for more than eight years. Massive, crashing waves sent off sprays of salt water, which splashed onto our faces and mingled with the rain and Leslie's silent, salty tears.

• • •

Back in southern California at McCabe's, a popular Santa Monica folk club, Leslie heard Cris Williamson sing her song "Native Dancer," with the lyrics:

Just a situation, with four walls and a floor,
She stared at the ceiling, she longed for the door,
Strange lands and separation, so far from home,
And so far, she's holding her own.[1]

Leslie had first met Cris in the Special Security Unit six years before, when Cris came in to sing for the women there. Two years before the McCabe's reunion, Cris had given Leslie the lyrics to "Native Dancer," which described Leslie's situation and that of anyone trapped by circumstance.

Now there she was, experiencing the song amidst a crowd in the "free" world, Cris's music creating a comforting ambience far from the tensions of the prison.

• • •

One day I asked Leslie what she most liked about the world, seeing it as she was for the first time in years. She said, "Me being in it." She was calm now, grateful to be alive, not taking it for granted.

• • •

The months on bail were healing to Leslie. Despite the pressure of the trial, and the need to evade the media outside court, Leslie appeared to adjust quickly to the absence of prison discipline and surveillance. With friends and family in reach, she created a quiet, private life and maintained her equilibrium. In conversation one day in the car, she reflected on how her prison mates expected to hear from her about "how weird it is out here, how strange, foreign, and outer-spacey. But driving through those fields, it doesn't seem like nine years since I traveled that road, with the eucalyptus protecting the crops from the wind. . . . There aren't enough hours, days are too short."

Third Trial

The third trial began in March 1978, in the court of Judge Gordon Ringer. Disappointed at the outcome of the second trial, Stephen Kay changed his strategy for the third. He focused on the fact that food, clothing, coins, and a wallet had been taken from the LaBianca home. Technically this made felony robbery an additional motive for the murders. Unbeknownst to Pat and Leslie, Manson had taken a wallet before he sent his team into the house, but robbery was certainly not on their minds. The wallet was left intact as a decoy in a service station bathroom, in what Manson mistakenly believed to be a black neighborhood. Manson intended that the police would assume a black person stole it.

According to California state law at the time, a first-degree murder conviction required that the accused's state of mind was capable and culpable of premeditation, deliberation, and harboring malice, and further, that the accused was able to reflect "meaningfully and maturely" on the gravity of the act. In the second trial, Max Keith had defended Leslie on the grounds of diminished capacity because she clearly had neither premeditated murder nor acted with deliberation or malice. Indeed, she had shown herself to be incapable of committing murder. Further, her behavior during and following the first trial, like that of her codefendants, demonstrated that she was then incapable of reflecting in any meaningful or mature way on the seriousness of the murders.

Instead of trying Leslie solely on murder in the third trial as he had in the second, Stephen Kay changed the charge to felony murder committed in the act of robbery, a crime for which state of mind was not legally relevant. This was a reversal of the strategy of D.A. Vincent Bugliosi, who, when he led the prosecution in the 1970–71 trial, had stated unequivocally that there had been "no evidence of ransacking or robbery." The LaBiancas' son testified in that trial that nothing was missing except the few clothes and coins.[2] Bugliosi wanted it understood by the jury that Manson's motive of Helter Skelter was what made the LaBianca murders part of the so-called crime of the century (singular), not a pedestrian robbery-murder. With Leslie, Kay had to settle for less.

The law was much less philosophical about murders committed in the course of a robbery, and conviction did not require evidence of malice, deliberation, or premeditation. Even though food, clothing, and coins did not constitute evidence of serious robbery from rooms filled with valuables, adding that charge gave the state the technical authority to convict her of the murder as a first-degree offense. To bolster Kay's efficiency in the courtroom, a second D.A., Dino Fulgoni (later appointed to a judgeship), was assigned the case to assist with the trial. This particular man was versed in psychology and would be useful when the diminished-capacity arguments were raised by a persistent Max Keith. Fulgoni's expertise was used to challenge the psychiatric testimony. The judge, for his part, explicitly instructed the jury to disregard Leslie's state of mind at the time of the crime or in the present. It was no longer relevant.

Stephen Kay told the press, "I think if I can get a jury that follows the law instead of emotions, I can get a first-degree conviction."[3] Once again Kay displayed for the jury the enlarged color photos of the murders at the Tate residence, emphasizing his charge that Leslie was part of a conspiracy responsible for both nights of murder. Technically, conspiracy was irrelevant to this third trial, because it was a single event of felony murder for which she was now being prosecuted. Thus, the Tate murders were likewise irrelevant. But the state showed a commitment to a reconviction, and the strategy succeeded. In the process, the state could sidestep the psychiatrists and other expert witnesses concerning Leslie's state of mind.

Just as Kay no longer had grounds for the conspiracy theory as it applied to the Tate case, Keith no longer had legal grounds for asserting the diminished-capacity defense. But he pushed it nevertheless. Leslie could not have understood the nature of the crime, he argued; her mind was altered because of the cumulative effects of LSD and Manson's power over her. Keith strove to win a verdict of voluntary manslaughter, which is defined as unlawful killing without malice aforethought.

On July 5, 1978, nine years after the crime and after six months of freedom, bail was pulled and Leslie, now age twenty-eight, was returned to court to hear the jury's guilty verdict. She was then taken back to jail, to await sentencing. The jury's foreman later told the press that jurors had agreed that Leslie "suffered some diminished capacity. But we just could not determine that it was diminished to the extent that was required to relieve her of responsibility for what she had done."[4]

The jury's unanimous conviction on two counts of first-degree felony murder did not clear up the question of individual responsibility versus cult coercion. The third trial, however, had the effect of officially separating Leslie's case from that of her three codefendants; legally she was no longer one of them. Superior Court Judge Gordon Ringer didn't equivocate: he sentenced her to seven years to life in prison. Given California law in 1978, the new sentence automatically carried with it the possibility of parole after seven years (which she had already served), and he encouragingly implied that she might well become an early beneficiary of that provision.

Leslie had other judicial reasons for hope. The release in fewer than ten years of Jean and Linda, her early prison mates in the old death row unit, offered encouragement as Leslie approached ten years in prison. More important, Leslie was no longer legally a death-penalty overturn; for her part in the crime of which she was now convicted, she would not have received the death penalty, even though it was then back in force in California. The conspiracy-to-murder charge was technically moot in the third trial. In 1971, Kay's then-boss, Vincent Bugliosi, had succeeded in convicting Leslie of seven murders (based on conspiracy). In 1977 and 1978, it took two juries and a severely compromised strategy on Kay's part to convict her of two of them. She was now officially separated from her association with Helter Skelter.

The Question of Retribution

I think it is disrespectful toward murder victims and their loved ones to quibble about the seriousness of any given murder. Prosecutors and the media are fond of ranking first-degree murder cases as bad, worse, worst. In court during the second trial, Stephen Kay repeatedly declared the Manson crimes to be "the most cruel and vicious murders in the bloody history of American crime." The media agreed; it routinely spotlighted one or another former member of the Manson "family" and referred to the "crime of the century."

The following are among some other horrible crimes that occurred in California through the 1970s and into the 1980s. A man was found guilty of the rape and murder of fourteen young women. Another predator-sadist was convicted of raping and murdering several young women, with the collusion of his submissive wife under threat to her own life. (She did finally call the police, and received immunity for her testimony.) More than forty boys were assaulted and murdered, and their bodies dumped in ditches alongside southern California highways. A man went on a rampage in a nursing home and raped an elderly blind woman. Dan White killed San Francisco mayor George Moscone and gay activist and city supervisor Harvey Milk in cold blood—with intent—but his charge was reduced to manslaughter owing to his "Twinkie" defense. (He claimed that low blood sugar caused his irrationality.) The Ku Klux Klan and neo-Nazis were overtly commiting and encouraging violence against

African Americans, Jews, gays, and lesbians. A young white woman in a northern California suburb strangled a black boy to death because, she said, something told her she was "supposed to kill a nigger." To hold up Manson, the head of his "family," as the worst perpetrator of all is to give him too much credit. His predatory contemporaries were no less cruel or vicious.

For many years Stephen Kay has routinely, by his own choice, attended parole hearings for those connected to Manson's crimes, traveling the state from one prison to another for that purpose, each time reiterating his plea to the board to withhold release. To buttress his cause, he enlisted the support of Sharon Tate's now-deceased mother, Doris, and her sister Patty—his neighbors in a comfortable Los Angeles neighborhood. The Tates gathered tens of thousands of signatures opposing parole for any of the former Manson disciples. In the past few years he has similarly harnessed the unrelenting grief and anger of some of Leno LaBianca's relatives to campaign against the release of anyone associated with the murders. He has given statements to the *National Enquirer,* a tabloid paper, to garner public support for his position. At the time of the second and third trials, however, none of the LaBianca family had spoken publicly.

The prison system as we know it is based on this principle of retribution. But there are families who have lost loved ones to the crime of murder who focus not on the punishment of the offenders but rather on forgiveness, accountability, healing, and reconciliation. These are exceptional people who are highly principled, and most often are people of deep spiritual faith. They seek to avoid living with the debilitating effects of sustained hatred. Instead they attempt to understand why the perpetrator of the terror inflicted on their loved one could have done such a thing. They will mourn their loss for their lifetime, but they mitigate their own pain through prayer and the hard emotional work of finding compassion for the offender within their own hearts.

My own attitudes were directly influenced by Herb and Ellie Foster, friends in Santa Cruz, California, whose young adult daughter was brutally murdered by a stranger at the same time that I was getting acquainted with the young women on death row. The Fosters, who were an inspiration to their community, not only found the strength within themselves to carry on without bitterness, they also became adamant critics of the inequities of the criminal justice system.

Students of crime and punishment are aware that, apart from pathological crimes of murder, and despite alleged equality under the law, criminal justice systems throughout the Western world selectively criminalize and predominantly incarcerate those who are already marginalized by racism, poverty, and other social and political inequities. The crimes of the wealthy, including profit-motivated corporations, very rarely result in imprisonment. Manufacturers of automobiles or elevators who knowingly make decisions to breach safety regulations, when "accidental" deaths result, do not end up in prison. Corporate CEOs whose businesses fail to ensure safe working conditions are not sent to prison when deaths ensue. Owners of mines who shirk on safety and pay for that "oversight" in mining tragedies do not go to prison. Most commonly, the corporation pays a hefty fine, which they can well afford, and that's the end of the story for all but the survivors.

The inequality of punishment systems also extends to much less significant crimes on an individual level. A poor black woman and an affluent white woman may be found guilty of the same offense, such as possession of an illegal drug, but it is the black woman who is much more likely to be sent to prison while the white woman remains with her family, perhaps participating in a community rehabilitation program.

These are the kinds of issues that informed Herb and Ellie Foster's refusal to succumb to any impulse for vengeance, and instead to successfully struggle to accept their personal tragedy with a loving and compassionate regard for the human condition, together with a commitment to work for social justice. As Quakers, the Fosters were affiliated with a religion that has a long history of seeking equal justice for all and reformation of the worst abuses of penal systems. Thus, not long after their daughter's murder, when the construction of a new and much larger jail was being proposed for their city, they ardently campaigned against it.

They were aware that when the number of available jail and prison cells expands, judges quickly fill these new cells with offenders who would otherwise have been granted probation. In this process, people have been increasingly incarcerated for minor offenses, which has led to a burgeoning prison-industrial complex in the United States over the past several decades. Given that prisons produce rather than alleviate violence, the Fosters did not want to collude with this defeatist trend.

The contemporary penal abolition movement is energized by many people who, like the Fosters, seek resolution through healing rather than harsh punishment.

The above notwithstanding, it is not at all difficult for me to comprehend why other families of murder victims would be disconsolate, preoccupied with their loss, and committed to retributive justice. I don't know that I could be so forgiving myself, if I were to lose one of my children—or grandchildren or anyone I love—because of another person's inability to contain his rage.

It is much less obvious, however, why Stephen Kay would have become so apparently obsessed with this case, that it should have played such a central and abiding role in his career. Certainly media sensationalism brought the Manson crimes before the public's view with an uncommon intensity, and Leslie's retrials brought Stephen Kay into the spotlight. But as I observed him in the courtroom, he wasn't performing for the press so much as he was singularly focused on what appeared to be a personal mission to vanquish any girl who would have been so immoral as to get involved with Manson.

One day when he seemed particularly determined to destroy what remained of Leslie's self-respect, I tried to grasp why he seemed so personally driven in the case. Kay's motive, as he presented himself to the jury, was to make America safe, to rid the country of an evil force. He spoke of Manson's tribe as unique among violent criminals because, in his characterization of Manson and his willing dupes, they were all working together to plot a revolution, and thus were a threat to an entire nation. This was a revolution that Manson thought he could get away with because he and his "family" would be safely ensconced in a bottomless pit in the desert. I wondered if Manson was flattered to have his preposterous revolutionary scheme taken so seriously by this earnest servant of the establishment. Further, while I didn't doubt the sincerity of Kay's patriotic fervor, his logic didn't fit with Leslie. Having severed her association with Manson several years before, she was not dangerous, according to every expert and by every measure, and he knew that from her records, court testimony, and, surely, from his own observations.

Leslie herself has never suggested an ulterior motive on Kay's part. She has never disparaged him in any way in any conversation with me, or tried to analyze his motives. When I was critical of his hostile treatment of her in court and in later parole hearings, she defended him. Leslie has great respect for the law, having trained as a legal secretary. He was, she said, just doing his job. After all, he was not on trial. I, too, don't wish to be unfair to him. But I believe it is reasonable to ask why he has pursued this case so diligently and perseveringly for such a long time.

During Leslie's second and third trials, in 1977 and 1978, when she was approaching age thirty, Kay repeatedly said to the court, and to the press, that he was committed to seeing her remain in prison until she reached age forty. This was consonant with Bugliosi's prediction in 1971 that the girls would remain in prison for fifteen to twenty years, substantially beyond the then-average of ten to twelve years for "serious" homicide. Had Leslie been released in 1989, at age forty, she would have fulfilled both prosecutors' harshest suggested sentence, twenty years. But in early 2001 she is fifty-one, and she is still in prison; and Kay, who appears at each parole hearing, has changed his tune. Now, at her hearings, he says that she should never be paroled. As I and anyone who knows her view it, Leslie has been thoroughly rehabilitated. As for Stephen Kay, one would think that by now he would be weary of this battle, so bravely fought almost single-handedly, and would be moving on to other priorities. Meanwhile, I do understand that, whatever his reasons for holding on, it is not my place to judge him.

When I described to Anne Near the ways Kay impressed me, she replied, "What you are searching for is what we need to know: how can we hear Leslie's story and not be the judge? 'Judgment is mine, saith the Lord.' And yet we have an irrepressible tendency to be judgmental. Perhaps it starts through a childhood attempt to know ourselves. We define ourselves at other peoples' expense. 'I don't want to be like my mom or my brother.' It becomes a function of growing up. Maybe we start being judgmental right in our own families." Anne and I agreed that, in her words, "Revolution must not lead away from but rather toward simple trust between people. No matter how profoundly you reach to articulate the need to be nonjudgmental towards each other, you still do not wish to live in a world where it's okay to go rob or otherwise harm your neighbor." Judgments rob innocent and guilty alike of their dignity, and their sense of safety and belonging. But who could not judge the actions of the young people who attempted murder at the behest of Charles Manson?

I learned a lesson from Leslie, from other women formerly associated with Manson, and from other women in prison who had been convicted of first-degree murder. Namely, a deed must always be the responsibility of the perpetrator (assuming intention and sanity), but the character of the perpetrator is not always reflected in the deed. It doesn't define her. It's not who she is.

The women involved with Manson were committed to a world without racism, war, or violence of any kind. They were each highly idealistic. A person of authentically strong ethical character who "loses her mind," in some way, may commit a heinous action without recognizing anything wrong at the time. Later she may not recognize herself in the action or in the beliefs supporting it.

Anne remarked, "It is puzzling that the women involved with Charles Manson could imagine that their act of killing could call forth anything good." It's not that they didn't have good teachers. Killing people to keep the peace is common; besides politicians and the military, the police in some cities employ that practice regularly. Battered women sometimes succumb to that solution. The death penalty is based on the fallacy that if we kill someone who has killed, others will not kill. It is clear from history that this is not the case. Whatever the justifications—and some are no doubt valid or at least understandable—violence ultimately begets only violence.

Carrying On

During Leslie's six-month sojourn into freedom, she contemplated her prison experiences. I asked her one day whether she had ever given up hope for her own future, and she conceded that yes, she had given up after seven years in prison, shortly before winning her appeal. She was becoming institutionalized, passive, and placid, and was guarded against emotional involvement. "You learn your own inadequacies, the insecurities you lay on a person." In 1977, when she was in the Los Angeles jail awaiting retrial, she had the impulse to just drop the case and go back to the state prison, "just lock myself up and forget it forever." It was an impulse on which she couldn't act because "so many people love and care for me. . . . You can't help but keep trying to be free, even if you don't stand a chance. You always fight for it. . . . The more attention I get from people truly trying to understand it, the clearer my own perspectives on what happened." Leslie spoke of imprisonment as "something I have to go through, need to do."

In August 1978, Leslie was returned to the California Institution for Women in Frontera. Early in 2001, she is still there.

Seven

DOING TIME

LESLIE NEVER SAID, "It wasn't my fault," nor did her codefendants. The way she bears responsibility for such guilt without hope of offering restitution, and lives without letting the guilt erode her character, is beyond my understanding. Leslie participated in others' violent deaths; she has intimate knowledge of being condemned to death, waiting to die, and then having her life suddenly returned to her. These experiences have given her an uncommon breadth of perception and depth of commitment to life.

Had her crime been committed a year or two earlier—or a few years later when the death penalty was restored—Leslie would have been executed. Instead she has built an active, useful life in a fortressed, high-security southern California prison that today warehouses over two thousand other bodies.

In both the sacred and the secular sense, Leslie is doing penance for participating in the taking of two lives and irrevocably harming their families. She is also doing penance for hurting her own family, and for sacrificing her own life. In recognizing the choices she abdicated as a youth, she has found her strengths, but not without struggle. She described herself in 1997 as the woman she would have become had she not met Manson. Many years ago she traveled through hell, rejecting society and then her own body, with anorexia. She used every avenue available to her within her maximum-security prison to recover herself until she was finally comfortable in her own skin.

The parole board suggested in April 1996 that outward expressions of remorse were key to her eventual release: to win her freedom, Leslie's suffering for the crime would need to be more apparent. Leslie learned from her parents, however, to confide her troubles with discretion, in private; she doesn't burden others with her own grief. She was raised to be polite, pleasant, and unselfish and she is, with a sense of humor that helps keep her sorrows contained by day. Her emotional containment is reinforced by the prison culture she has inhabited for thirty years, which discourages open expression of deep emotion.

In her January 1977 interview, Barbara Walters pressed Leslie to be explicit about how she handles her guilt. It was a painful, halting moment in the interview. Leslie was aware that anything she could say about the remorse she carries within her would be interpreted as self-serving. Any words she could speak would trivialize the magnitude of what she did and of what she feels. Silence was her appropriate response.

In my conversations with Anne Near, there was never a moment when sympathy for Leslie overrode our awareness of the anguish suffered by the LaBiancas. As Anne pointed out, "The prisoner pays her debt to society, at enormous cost to society, but society does not repay the victim." Speaking generally, the complication here is that most offenders are also victims. For me, the question is whether we must practice vengeance. If yes, then how can we also say we believe in rehabilitation or redemption of the person who offended? Here is a person, Leslie Van Houten, who participated in a crime that permanently inscribed deep shame on her heart, mind, and soul. Many years ago, in spite of the negative and punitive prison environment, she used her remorse, intelligence, healthy body, and strong spirit to rehabilitate herself. Yet the parole board, at the urging of Deputy District Attorney Stephen Kay, has prolonged her sentence indefinitely.

The idea of rehabilitation comes from the ancient tradition of banishing criminals naked into the wilderness, with only their shame as a cloak. Outcast, they repent and eventually return fully clothed, with their dignity restored. The word *rehabilitation* means putting your clothes back on as symbolic of restoring your good name. Everyone who knows Leslie and has seen her over the years agrees that this restoration of dignity has occurred for her. She is in prison to satisfy society's desire for vengeance, and she accepts the punishment with equanimity.

Since being moved in 1976 from the old death row into the main prison, Leslie has used her incarceration as an opportunity to do good work. Being confined for three decades in a harsh prison environment is an indisputably painful and prolonged punishment. It frees her from the need to punish herself beyond that of living with her accountability for the crime. Daily, she confronts grief for her victims and their family, her grief for her own family, her anguished conscience and shame, the psychological battering and physical deprivations of her crowded prison environment, her infamy. As a friend once said of the public perception of Leslie, "She'll be a 'Manson girl' all her life. Let her infamy be her punishment. That's punishment enough. She doesn't need to be in prison."

In the United States in the 1990s, governors were elected who supported an increased use of imprisonment for minor crimes. They appointed parole boards that have expanded the prison industry by withholding release from nondangerous (as well as from presumably dangerous) lawbreakers. This overtly brutal and reactionary approach, generally supported by the public, prolongs a cycle of vengeance in which the guilty are demonized.

As Jeanne Gallick wrote to me in regard to Leslie's three decades of imprisonment:

What ideology does she represent, so threatening to the status quo that she is denied parole year after year? Certainly there is no legal justification for this cruel punishment. They need to keep the whole story on the demonic level. The whole prison system [and the public at large] is so ready to demonize people [not just those who have killed], so as to turn public attention away from the real causes of so many crimes, such as poverty, low wages, institutionalization, racism. . . . It's a lot easier to put a woman in jail who breaks the mold than to work on the conditions . . . at the roots of her crime in the first place. The Manson case is a good example of how this demonization works.[1]

A prison may occasionally satisfy a prisoner's own need to be punished. But in my experience, those imprisoned women who feel a need for punishment recognize the prison experience less as an opportunity for atonement and forgiveness and more of an opportunity for state employees to inflict unmitigated, unrelenting degradation on caged women, regardless of the seriousness of their offenses or the levels of their remorse. Because a majority of women in prison have been abused from childhood, prisons become a perceived extension of that abuse, even if the prisoner is open to repentance. To the unrepentant, the harshness of prison justifies their lawbreaking.

This is not the case with Leslie or her codefendants, Susan and Pat, all of whom are deeply remorseful and who have succeeded better than most at adapting to prison by being useful to their community of women. Within the prison they live independently of one another, their close association severed when they moved away from Manson. But they have been united for two and a half decades, as of 2001, in their repudiation of their actions with him.

In the history of modern punishment, it has been rare for anyone to be held in prison for as long as thirty years, except for the relatively few whose crimes were heinous and who are still so dangerous that they must serve a literal life sentence behind the walls. Three decades of unrelenting punishment, save the six-month break in 1977–78, would be considered cruel and unusual for anyone known to be no longer a danger to society. After even a decade, long-termers have long since passed the time when their sentences have made an enormous impression on them as punishment; they are simply a given. The prison is where they live. This is their life. And so a life is made of it.

If the motive for the punishment is not rehabilitation but vengeance, the prisoner's personal guilt is lost to the public's abstract desire for punitive action for its own sake. Juries, judges, politicians, law enforcement authorities, and policy makers ostensibly inflict punishment because of their respect for the law. But given their various levels of discretionary power and the inconsistencies in their judgments, it is clear that more subjective factors are at work. Talking with Anne in 1981, at which time Leslie had been in prison almost twelve years, we contemplated vengeance as a giving up on the part of society, a surrendering to the rule of rage. We agreed that vengeance is an archaic, atavistic, vestigial kind of thing, a caudal appendage.

We don't need a tail anymore. Maybe we did once, when we lived in the trees (if we still believe in Darwinian evolution), but we don't need it now. It doesn't help our lives together. It's not functional or rational. Charles Manson is a vivid example of the product of cyclical, reciprocal vengeance. Manson and the state reflect each other. A truly civilized society would reject archaic, vengeful tactics not only of a murderer like Manson, but of a state that claims to defend civility.

Inside Connections

As a general rule, people who are imprisoned together do not pry too deeply into one another's crimes, though they learn that information over time. In many prison cultures it would be considered rude to ask a stranger what she did to land in prison. But women in the main prison at the California Institution for Women thought they knew everything about the "Manson girls" long before they were all transferred out of the Special Security Unit. Every little tidbit about them spread through the grapevine. Some women had been in jail with them in Los Angeles. Everyone knew the media versions of the crimes, but they were more interested in information about how the girls passed their days, what they were wearing, whether they'd shaved their heads again, or what they said to visitors.

Through the internal mail system and with help from supportive staff who served them as occasional messengers and couriers to the main prison, Pat, Susan, and Leslie were able to actively contribute to *The Clarion*, the prison newspaper. They aligned themselves with the Long-Termers Organization, and otherwise joined their voices to activities of the institution from the isolation of their cells. They gained respect from other women for their steady perseverance and positive outlook even while still in the isolated SSU. They were doing the hardest of time: facing first death and then a life sentence.

The women in the main prison worried about the girls' physical conditions when they were still in SSU. Many had been through the torment of rack and knew how terrible it was to be locked alone in a grim cell twenty-three or twenty-four hours a day, seven days a week, under constant surveillance. The main-prison women weren't judgmental. They seemed to understand that "the girls weren't themselves" when they went along with the unspeakable crimes of which they'd been convicted. They seemed to understand what it is for a woman to surrender to a powerful man's force, and they had theories about how the three young women had been brainwashed to do what they did. The main-prison women spoke sympathetically, saying things like, "It's a rotten shame, what those girls did, what they've got to live with over there," and "Goes to show you what'll happen when you'll do anything for a dude," and "You just can't trust psychedelics."

The "Manson girls" had given over their minds to the dude and the drugs. Psychedelics can bring on both paranoia and trust—trust in whoever is there to protect against the object of paranoia. Charles Manson, they had believed, was there to protect them from the whole world. Over two years after Leslie's reconviction in her third trial, she was interviewed for the *Los Angeles Times*. She makes a case for the dangers of letting someone else do our thinking for us. "My responsibility . . . was in allowing another person to have that control over me. It's a classic mistake people make when looking for someone who has the answer."[2]

It wasn't only the other prisoners who formed sympathetic regard for the women who were kept isolated from them. The main prison staff—black, brown, and white; men and women—likewise routinely inquired how they were doing when I returned from my visits. And the administration took a direct interest in their welfare. The tough associate warden showed wistful compassion for them one day when he told me that he didn't see how they could get used to being locked up in that small place, year after year. He said the whole thing was a terrible shame, and he too blamed it on drugs. Unlike the women I talked with (prisoners and staff), he ignored Manson's role in it. Leslie and the others have argued that blaming the drugs diverts responsibility from Manson, who controlled their every action. The drugs did make them more vulnerable, but with or without drugs, they obeyed. A hypnosis researcher concludes of Manson, "True, he had the advantage of LSD and marijuana, which he doled out to his 'Family' as required; but the old hypnotic spell was still his chief forté."[3]

Leslie has been consistently pragmatic and constructive in her approach to doing time. Always working on specific projects and goals, while still in segregation her short stories and Pat's poetry were published in a book of (primarily male) prisoner writings.[4] When she joined the main prison population after years of solitude, she became immediately useful, first in the clinic and then as the assistant to the director of the school program. Leslie has volunteered for years in the literacy program, and in the production of audiotaped readings for the blind. She responds to every opportunity to liven the environment, such as working with other talented women to provide entertainment for their well-attended, annual AA party. As she has aged, and the prison has become more crowded, tense, and chaotic, she has found it more difficult to sustain so many volunteer activities in addition to her prison job, correspondence, and perennial preparation for parole hearings. She suffers, ironically, from too little time alone.

Outside Connections

One of the effects of Leslie's second and third trials in 1977 and 1978 was to garner active support for her release from old and new friends, friends of her mother, and friends of friends. In January 1980 they organized a group, Friends of Leslie, one purpose of which was to indicate to the parole board "that she has a wide base of support among the general public."[5] Members of the group gave talks to community organizations, spoke to the media and to church groups, and gathered hundreds of letters supporting her release in 1981.[6] Attorney Paul Fitzgerald wrote in a June 1980 newsletter, "She is a stable, responsible, trustworthy person . . . [surrounded by] family, . . . a wide span of friends, and professionals across the community—lawyers, journalists, professors, psychiatrists, [ministers, artists], scientists, prison staff—all of whom believe in Leslie."[7]

Within the group were the individuals who had helped raise the cash to secure Leslie's bail bond in 1977. Impetus for the pursuit of Leslie's release on bail came initially from the captain in charge of the Sybil Brand Institute. Leslie's friend Linda had come for a visit, and when the visit was denied for pointless bureaucratic reasons, she had resourcefully made her way to his office, to appeal to reason.

He appreciated her observations and took the time to personally escort her on a tour of the entire jail, to places visitors rarely see. He showed her an empty cell that was the duplicate of the one in which Leslie was segregated. While walking around the large maze of the jail, the captain expressed his strong opinion that Leslie should be free on bail during the upcoming third trial. He had been a guard when she was jailed there during the first trial, seven years before, and he saw that she was a different person from the Manson groupie he'd guarded then. His confidence was contagious, and Linda got the ball rolling with ready assistance from other friends of Leslie.

In over six months' freedom between her second and third trials, from December 27, 1977, to July 5, 1978, Leslie had demonstrated her reliability. In 1981 Leslie wrote, "I wish others here could have some of the acceptance and love that so many of you share with me. God bless you all for being people who seek solutions."[8]

At the mark of twenty-five years of imprisonment, in August 1994, CNN aired an interview Larry King had held with Leslie at the prison. Several months earlier Diane Sawyer's late-1993 interview of Leslie and Pat had been broadcast on ABC's *Turning Point*. Leslie's reason for accepting the interview requests was to be able to say again to "the kids," publicly, that it is in no way cool to follow Charles Manson. In her opening, Sawyer described Pat and Leslie as "the girls next door," and continued, "Long before David Koresh, long before Jim Jones in Guyana, Manson awakened this country to the dangers of cult psychology." Leslie finally acknowledged in that interview, with deep sadness, that she did know as she entered the LaBianca home that "there would be killings."[9]

In Leslie's interview with Larry King, he asked her how she viewed Manson after not having seen him since their trial twenty-three years earlier. She said she saw him as "an opportunist of the cruelest, most vicious kind, for his own aggrandizement—I feel very responsible for helping create a monster. A follower is as responsible [as a leader] for allowing a leader to lead them foully. . . . I didn't take Mrs. LaBianca's life, but I feel as responsible as if I had."[10]

Parole Hearings

Prior to the 1980s, parole hearings were conducted annually, often perfunctorily, for every prisoner serving a life sentence in California state prisons. In 2001, after denying someone parole, the board can postpone a prisoner's next hearing for up to five years. Media interest in Leslie's case is revived whenever she appears before a parole board. Preparing for, enduring, and recovering from hearings—which, each time, require a detailed retelling of the crime—has been a painful and preoccupying part of Leslie's life on an ongoing basis. The hearings are effective as punishment and degradation, two of the purposes of prisons.

As of 2001, Leslie has been effectively reconvicted thirteen times by politically cautious boards, the parole denials generally rationalized in terms of the seriousness of the crime. Leslie's supporters, since her hearing in 1978 soon after her new conviction, have been pleading the following points in letters to the board:

1. When resentenced in 1978, Leslie had already served eight years in prison, and legally qualified for parole.
2. Psychiatric reports support the view that she has excellent mental health.
3. Community release and parole are much less expensive than incarceration.
4. She was, in 1978, out of prison for over six months, with no problems, no thoughts of escaping or doing harm, and no contact with the press outside the courtroom.
5. She can make a living as a computer programmer and word processor, an editor, a legal secretary, a researcher, or as a skilled artisan. If allowed the opportunity, she would be an excellent counselor.
6. She has the loyal support of her family and close friends.
7. She has the support of people from every generation and walk of life, many of whom have known her for decades or all her life.
8. To the extent that prisons can be helpful to someone who has committed a serious crime, seven years, more or less, is usually the limit in terms of effect. After that, it's "dead" time.
9. Leslie lives by strong morals, she is of good character, she works well with other women in the prison to collectively improve their situation, and she gets along well with her job supervisors and other staff.

The notion of rehabilitation has been generally out of favor among prison policy makers since the 1980s, though parole boards espouse rehabilitative principles as an expedient. When extended punishment—as vengeance—is the only reason for withholding Leslie's release, parole boards lean on their assumption of what the public wants. During Leslie's third trial, in 1978, Judge Gordon Ringer received ninety-two letters from the public with opinions about her sentencing; ninety of these strongly recommended that she be released. When, instead, he sentenced her back to prison, he noted that "Leslie was ready to reenter society," but he remained "fearful that society was not ready for Leslie."[11]

When it became clear to the parole board in the early 1980s that Leslie was rehabilitated by any definition, with political honesty they changed their rationale for not releasing her. Instead of talking about her need for more programming as a reason to deny parole, they focused on the need for a punishment that fit the crime. They said they were fulfilling their responsibility to society. Yet there was no public outcry against her six-month release on bail. When she was reimprisoned, letters to the parole board made offers of providing a home, a job, and other primary assistance upon her release. As her lawyer Max Keith said in her second trial (1977), "Neither society nor my client will benefit from her return to prison." In fact, the question of her parole is a matter of politics, not public safety.

Two scholars who have studied cults for over twenty years, Flo Conway and Jim Siegelman, arranged for an interview with Leslie in the late 1970s because at that time, of all those involved with Manson, she was the most likely to have recovered from Manson's spell, and to receive an early parole. They were working with the theory of sudden personality change, or "snapping," to refer to someone whose personality is radically altered through indoctrination. They wondered if that was what had happened to Leslie. Their impression of Leslie at twenty-seven was that, in contrast to the media images from the first trial, when she was twenty, "Leslie seemed sober and thoughtful. . . . It seemed to us very possible that she had indeed broken free of Manson's spell. . . . She recalled with great clarity the paths by which she went into and came out of her nightmare existence in the Manson Family."[12]

Like her psychiatrists, wardens, guards, family, friends, lawyers, and everyone who has known her over the years, I never saw a monster in Leslie (or, for that matter, in Pat or Susan).

Beginning in the early 1990s, under Governor Pete Wilson, political pressure stopped virtually all releases of individuals in California with homicide or lesser violence on their record, whatever the circumstances of the crime, however long they'd been incarcerated, however thoroughly they had been punished or reformed, and however contrary to the principles of justice. Having anticipated the possibility of getting out in 1978, Leslie nevertheless did not criticize the parole panel that denied her release. Her response in court to the new life sentence (supposedly with the possibility of parole) was to acknowledge the irreparable pain she caused the LaBianca family and her own family; she said to the judge, "It's a shame that I have to live with. . . . There is no mending."

In the mid-1970s, soon after she was transferred to the main prison and at a time when her spirits were at their lowest ebb, Leslie was charged with her one prison infraction in over thirty years: she was found with a small amount of marijuana she had been given by another prisoner. Drugs of all kinds find their way into prisons; I know of cases where people who had never used heroin on the outside became addicted while imprisoned. But Leslie was so appalled by the experience of being charged and punished for an illegal offense while already a maximum-security prisoner, that she immediately went back to being a model prisoner and never again committed an offense against prison rules. Fortunately, the board did not blow the incident out of proportion.

In 1979 she was told by the chair of the parole hearing, "We are finding you unsuitable [for release] because the time already spent has not yet outweighed the gravity of the crime." She was complimented, however, on her success with her college courses, and told, "Keep it up; you should have a great deal of hope." Contradicting their own decisions, board members for the past two decades have consistently encouraged her to maintain hope for release. Each time she has met with the board, through 2000, her hopes have been dashed, then raised for the next hearing. In 1985 she was told that her parole date was "closer than you might think." In her 1996 hearing Leslie was given two years to serve before her next hearing, which for someone serving life is encouraging. In 1998 she was given a one-year review, which is tantamount to preparing someone for a parole date. Because hope can be a torture, before every hearing Leslie has prepared herself and her family for denial.

Leslie makes favorable impressions on parole board members, who work in rotation and regularly include new members. She is also routinely degraded, however, by one or another of them. In one of Leslie's parole hearings she was asked, as usual, by a member of the board—who had trouble remembering her name and said he hadn't read her file—to relate the details of the murders. As has been true of parole board members through the years, he was incredulous that she could be so well spoken and rational. He wondered if she could be like "that Sybil girl, the one that was on TV."[13] He figured that Leslie, too, must be a "split personality." He voted against her release. At another hearing, in 1980, a board member had likewise insinuated to a reporter who was impressed with Leslie's demeanor that she was "similar to that girl with eight personalities." Certainly the short-term identity Leslie assumed under Manson was distinct from her own personality, which she has exhibited consistently, all the while under surveillance, for over a quarter century. Leslie doesn't suffer from multiple personality disorder, either from a clinical perspective or in the lay observation of anyone who knows her. For decades she's been an unusually steady, reliable woman with one very clear and consistent persona.

In her early years of imprisonment, Leslie had engaged in correspondence with men she met through an informal network of prison journalists whose different institutional newsletters were circulated throughout the prison system. The prisoners' shared creative writing and intellectual exchanges produced pen pal friendships, which eased the monotony of the passing hours, days, weeks, months, and years. Being able to communicate with men in this way, albeit platonically, also helped to normalize life for Leslie and other women.

Like many attractive imprisoned women whose cases make headlines, Leslie had received mail from interested suitors for many years. Some of those suitors were themselves imprisoned. And like many women in the prison, Leslie was so young when she entered prison that she hadn't experienced adult romance prior to incarceration, apart from her so-called relationship with Bobby Beausoleil within the Manson clan. Thus it was startling when, late in 1981, she wrote to her friends about having fallen in love and about her plans to marry. Bill was a man who was still incarcerated when they began corresponding; when he was released, he began visiting her in the prison and she found herself attracted to him. He was good company and he was respectful toward her. She felt hopeful that this was a man with whom she could have a lasting relationship whether or not she had to remain in prison. When all the required permissions were signed and arrangements made, Leslie and Bill were married in a small private ceremony within the prison. They were then granted the occasional privilege of private visits in the family apartment.

Very early in the marriage, Leslie became uneasy and realized that the marriage complicated her life more than it eased her loneliness. Her foreboding was intensified when she realized that Bill was not the decent, sane, law-abiding man she had trusted him to be. Most seriously, the prison authorities discovered that, without Leslie's knowledge, Bill was formulating a preposterous plan to help her escape—an idea that she herself would have never entertained. Disillusioned, she abruptly ended the relationship.

Bill was returned to prison and, at age thirty-two, Leslie returned to her prison routine with a more realistic acceptance of the constraints that imprisonment imposed on her emotional as well as her physical life.

On April 22, 1982, Leslie was denied parole primarily on the grounds that she had been irresponsible to have married a man who had been in prison and who continued to break the law while on parole. Leslie's punishment for her poor judgment in trusting and marrying this man was that she had to wait three more years for another hearing. The parole board did not give her credit for taking the initiative to end the relationship. Nor did they comment on the fact that her decisiveness was in sharp contrast to the days when she had acquiesced to male authority without question.

In September 1986, in response to my inquiry, I received a letter from the California Board of Prison Terms explaining why "Ms. Van Houten was found unsuitable for parole at her July 11, 1986, hearing." They cited four reasons, each of which was fraught with flaws as to relevancy or factual accuracy. For me to point them out would be redundant. In their unedited words, their reasons were:

1. Commitment Offense. The butchering of the Tate murder victims and of the LaBianca couple was without equal in the history of criminal record.
2. Previous Record. The unstable social history and prior criminality include the prisoner's parents who were divorced when she was 14, [Leslie] started using dangerous drugs, such as LSD, Benzedrine, mescaline, and marijuana. She became pregnant at the age of 15 and experienced an abortion.
3. Institutional Behavior. The panel considered the prisoner's lack of participation in a beneficial self-help program, specifically the area of Narcotics Anonymous or Alcoholics Anonymous. The prisoner has failed to demonstrate evidence of positive change in her selection of close relationships, as evidenced by her quick and unsuccessful marriage, that lasted approximately eight months. He was a parolee at the time.
4. Other Factors. The panel was not satisfied with the lack of detailed information regarding the prisoner's parole plans.

The letter concluded with this reassurance: "The panel commended Ms. Van Houten for her good work record, lengthy record of disciplinary-free prison conduct, volunteer work as a tutor, and positive attitude and performance."

In her spring 1996 parole hearing, she chose to represent herself rather than rely on a lawyer as she had in previous hearings. She calmly stated that after twenty-six years she believed the time had come for her to leave prison. Her plea was eloquent, but it was rejected. In this hearing, Leslie reflected quietly on the crime, responding to one board member's question about what she thought the LaBiancas must have been feeling as they realized they were being killed. She answered, "Terror. To die in terror. Probably everyone's worst nightmare." A decade earlier, the board panel had insisted she join Alcoholics Anonymous or Narcotics Anonymous. She had resisted having to join, but in this hearing she told the board that she appreciated being in AA, despite having no experience of alcoholism. She described how the group talked about reaching "a point of pitiful and incomprehensible demoralization. . . . Certainly for me, my point was the LaBianca home, my reason for going."[14] Watching a videotape of the hearing, I saw that, when compelled to speak of the murders, Leslie's remorse was deeply evident, etched on her face and audible in her voice.

One of the reasons offered by a member of that panel for the unsuitability decision was the charm factor: anyone as charming as Leslie must surely be manipulating others, and must therefore be untrustworthy and perhaps dangerous. This man used *charm* in its original meaning—casting a spell. In 1994 I was interviewed by Vickie Gabereau on CBC national radio about a book I'd published on women in prison, and she asked about the "Manson girls," wanting to know what kind of women they had become. When I said they were charming, we both laughed nervously at the incongruity of how that sounded. It is difficult to reconcile the qualities of warmth and likeability—which is what *I* mean by charm—with the scary media images of the three girls during the 1970–71 trial. People who kill or assault, or who in this case attempted to do so, may indeed be charming. But there is no correlation between charm and violence: most charming people do not harm others, and people who do violence are by no means always charming.

In the 1996 hearing, Leslie responded to the charm charge by saying that she engaged in violence just once in her life—August 10, 1969—whereas she has always been considered charming. Charm may conceal inner pain, shame, degradation, and remorse. But it is Leslie's calm demeanor that perplexed the board member, who judged Leslie insufficiently remorseful to deserve parole. In the days of the witch hunts, professional "prickers" were brought into European courts to test a woman's sensitivity to physical pain. If having the needle stuck into her body did not produce tears, it was believed she must be a witch, therefore guilty, therefore to be executed—or, in this analogous case, held in prison indefinitely. The irony is that when a woman does, against her will, break down and weep in shame in front of the parole board, she may be denied parole on the grounds that she is faking remorse and trying to gain sympathy by using one of woman's oldest "tricks."

At that 1996 session, the board commissioner continued to badger Leslie, then age forty-six, about showing remorse, about whether her feelings were for herself or for the victims. She replied sadly, "I naturally mourn my own life that never has been. But most of all, I think about the children who are being born into a family that has to live out the legacy of the crime, the LaBianca children's families. I think a lot about that, how unfair."[15] A 1996 televised biography of Charles Manson included a clip of Leslie saying, "The older I get the harder it is. Mrs. LaBianca was younger than I am now. I took away all that life.... Manson took a lot of time taking middle-class girls and remolding them. Part of my responsibility is that I helped to create *him*."[16]

Continuing her statement to the board, Leslie pointed out that she was nineteen when the crime was committed. She went on. "Most people have changed and matured within twenty-seven years. Most people have become parents and sometimes grandparents in that period of time. I've had not just the process of aging, but I've had twenty-seven years of intervention, therapy, and self-help." But they persisted with the issue of her emotional containment. They wanted to see her in her suffering; they wanted her to summon and expose her raw feelings—while sitting alone, facing a formal, adversarial board that held her destiny in their hands. Her diligent, omnipresent prosecutor, Stephen Kay, was seated across the table from her. All the while, under bright lights, the cameras would record her testimony and any emotional display for cable television. This was what they were asking from her. But even if she lost her composure, it would have to be controlled; if she became upset, the board could deny her parole on the grounds of instability.

In its decision, the parole board focused on the crime, not on Leslie's good behavior for nearly three decades in jail and prison. In that 1996 hearing, the presiding commissioner officially stated, "In arriving at a decision, we will consider the commitment offenses, your prior criminality, and your adjustment since you've been incarcerated."[17]

Leslie had no criminal record prior to meeting Manson. Her prior illegalities consisted of possession of small amounts of LSD and marijuana, though she was never charged with a drug offense, and charges against the whole "family" for the theft of dune buggy parts, which were dropped. In terms of "adjustment," she overcame anorexia long ago, in her twenties, and has been exceptionally well adjusted as she has matured from young womanhood through middle age. Everyone agrees she has a healthy outlook—family, friends in and out of prison, psychiatrists, prison staff, lawyers, and so on. Seeing that she has satisfied the criteria for having no serious "prior criminality" and for having made a good behavioral "adjustment" to prison, the board continues to decide her fate on the basis of two crimes: one with which she was involved, and the more sensationalized crime in which she had no involvement.

In a letter to the parole board in 1996, prior to the hearing, Leslie's older brother asked, "Why is it year after year you keep making up new reasons she can't be paroled? Why is it year after year you keep making up new goals for her to achieve, and she does, and then you make up new ones, and new ones, and it goes on forever? This is very cruel and unusual punishment. I have hope that someday, some board will return Leslie to her family. I hope you are that board." The board panel members were angry about the letter, and grilled Leslie about whether she shared her brother's attitude. Leslie, simply and quietly, stated that her brother was frustrated because he loved his sister and wanted her home. They were then gentle with Leslie, who remained calm and well spoken. They expressed respect for how she was living her life in the prison. They gave her new goals to achieve. They denied her parole.

At Leslie's May 28, 1998, hearing, she was received respectfully by the board, who were very encouraging to her despite Stephen Kay's persistent advocacy for continued imprisonment. The board listened to her very carefully as she responded to their questions. They gave her reason for hope that the year 1999 would be her last year in the prison. She was granted a one-year review, scheduled for July 1999 and signifying the approach of a release date.

Rosemary LaBianca was Leno's second wife. Her daughter, who with her half brother had discovered their murdered parents, has never called for continued incarceration. In fact, she testified at one of Charles Watson's hearings, decades after the crime, as to her belief that he had earned the right to parole. (He remains in prison as of the year 2001.) Leno LaBianca's first wife, with whom he had children, and several other relatives have recently opposed the release of any of those involved in killing the LaBiancas. In 1999 Leno's niece, who had been in contact with Kay, was quoted by the *National Enquirer* as follows: ". . . for crimes like these, there can be no forgiveness. . . . Leslie Van Houten is a cold-blooded killer. She should never be allowed out of prison."[18] The tabloid accompanied the story of Leslie's then-upcoming hearing with a plea to readers to submit to the parole board a detachable coupon protesting her release.

Leslie's hearing scheduled for July 1999 was postponed at Leslie's own initiative. I know of no other case where a prisoner with the prospect of parole has requested a postponement of a hearing. I was particularly surprised because, with her friend Linda's assistance in gathering documents, she had prepared extensively. Her reason for requesting postponement was that she had learned that a man was copying the cable-telecast videotapes of her hearings and selling them over the Internet at a profit. Because she did not want to collude with profiteering from the LaBiancas' murders, she informed the board by letter, well in advance, that she wouldn't participate if it was being telecast, knowing that pirated tapes would be sold. When she arrived for the hearing, the lights and cameras were set up. She refused to participate in what she described as "a circus."

Stephen Kay announced to the disappointed media crowd, which was waiting in the prison parking lot, that Leslie was faking her reason for postponement. He said she just didn't want to face Mr. LaBianca's niece, who had accompanied Kay to the hearing to protest Leslie's release. This was patently untrue; Leslie's letter to the board was mailed before she heard that a family member might be in attendance.

The board agreed that Leslie's concern about the tapes should have been honored, and assured her that the situation would be rectified at her postponed hearing, rescheduled for summer 2000. Leslie returned to her routine, but with the pleasure of a new job as assistant to the chaplain.

Leslie's June 2000 hearing was significant for two reasons. First, prior to the hearing, Margaret Singer, a leading U.S. expert on contemporary cults, met with Leslie after examining all the relevant documents in her case. In Singer's report to the board, she verified that Leslie's experience was a classic case of cult indoctrination and recovery. After thirteen hearings, beginning with her first one in 1978, a board panel finally officially acknowledged that Leslie had indeed been the victim of cult brainwashing.

Secondly, Leno LaBianca's middle-aged niece and two nephews accompanied Stephen Kay to the hearing. Normally, only immediate family members and next of kin are permitted to attend hearings, but the board made an exception in this case. Kay's purpose in bringing them, of course, was to strengthen his usual arguments against her release. Leslie, however, welcomed this opportunity to apologize directly to representatives of the LaBianca family. For decades she had envisioned and hoped for this encounter, but her own request to meet with the family had been previously denied by the authorities. Now she could express to them her profound remorse, just as they could directly confront her with their pain and their anger. It was, of course, extremely difficult for everyone, but for Leslie it was also a relief to have this communication on a human level.

As for granting Leslie a parole date, the board ignored the abundant documentation and experts' evaluations that had been submitted in support of her release. She was again denied parole.

• • •

In 1999, Leslie wrote to me of how "each moment and action is a prayer. . . . That I am so smiled upon gives me great joy."[19] One day, I trust, Leslie will be free to tell her own story, to explain firsthand why that contradiction could occur in one person—the very decent, thoughtful woman who, in her youth, became someone else for a few years. Through the decades I've known Leslie, I've seen her evolve from a deluded slave of a seriously damaged man to a mature, multidimensional woman who contributes to her community. For her actions one night in 1969, she was condemned to suffer, whether or not she's in prison.

Eight

REFLECTIONS

LEGAL SCHOLARS IN THE UNITED STATES observe that dominant world religions as well as localized cults (which can be characterized as new, usually transient religions) are heading toward an era of greater legal accountability.[1] When the Manson murders were dominating the news, little was known about cults. In 1978, almost a decade later, a dramatic example of mind control by a cult leader helped bring the issue out of the shadows. Jim Jones, a preacher with a following in northern California, left the United States with a large flock of his devoted followers, to form a colony called Jonestown in a jungle region of Guyana, South America. There, on November 29, 1978, he orchestrated a mass suicide–murder, taking the lives of 912 people, including 276 children, before killing himself.[2]

Like Charles Manson, Jim Jones had absolute, totalitarian control over his subjects. Leslie recalls reading a *Rolling Stone* article in which Jones revealed how very aware of Manson he had been. Echoing Manson, Jones preached of an imminent holocaust and of a coming race war. He also availed himself of the sexuality of his followers. And he did not allow anyone to question him about what he was doing and why.[3]

Subsequent real-life dramas that resulted in many deaths of cult members brought home the message that closed-minded, unmitigated devotion and obedience to a person or a dogma is a dangerous thing. For example, in 1993, after a fifty-one-day standoff with the FBI in Waco, Texas, over seventy men, women, and children devoted to David Koresh, leader of the Branch Davidians, were shot or burned to death. And in March 1997, Marshall Applewhite, the sixty-five-year-old leader of the Heaven's Gate cult, brought himself and thirty-eight other men and women, age twenty-six to seventy-two, all characterized by the media as "very ordinary," to their carefully programmed suicidal deaths in San Diego. They had plans to shift to a higher plane, just as Manson envisioned paradise for his followers through death (of others).

There is no reason to doubt that virtually all human beings are capable of destructive and self-destructive impulses. It's a factor of chance circumstance. In 1981 Anne Near and I contemplated whether everyone is capable of murder. It was significant that Leslie had shown herself to be incapable of it, at least in that place at that time.

Still, one evening I started to say to Anne that we should assume that every person contains within him- or herself the potential for any form of behavior. She added, "Except frequently so well repressed." Then she completed the thought. "The whole spectrum [of potential action] is a possibility we must acknowledge, especially when seeking to learn from the tragedy of violent crime." An old theme in Christianity is admonishing the flocks against being fooled by the seductions of false prophets. (See Matthew 7:15–16.) The implication is that it could happen to anyone. The need to warn everyone about evil lurking everywhere suggests that everyone is vulnerable to committing heinous sin as well as being a victim. In talking about Leslie in this context, Anne and I talked again about making judgment:

> *KF: We could get closer to the heart of the matter if we could wipe away those elements of distrust which are born from judgment, and from the fear of being judged.*
>
> *ANNE: "Judge not that ye be not judged." A rediscovery.*

This exchange with Anne Near took me back to notes from a conversation in the Special Security Unit in 1973, when the women talked about "discovering the power within [themselves] for destruction." We were talking about the prison psychiatrist, who was always trying to get them to reveal "the monster inside." In exasperation, each woman would echo the others' remarks: "Doesn't he know *everyone* has a monster inside them?" "It isn't something you just pull out when someone wants to look at it." "He can't appreciate that what we are, what he sees in front of him, is also real." "They want to watch us dig out for display the rage and frustration that they believe is inside us." But they hadn't acted out of rage. They had acted out of blind obedience.

Everyone was amazed at the women's calm equanimity, day after day, year after year. Most staff accepted their peaceful ways as an unexamined blessing; cynical professionals, the brain explorers, sought to shatter the women's calm with invasions into their interiors, lusting after the dark side of their psyches.

Both formal, legal, professional judgments and informal social judgments are based on the presumption that the person issuing judgment would never commit the offense. The alternative would be hypocritical.

Forgiveness is not about lowering standards, but about suspending judgment for self-protection. It's an error to assume that we have structured ourselves or our lives in such a way as to be perpetually protected from the whole range of human possibility.

The killer is often the boy next door. We see his neighbors on television saying some variation of "He is such a nice fellow. I never would have thought him capable of such a thing." Anne Near went on. "Young men who were sent—or even volunteered to go—to Vietnam and found themselves setting fire to villages were not 'that kind of people.' They were not that kind of people at all!" But they willingly obeyed their authorities. Anne said, "It seems possible for people to perceive themselves in a comparable state of war and follow orders that supersede their normal behavior patterns. They begin to follow orders. The German people horrendously—but not *only* the German people—succumbed to this human possibility. The Manson people, in a very strange context and feeling that everything was disintegrating into chaos, began to believe it was war, began following orders."

A lifetime activist for peace and justice, Anne pointed out that acts of war cannot so easily be distinguished from murder as the military would pretend. Courts-martial of soldiers who have committed homicide during a war show ironic layers within which the act of killing (and rape) is justified according to the particular authority, the players, and the rules of the game. In a grim litany, Anne and I talked one day about the crimes of Hiroshima, acid rain, pollution of streams, the bombing of Cambodia, germ warfare, government agents shooting students at Kent and Jackson state universities, crimes of the corporate world, and women beaten by their husbands. These are crimes that most people understandably don't want to be thinking about.

> *KF: People I encounter don't want to look at the guilty person because I think they're afraid for themselves. Fear can be a counterproductive effort at self-protection. Beneath the hostility and distancing, I see an almost instinctive or archaic recognition that we're all in this together, that the ultimate spiritual reality is that we are all connected and share this universe, not only as companions, but as mutually responsible partners in life. What one does affects the other, an old spiritual theme.*
>
> *ANNE: Eugene Debs wrote, "As long as there is one person in prison, I am not free." It's literal.*
>
> *KF: That anyone at all must be locked up is a significant statement of failure—generally of both the individual and society. Do we or do we not have a mutual responsibility?*
>
> *ANNE: We cannot absolve ourselves.*
>
> *KF: We can't pretend that somehow we're excluded.*

It has given me pause to consider this particular conversation in light of Manson's own beliefs. For example, Charles "Tex" Watson described Manson's philosophy this way: "We are all one, all part of the same organic whole, no separate *me* or *you*, just ripples in the one wave that is life. True freedom means giving up ourselves, letting that old ego die so we can be free of the self that keeps us from one another, keeps us from life itself. 'Cease to exist,' Charlie sang in one of the songs he'd written.... The girls repeated it, over and over—*cease to exist, kill your ego, die*—so that once you cease to be, you can be free to totally love, totally come together."[4]

This age-old affirmation across many cultures of the connectedness of all life was betrayed by Manson's war plan. And however routinely horrific the crimes in the world at large may be, as Anne said, "It doesn't add up to 'what Leslie and the others did was not so bad.' " We have to acknowledge that here is a terrible crime and here is another terrible crime, and over here is yet a third.

To this day Leslie asks not to be excused or granted immunity from judgment. But she does want to be seen as she is now. The state's perennial judgments against her release hark back to August 10, 1969, to the night in her very young life that has determined the rest of her life. To the parole board, the past thirty years have counted for nothing.

Leslie's humility is most evident in her appreciation of every opportunity the prison offers. She is responsible and is a good friend to other women in her prison community. She took classes and tutorials through the University of California and other higher education institutions when they were offered. She served as the teaching assistant for philosophy and psychology classes brought in by a college, and completed her B.A. degree from Antioch. She has also been active in service work in the prison at large. With the few other well-schooled women in the prison, Leslie has taught basic reading and writing skills to women for whom public schooling has been a failure. Leslie has also volunteered in programs that help people outside the prison—she has made quilts for the homeless and read onto tape for the visually impaired. She served as editor of *The Clarion,* the prison newspaper, as a means of activating good writers in prison. She is supportive of other women in her cell unit and through various prisonwide organizations. She is not without sorrow, anger, and frustration. For many years she kept in physical shape by releasing tension in the gym, but several years ago the equipment was removed from the prison. She seeks counsel and spiritual guidance, and has been welcomed by First Nations women in sweat-lodge ceremonies and healing circles. She works with other women to find "ways to help each other find effective means of coping with the stress and anxiety that overcrowding causes."[5]

Leslie has also found other "meaningful and satisfying things to do within the confines of my environment."[6] She has worked, with an outside attorney, as a jailhouse lawyer, helping another woman with her case. She studied the history of quilt making, and does cross-stitched samplers, designing her own pieces. Like any prisoner, to earn her keep through decades in the main prison she has worked steadily at various prison jobs, and has managed to make most of them meaningful. She was first the head clerk in the medical clinic. Later, after five years in the education office, the maximum time a prisoner can stay in one work assignment, she became a nighttime clerk for the administration and helped put out the daily prison bulletin. Night work afforded her some welcome solitude during the day, when most other prisoners were at work. Because she's skillful, reliable, and congenial—and because she has seniority—she has had favorable work assignments since arriving at the main prison in 1976.

Leslie doesn't take anything positive in her life for granted, or assume any comfort as her prerogative, her due, or her right. She has lived her entire adulthood as if grateful to be able to live out her sentence, the difficulties of that life notwithstanding. She would like very much to be reunited with her family while her parents are still living. She would like to live in a larger world. But she has learned to live the life she has been given, in the midst of a crowded prison. Leslie reflects:

> *Sometimes I feel like people hold me responsible for the fact that I didn't go to the gas chamber. Sometimes it would have been easier if I had gone. When I need strength to go on, I draw it out from within myself. I do that alone.*[7]

Leslie's perception of a public desire for capital punishment in the USA is accurate. In every public poll, a majority claim to believe in the death penalty as a just punishment and as a deterrent to others. In the USA, the only Western nation to retain the death penalty, it is a minority who espouses the practical as well as ethical reasons to oppose capital punishment. Retribution makes sense only to the extent that it culminates in remorse, penance, and reconciliation with society—which can't occur if the offender is killed. Innocent people have been executed throughout history owing to human error or corruption. If the state wants to communicate that killing people is wrong, it is hardly setting an example when it performs executions. Given the necessary legal appeals in cases where the sentence is death, and the expense of incarceration during the long delays between sentencing and actual execution, the death sentence is sometimes more costly to the state than keeping someone in prison for life would be. It is conventional wisdom to believe that the death penalty is a deterrent to other would-be killers, but murder rates in the United States are consistently highest in those states that conduct the greatest number of executions. Often, when the execution rates go up, murder rates follow suit.

The majority of U.S. citizens believes that, for the most heinous violations, "the punishment should fit the crime" (therefore, murderers should be killed). But if the purpose of the punishment is to inflict pain, it is generally a greater punishment to hold someone in prison indefinitely. When asked why she seemed so little affected when she was sentenced to death on April 19, 1971, Leslie explained, "The death penalty for me at the time almost justified my not having to deal with what I had done. It was the eye for an eye."[8]

Although generally emotionally charged, debates about capital punishment are academic until one meets someone who has been sentenced to death. Few people advocate death for individuals with whom they are acquainted, however much they believe in the ultimate penalty in principle. No one I know who has met Leslie, including death-penalty advocates, has believed that she should have been executed for her crime, or that the world would be better in her absence.

For Leslie, the prison has simultaneously served its purposes as a harsh punishment for her crime and as a place to reflect on the crime and its effects. She has endured her punishment with dignity, using her time as positively as possible. Within the walls of her confinement, Leslie has recognized her part in an orgy of human destruction. Her sorrow is a matter of conscience, a purely solitary force. She has re-created her life through the daily, hourly act of serving penance.

In the early 1970s Leslie, along with her codefendants, was demonized by the media. But she also gained sympathy from some serious journalists who were paying attention. This positive attention accelerated during the second and third trials in the late 1970s. Even world-weary journalists whose cynicism was unbounded found positive qualities in Leslie, especially the old guard who had covered the original trial and were stunned by the change in her, less than a decade later. The mainstream print media in California, through the words of half a dozen reporters working primarily for the *Los Angeles Times* and the *San Francisco Chronicle,* used these words to describe Leslie during the retrial period (1976 through 1978): charming; smiling; vivacious; open; aware; exceptional; gracious; animated; thoughtful; responsible; trustworthy; remarkable, mature young woman; warm and caring human being; a person of great sensitivity; undergone an extraordinary transformation; stable; law-abiding; not the least bit dangerous; productive; legal secretary; skilled artisan; completely rehabilitated.

When Leslie was a child she attended Sunday school, and with other dedicated young people she became a junior deacon. This job included collecting and counting the offerings, and taking flowers to the elderly and the ill. Dwight Blackstock, who went to Sunday school with Leslie and was also in the group, later became a Presbyterian minister. He recalls of those days when they were friends: "Leslie and I, along with the other junior deacons, learned how to demonstrate love and concern for others."[9] Eight years after Leslie's imprisonment, Blackstock became her prison pastor, and was soon a strong advocate for her release. After some visits with her, he said, "It became abundantly clear to me that Leslie is an exceptional person. She has not only a tremendous intellectual capacity, but also an abundance of love and sensitivity.... I found Leslie to be a woman of integrity and quiet faith."[10]

Leslie learned from solitary confinement to be her own best friend. One of her favorite authors from the 1960s, Carlos Castaneda, said that an ordinary person is one who regards each moment of life as a blessing or a curse, whereas a warrior faces each moment as a challenge. Leslie rises to the challenge of making the passing of prison time meaningful, despite the sometimes desperate conditions and unrelenting pressures of prolonged confinement. Long ago she was returned to herself, transformed from virtually complete subjugation by Manson to an unfettered independence of mind common only among exceptional human beings in a free society.

The only useful response to any deep lapse of human decency is to attempt to live each day thereafter with honor. Guilt without honor is a degraded condition. Guilt that obsesses, distorts, and disables is of no use. Leslie's greatest victory has been to accept responsibility for her crime and to accept the omnipresent grief without losing her capacity for self-respect. She has transformed her guilt into constructive activity, making herself useful to her community. Victor Hugo developed this theme beautifully in *Les Miserables,* though the crime of his protagonist is morally antithetical to Leslie's crime. The fictional character of Jean Valjean spent nineteen years in prison for stealing a loaf of bread to feed his sister's seven starving children. The prison corrupted him. When released, he could feel only for himself. Through the actions of a priest who possessed saintly wisdom, Jean Valjean recovered and, in the manner of his mentor pastor, became once again a noble, humble, kind, honorable man. He regained his gratitude for life.

This gratitude is what I see in Leslie. She will never be able to free herself from the consequences of her past actions or from the weight on her conscience. But despite her everlasting guilt-born sorrow, despite the day-by-day agonies of being imprisoned, she is grateful for her life and she lives each day with honor. She knows that getting out of prison and finding freedom are not the same thing.

Part 2: Leslie's Letters

Nine

MARKING TIME

THIS CHAPTER CONSISTS OF EXCERPTS from letters and notes I've received from Leslie. They are published here with her permission. Aili Malm, of Simon Fraser University, helped me choose which letters to include, to give a fleeting chronicle of Leslie's life in the prison from 1972 until 1998. She has sent beautiful note cards and typed or written letters on whimsical or elegant stationery, sometimes handmade. My purpose here is to give Leslie her own voice and to give readers a chronological account, in her own words, of how she has lived her life sentence.

I have omitted most of Leslie's frequent references to mutual friends like Linda, Nancy, Sue, Liebe, and her own family or mine. The focus is on Leslie herself. This is misleading in that it is all about her; in life and in letters, she is not self-centered.

The letters catalog years marked by parole hearings and a rising prison population and overcrowding.

All incoming and outgoing mail is read and censored by prison officers, which affects the content of letters. One must, therefore, read between the lines. I've inserted commentary here and there, in brackets, to help the reader place the letter in the context of what was happening in Leslie's life at the time the letter was written.

These excerpts from her letters are an accurate representation of how

Leslie converses, whether or not she is under surveillance. I wish her animated voice and facial expressions could also be reproduced here. She uses words carefully to say what she means, directly. She does not exaggerate or indulge in self-pity.

Leslie does have bouts of low spirits—sometimes for months after a parole hearing—but she always returns her focus to positive strategies to improve her state of mind. She is bothered by people who chronically whine and complain about their own lives, or who avoid responsibility. She understands with keen awareness that we all have to carry our own burdens. This does not preclude sharing tears, advice, perspective, and practical assistance with those close to her. It just means that she has deep respect for other people's emotional space and works at maintaining a positive outlook. She tries to be useful under difficult circumstances, if only by maintaining a kind disposition.

Special Security Unit: 1972–1976

[All letters from Leslie dated between 1972 and mid-1976 were written from the Special Security Unit at the California Institution for Women, Frontera. We corresponded infrequently during those years because our visits were so frequent.]

September 12, 1972 (age 23):

Not much has happened around here [since we last saw each other]. The yards are beginning to look prettier and I'm beginning to feel more physically in shape.

Today some kind of siren went off and we spent time watching [staff] try to stop it. Rather odd thing to hear a siren. I felt like I was in a gangster movie and Cagney just escaped.

January 31, 1973

You know that expression "You made your bed, now lie in it"? Well, that's just what I have to do. My ickiest part of the week is changing the sheets on this iron slab. (An iron slab is better than springs.) I would just like a sleeping bag under the stars.

February 28, 1974 (age 24)

I am sitting, very studious, at my renunciate furniture, hair in rollers, listening to opera [on the radio]. [Why opera? because of the] longer lapses between commercials.

You've gotten on me to [do creative writing], and Pat as well. But there has always been the hang-up of "what for?" I'm still not sure of the purpose, but I do know I can leave this environment and its vibes, and go into a surprisingly fun world of words and imagination. [Leslie and Pat had just been published in an anthology of prison writings, edited by Frank Andrews.]

April 28, 1975 (age 25)

[Please send] a letter for our files, listing all the [University of California workshops] we've taken, and credits. [Soon after, Leslie enrolled in the Antioch in-prison college program to work toward a degree.]

March 1, 1976 (age 26)

[Leslie is now given time each day in the main prison, where she has a prison job with the school and *The Clarion,* the prison newspaper.] I feel good today. I wrote an editorial and it's pretty good. It's on waiting in lines for things like canteen and packages.

I moved to a new office. I do more work since I moved. It's fun, and I hope to get [the office] functioning smoothly soon, with pictures on the walls. . . . I'm doing my first Clarion interview on Monday, with [the assistant warden].

May 22, 1976

[Leslie now lives in the main prison.] Just to walk and talk with people is so good. It's been a long, long time [six and a half years].

December 15, 1976 (age 27)

I'm on my way to the [Los Angeles] county jail so that I can start trial again. I'll send you my booking number so you can visit.

Sybil Brand Institute: 1977

[Prior to the second trial, Leslie was returned to Sybil Brand Institute, where she had been incarcerated from late 1969 to mid-1971. Whenever Leslie was not in the jail's visiting room or in court, she was locked in a maximum-security, heavily guarded cell isolated in the basement of Sybil Brand. We had frequent in-person twenty-minute visits (in a cubicle with phones, separated by a glass partition), and we wrote back and forth to fill in the gaps. Communicating with her friends and family members helped Leslie to keep track of details and stay grounded throughout the intensity of the trial, from January until September 1977.]

January 3, 1977

I have been adjusting to my new situation and getting my head together for court. I'm in isolation but that's fine with me. It's quiet and I'm beginning to do some writing.

January 16, 1977

I gave an interview with Barbara Walters. It's not all that bad here. I get out [of solitary] an hour a day and two hours every other night [to visit with other prisoners in the dayroom].

April 16, 1977

The jury is selected and now it's time to start trial. There's really no guessing as to how things are going to go.

June 13, 1977

I'm on the stand. I'm relatively calm. I haven't lost weight. I figure about three more weeks of court.

July 20, 1977

I'll see you Tuesday. We've been friends for five years now. Remember the banana-split birthday party?

August 16, 1977

I'm thinking how strange it is that on the eve of my 28th year, I'm beginning to feel comfortable as a woman, becoming my own woman.

August 31, 1977 (age 28)

I'm in a weird space right now. Tomorrow I may hear something [verdict].

I now have permission to crochet and embroider dolls' faces. They give them to little people in hospitals. I'm crocheting a blanket for myself.

I'm not the same person I was eight months ago. What do you see when you look at me?

. . .

[In September 1977, Leslie's second trial ended in a hung jury. Her request to plea-bargain was denied. A third trial loomed ahead.]

September 15, 1977

Naturally the news was a hard blow [hung jury and denial of plea bargain, which necessitated a third trial], and even now I haven't accepted it fully. It's going to take time.

October 4, 1977

As always, mama is a beautiful champ. Smiling and keeping strong. I'm proud to be her daughter.

October 6, 1977

This evening [during her two hours in the dayroom] I talked with the four "aliens" [undocumented workers], one from Guatemala, three from Mexico. We had fun playing charades—drawing pictures to start learning words: sun-sol, teeth-los dientes, etc.

October 25, 1977

The judge [Gordon Ringer, who would preside over the third trial] is not what I expected [in pretrial proceedings]. Small man, little or no hair, glasses. [His] courtroom has loose vibes, friendly bailiff. Many attorneys feel J. Ringer is a really fine legal scholar.

NOVEMBER 24, 1977

I've been going [on assignment] to the sewing room to work on a [fabric art] banner. It's going to hang in the sheriff's office. What a trip, huh?

I went to a dentist to get my teeth fixed: eight cavities, one cap. I have to go back.

I have gained eight pounds. Last count I weighed 120, a first for me. I'm glad. [Leslie, about five feet seven, was recovering from anorexia.]

DECEMBER 8, 1977

I don't know how I'll make it through another entire trial.

Out on Bail: 1978

[Following are excerpts from a letter written during Leslie's third trial, when she was free on bail in Los Angeles. I was teaching at Sonoma State University, about seven hundred miles north of Los Angeles, where Leslie was staying with a friend for the months of the trial. For several months we had frequent contact, as described in Chapter 6.]

EARLY JUNE, 1978

It's almost over. I'm feeling pushed, tense, nervous. There are many exciting things to plan if all goes well. I went roller-skating and I played Frisbee.

The trial is beginning to wind down. This afternoon is the tape, a very boring four-and-a-half hour tape of me not talking to the police [in 1970]. I'm beginning to feel calmer, a bit freer since I finished testifying. It's all a matter of waiting now.

I'm trying to write while the tape plays, and it's difficult to free my head from what I'm hearing. Lots of old cobweb memories.

Back at CIW: 1978–1998 (and in early 2001 she remains there)

[At the conclusion of her third trial, on July 5, 1978, Leslie was convicted on two counts of felony murder and returned to the California Institution for Women. For a short time she was kept under observation in the Psychiatric Treatment Unit, which is maximum security, but she was allowed to go to the main prison by day for work and for interaction with other prisoners. She had good cause to believe she would soon be given a parole release date. Her return to prison came as a sudden jolt from unbridled hope to the beginnings of resignation, although it was a few years before she was reconciled to a long life in prison. From the start of her new life sentence, she made room for optimism. She trusted that one day she'd be granted parole, that she could give that to her mother and father in their lifetime.]

September 24, 1978 (age 29)

Although at times I am extremely lonesome, I've decided I will fill those spots with learning-reading-writing and concentrating my energies into positive channels.

November 14, 1978

I see prison as a place where people are forced to look at themselves. The longer you're here the longer you have to look.

So many are here because they just couldn't make it. Drugs the #1 escape.

To me the prison is a place to learn about yourself so you can cope with the world outside. [It was good] to live outside with good people who try to not break the law. The legal system is incredible—a lot of beautiful ideas.

I am OK. I'm feeling positive—well, it's touch and go, but I'm more optimistic with each day. [She writes that she really likes her clerk job in the medical clinic.]

The evenings are hard but I have my blank pages to fill up and a zillion threads to play with, so I'm OK. I cry a lot when I'm alone because sometimes it hurts a lot. The pain is a healthy one because it keeps me focused.

You'd really like my cell. I really love it the way it is. I don't know how to explain—rainbow and earthy hues. Most things functional. I keep it as clean and crisp as possible. I'm as settled in my patterns as Pavlov's dogs.

December 12, 1978

I spent the evening in the record room with Pat, listening to Cris [Williamson] sing. Pat was sewing a worn nightie, I was finishing a strange skirt. Another woman was there and it was nice to hear her sing along with Cris. She's been to Cris's concerts.

Today I played catch, volleyball, and basketball. We were all so bad at it that it was fun and funny. . . . helps ease my nerves for the upcoming Board date. I get so scared just thinking about it, really. But time is passing.

December 31, 1978

How are you? I'm OK, waiting for 12 o'clock to arrive so I can go to sleep after all the noise. My New Year's goals are: getting heavy into school; being organized; putting out good wherever I can; most of all, being true to myself, not allowing the negative environment to affect my inner heart.

[Leslie's mother continues to visit her every Saturday.] Mama is fine. She's holding up well. That helps. I worry about her so much.

February 12, 1979

[In early 1979, Leslie was again denied parole.] Well—I went to the Board and I received a year review. I'm going to try to get closer to a B.A. My head is OK. More than ever it is clear to me that this is not my home.

April 3, 1979

I saw daddy recently and that was great!!

July 2, 1979

I'm reading *The World According to Garp*. I've also been working on yoga. I'm beginning to step outside my blues, remembering there is an entire rainbow. But I miss everyone and I miss the beauty of the world, the variety of people [on the outside].

I've lost some weight again. I'm trying to stay at 120; 130 was pretty heavy stuff when it was all packed on the rear. People were saying that when I bent over I blocked out the sun!

SEPTEMBER 13, 1979 (AGE 30)

I've been working on a one-act play. It has four characters and deals with a teenage pregnancy. It's great fun, also a little painful. My [Antioch College] advisor feels I should have my degree in a year and a half.

DECEMBER 14, 1979

I am taking advantage of my confinement to study as much as possible. These last few weeks I've been studying poetry and writing it. I'm not comfortable with poetry, but I'm getting the sense of words. Next week I begin the short story.

I go to the Board on January 17. [Her lawyer] feels quite confident. I feel quite nervous.

JANUARY 19, 1980

I had my hearing and once again I'm dealing with deep disappointment. But I think that, in spite of the letdown, good things happened. We're going to challenge the decision. [One of the board] insinuated to a reporter that he saw me as similar to "that girl with eight personalities." They don't understand how I can be normal now and have been part of the crime ten years ago.

I'm OK and Mom's OK, so that's the main thing.

[The appeal on parole was denied.]

FEBRUARY 5, 1980

I've learned to live with my guilt.

One evening when it turned dark early, I was walking across the [prison] compound alone, and I realized this is one of the few places a woman can walk alone and not worry about rape.

MAY 27, 1980

I work in the school building now, as a clerk. It's great. I have time to study. My days are markedly more relaxed than when I was working in the clinic. I am hoping next quarter to begin a course on the essay. I'm uncomfortable with that form and would like to get over my shyness.

I think I have pretty much worked through my bad cycle.

June 15, 1980

[About her excellent instructors and the writing process:] As I learn my tools, so also I must learn my soul.

December 18, 1980 (age 31)

Another year is gone. Another year of lessons learned. . . . I am going through changes, and would but I could come and talk to you. I need a sorting. . . .

October 18, 1981 (age 32)

This last Board hearing really wiped me out. I am trying to mend. I finished my B.A. (in creative writing). [When in her cell after work, she's focusing on new writing projects.] I am also giving a lot of attention to the Long-Termers Organization. [And] I want to bring myself up to reading a book a week. [She also, very significantly, writes of falling in love with a former prisoner, a man who had been visiting weekly after a period of correspondence between them.]

November 3, 1981

Perhaps you should sit down when you read this. I'm getting married. Yes, I am. He is good to me and I feel very happy when I'm with him. Please don't worry. I'm in control of my senses.

• • •

[In 1981 I received my Ph.D., and the following year returned home to Canada to work at Simon Fraser University in Vancouver. Our visits became infrequent; our correspondence continued.]

February 14, 1982

I'm really surprised at how much our marriage has affected my life, much more than I had anticipated. I'm getting ready for another three-day visit [with her husband, in the prison's family apartment]. I feel strong but I also feel unsettled.

. . .

[Soon afterward, Leslie learned that her husband had continued lawbreaking activity while on parole and she immediately dissolved the marriage.]

UNDATED

I try to remember the deep need I had for this relationship and the greater understanding of myself that it ultimately gave me.

MARCH 13, 1982

In April I will begin [to co-lead] a series of workshops geared for women who have finished their GEDs but who feel inadequate [to proceed with college classes].

JUNE 1, 1982

Things around here have become very tense with the overcrowding. There are close to 1,100 women here now. That's in contrast to the 600+ when you were first here [ten years before]. But I have my room, and it is private and special.

. . .

[Because of harsh sentencing for drug possession offenses, the population of CIW peaked at over 2,500 in the 1980s. With the construction of a chain of new California prisons for women, the CIW population leveled off at around 2,000 women in the 1990s. There are now, in the year 2001, over 11,000 women incarcerated by the state of California.]

CHRISTMAS DAY, 1982 (AGE 33):

Another year is passing us by. Each year I feel I should measure my life less on what I accomplished than on what did I learn.

JULY 5, 1983

[Double-bunking has reached Leslie's cell. The six-by-nine-foot cell must now accommodate two women who are strangers to each other.] It's 7:30

A.M. . . . I'm alone in my room for at least half an hour and I'm feeling good. I must tell my new [cellmate] that it is only fair that she give me some time alone like I try to give her.

AUGUST 19, 1983

I've been reading a lot of Tennessee Williams and Jean Paul Sartre. The other day I looked around my room and saw I was surrounded by old men. I have Einstein, Schweitzer, and Picasso all on my wall. They all have strong countenances and a sense of having done something with their lives. So it's not that I am in love with old men, it's that I want them to motivate me.

CHRISTMAS 1983 (AGE 34)

Time seems to be moving quickly. There isn't the time in a day to do the things I want to do.

MARCH 25, 1984

I have been learning word processing in the mornings, and going to work [as a clerk in the school] in the afternoons.

We are at a 1,300+ population. It's so tense from overcrowding I can't describe it. I leave on the radio to put out the rest of the world. [When alone] I need the "talking postcard"—my five-inch TV. [Still, the tension is] taking its toll on me. I'm not as randomly friendly as I was.

Do you think if you presented me with questions, all kinds, and I wrote you lengthy, honest responses, we could begin that as a basis for a book? [By this time Leslie and I had been talking for years about "a book," with ever-changing notions of how best to construct it.]

JUNE 5, 1984

It was so wonderful to see you.

[In response to my question about the long-ago prison lines editorial:] Different lines have different conversations. Canteen line is usually just talk about how much everything costs. Mailroom line . . . always [has] one ill-informed radical who talks about what she can't wait to do when she gets out in the next thirty days, and puts on a tone of militancy against all the rules and regulations. Lines for attorney visits are notorious sob stories.

This place continues to go from bad to worse. The overcrowding is bringing on strong alienation between people. I have become rather abrupt and rude as a means of shielding myself from an onrush of lonely, lost souls. I read Tom Wolfe's "O Rotten Gotham," [which is] very appropriate to the situation. By the end of the day I am too exhausted to deal with it. I come to my room and knit and listen to classical music. Talk about surrealism.

[She continues to work on group projects.] One is a proposal for rap sessions between Viet Nam veterans and women convicted of murder. There is a workable chemistry. I've experienced it.

• • •

[Leslie asked for and was denied the chance to study for a degree in computer programming. Prison rules at the time forbade computer classes beyond word processing, unless the prisoner was two years or less before release from prison.]

August 8, 1984

With the overcrowding [and double-bunking] we are being required to cut down on "property." I'm really enjoying the lack of clutter.

The stress here has been draining. That's another reason I like the empty space of my cell.

[When she's released] I'm going to live on a small farm with a porch and a garden and no neighbors to speak of. Like those places we saw up north, with the rainbow that day. Do you remember?

December 1984 (age 35)

I so love this time of year. One of my ways of coping [with the increasing prison tension] is to do needlework. I've started to do the more traditional style, cross-stitch and all. I want to begin designing my own samplers. I've also been learning to knit. Needlework gives me a release and a pleasure.

[She writes of nieces and nephews, including a new baby.] Mom is in heaven. She'll be retiring soon. I'll be seeing Sue and Liebe this weekend. They have been good friends. [Many of Leslie's letters have included references to her important friendship with Sue and their regular visits.]

I've decided that when I parole I'm heading for the country. No more big city for me. I want some peace and quiet.

January 30, 1985

I won't have time for a long letter—overcrowding really depletes private time.

I'd love to belong to a healthy community with ice cream socials and picnics.

September 6, 1985 (age 36)

Life here has been extremely stress-filled, under conditions no human being was designed to live under. We are completely double-bunked and they are having to look to ice rooms to house even more women. I am [now] rooming with a woman I knew many years ago. It's not easy but we seem to do OK, better than most.

I now work as a night clerk [for the administration]. I really like the hours because I am a little less stuck in the rat maze. There are so many crowds of people bombarding each other all the time.

I've also been teaching embroidery, which has been fun.

December 12, 1985

I've taken up weight lifting. It's great for burning tension and at the same time toning up. I'm doing what is called sculpting. It's really great. [In the mid-1990s, the exercise equipment was removed from this and all other California state prisons. The rationale was that men who bulked up became aggressive and dangerous. In the interest of gender equality, women likewise lost their equipment.]

I'm doing much better coping with crowding. My new roommate and I get along well.

June 6, 1986

There are dormitories now in the recreation rooms in every unit, as well as 112 women living in the auditorium, no relief in sight. I have a roommate I live with well, and that's a blessing.

My new hearing is scheduled for July 11. I try not to think about it.

* * *

[By the mid-1980s, Leslie's skill at introspection in the midst of chaos was being challenged, as was everyone's, by ever-increasing numbers of women coming in, each new prisoner adding to the bedlam. Their charges were disproportionately for drug possession. Unlike the 1970s, when the average age of women in prison was thirty, the newcomers were predominately in their early twenties, and they were rowdy. Prison numbers were also increasing because women were serving longer sentences for crimes that previously had short sentences.]

September 8, 1986 (age 37)

This is about the third letter I have started to you today . . . not today, this week. It's very difficult to concentrate. Prison has become one big bomb blast to the nervous system. There are people everywhere, aggravations at every turn. There is no room to move around, to think, no time of silence, to reflect.

This all sounds so negative. It is. It takes a certain attitude to survive. I am managing to deal with all of this. It just takes a lot out of me. I fight to stay alive, meaning my spirit. I think I'm doing OK.

March 16, 1987

Two evenings a week I attend AA. The Board required it and at first I was resentful, but now it is OK. I appreciate the honesty of those who are part of the program and share their stories. They are not easy to tell.

* * *

[In June 1987, the *Friends of Leslie* newsletter gave attention to her upcoming July hearing with the parole board. Leslie wrote to her supporters:]

One of the foundations of AA is the Serenity Prayer, a portion of which I find myself using again and again: 'Grant me the serenity to accept the things I cannot change, courage to change the things I can . . . ' There are 2,500 women in a [prison] designed for around 900. . . . [W]ith the message of the Prayer, I find renewed strength.

* * *

July 31, 1987

[In July, despite Leslie's joining AA as recommended, parole was again denied.] False encouragement from [the board] only to be slammed down—acting as avenging angels for the deceased, all justified. I must just move forward a moment at a time.

December 19, 1987 (age 38)

I'm looking forward to 1988.

My roommate and I are now working on our third year of living together. It's amazing how we manage to adapt. It feels strange now to be in the room alone. I go to the field and sit quietly sometimes.

April 2, 1988

I have started writing again, a short story about an old woman in here who has given up. Her spirit has died and now her body follows. The teller of the tale cannot accept the surrender.

There are those of us who keep an eye out for each other, so it's not as bad as it could be.

December 6, 1988 (age 39)

I am going to the Board again this February. The D.A. said I had no heart. I'm preparing a statement. I'm not certain I'll be able to read it, but I'm going to try.

February 12, 1989

I have disappointing news. The Ninth Circuit Court of Appeals recalled its decision to take me to the Board this year. No one knows why. Congratulations on reaching 50!!! [I was 33 when we met.] [She writes of the pleasures of the "children in my life"—her nieces, nephews, friends' children.]

· · ·

[I wrote to the Board of Prison Terms, inquiring as to why her hearing date was recalled. In their reply they thanked me profusely for writing, reminded me that "The Board of Prison Terms is always interested in comments from family members and friends of inmates." The letter then said, "She will receive a parole consideration hearing in July 1990" (which they later pushed up to December 1989).]

NOVEMBER 7, 1989 (AGE 40)

I pay close attention to stress. People were not designed to live so closely. The [new prisoners] are different. They are young and aggressive and, most of all, they are scared.

The Court has now scheduled a hearing for December.

Here I am, at 40, growing up. I spend my time [before and after work] reading, writing, working out regularly, and doing needlework. I work hard at my state job [clerking for the prison administration]. Time passes and my days are full.

DECEMBER 2, 1989

[Preparing for] these hearings is difficult. I've just had so many disappointments and I keep praying I'll be able to handle yet another one. It keeps getting harder. I'm not certain what I'd do if I didn't have people who care for me.

In here or not, this is a good time of the year, a time to honor good tidings and birth.

• • •

[In an unusual move that gave hope, the board requested that the prison officials bring in a psychologist who was independent of the prison, to analyze Leslie's state of mind. His findings were entirely positive.]

JANUARY 20, 1990

As you know, I received a two-year layover. All in all, the hearing went well and I feel positive. I was found rehabilitated; they acknowledged the findings of the psychiatrists.

The most important thing for me was that I was calm going in, I was able to handle myself effectively in the hearing, and I haven't felt like scum since the hearing. I have never before been to one of these things where they didn't manage to make me hate myself.

April 7, 1991 (age 41)

I stay busy [before and after work]: AA/NA, therapy, special programs, reading, writing, handwork, and recently, painting. Except for the obvious, I can't complain. My days are relatively stressless and I have a little routine mapped out that keeps me busy in ways I like or find rewarding. I still do my weight lifting. It lets out a lot of the physical side of tension. My current philosophy is to go slow and steady, and enjoy what I'm doing as much as I can while I'm doing it.

Things here have eased up a bit. There are only 1,900 women now. They opened several other prisons [around the state].

It's sad to see all the anger in the young women coming to this place. No indication of ever having known love. Such hard lives for such young people.

There's quite a bit of therapy here now for survivors of incest and also battered women. Most of what is available, the women have been doing themselves.

January 5, 1992 (age 42)

I went to the Board on December 30th. I received another two-year layover, and while that was disappointing (though I did not expect other), it was a different kind of hearing, in as much as there were no low blows other than from the [Deputy] D.A. [Stephen Kay].

I am doing OK. I don't live as I'd like, of course, but I do manage to give my life quality.

It's been raining here all weekend and I've enjoyed lying in bed finishing a Henry James novel.

This year my roommate paroles. This will be an adjustment for me. We've lived together [in a six-by-nine-foot cell] for seven years. It's going to be odd not having the same person around all the time.

February 10, 1992

Where I work there is a window, so I can sit and look out and listen [to the rain] and feel the coolness. It has been so dry here.

There isn't enough time in a day to do what I want to do. I try not to be a recluse.

April 2, 1992

I really love the Southwest . . . the contrasts, silence, colors. I would love to live there with the incredible sunsets and sunrises.

June 9, 1992

. . . three days with my dad [in the prison's family apartment—a rare privilege] and we had a wonderful time together . . . close, comfortable. We just watched a lot of sports and ate a lot of food and talked. I am so thankful that I know peace with both of my parents. [Since 1996 women serving life sentences may no longer have visits in the family apartment.]

I'm involved in a new project. A group of us are now sewing blankets for the homeless.

Last night I worked with two women [who are] learning to read. It's really great when it all starts to click, and they spell and sound out words with four syllables. We had a lot of fun.

December 1992 (age 43)

I decided this year I am not going to set expectations on myself [no New Year's resolutions]. This is going to be the year that I learn to relax and give myself a break. I really push myself.

I am surprisingly at peace with myself and feel stronger and more positive than I ever have.

April 27, 1993

I keep saying I need solitude, but it will not be mine for a while, so I need to find it somewhere in the noise.

October 18, 1993 (age 44):

I [and Pat] have agreed to be interviewed by ABC. The program is Turning Point, to be aired sometime in the spring. Diane Sawyer will be the interviewer. It seems so odd that in my last letter to you [in August] I was adamant about not doing interviews. I believe this is a good opportunity for me to make an attempt to address some of the misinformation.

The producer wanted to know if we related to "women's lib." Pat said the first time she remembered ever being aware of women's issues was "when the History of Consciousness program came from U.C. Santa Cruz into our little area" [in 1972].

I remember your frustration in trying to get across that the ends don't justify the means. I also remember that [in 1972] we were childlike. [The Santa Cruz people] coming in was always exciting.

Up to this point my silence was an attempt to show respect to the LaBiancas' next of kin, my family, and others affected by the memory. I have also felt that the negative was too overwhelming to even attempt to confront. But if the public has a [distorted] view of things, it's partly my responsibility.

NOVEMBER 29, 1993

[Leslie taped the interview on November 15]. It was hard, but straight on. Diane Sawyer is a gracious woman and I appreciated her downplay of her celebrity status. I realize that I can speak the truth and not feel like I am somehow justifying or excusing myself.

I talked about a new generation of fringe teenagers who think it's cool to wear [Manson's image] on a T-shirt. Manson is using the D.A.'s rhetoric to pull in kids.

DECEMBER 1993

If each of us maintains the true spirit of this season throughout the year, we will have made [the world] a better place.

I felt that because the crimes were such a negative statement to end the '60s, that I have had no right to speak on social issues. It feels good to be discovering my voice.

JANUARY 20, 1994

I received another two-year review.

My spirits are good. I know what I need to do.

MAY 4, 1994

I really appreciated your feedback from the TV show. Reactions have been interesting. For people who know and love me, it was too much [talk about] Manson and the crime. From strangers I get a great deal of support and understanding. I have received close to 100 letters. I am attempting to respond to them as time permits.

November 12, 1994 (age 45):

I was on Larry King [Live]. It has been aired twice now. It was a taped interview with me for the first half-hour and then [live studio] discussion with my dad, Bugliosi, my lawyer, and Patty Tate [Sharon's sister]. I appreciated his [King's] method of interviewing. It was not edited. He came out here, we spoke, and he left.

I'm in Data Processing now. The Board wanted me to get this training. I'm learning how to program computers and it's interesting.

December 1994

I love this time of year. The caroling group [is] all ready to sing for the Yard this Friday and Saturday. We are 35 strong this year, with three-part harmony. On Christmas Eve we will put on a show for the Psych ward, great fun. The women there are so free of inhibitions and get very involved with us.

Let's pray together in our own way for peace, understanding, acceptance.

July 2, 1995

Governor Pete Wilson has stopped [virtually] all paroles of life prisoners. Women who had dates have had them taken away.

We have recently lost all group therapy for life prisoners, and at the same time the Board continues to recommend therapy. A new common reason for denial of parole is that we have not "dealt" with our crimes. The panel denies parole because the prisoner needs "more insight." [She has learned of an intensive therapy regimen being used in a men's prison in British Columbia, and asks for information about it.]

There is no interest in women [in the prison system]. Every time my roommate writes someone for legal advice she is told they'd love to help but they are busy with San Quentin, etc.

I'm learning to program computers, I'm still involved in tutoring and other volunteer work; I'm doing OK.

Many of us are learning to turn to each other for strength, and we are encouraging each other to overcome helplessness and hopelessness. We are finding the strength of friendship.

SEPTEMBER 24, 1995 (AGE 46):

[Beginning in 1995, Leslie and I were able to speak on the telephone from time to time, and have continued to exchange occasional letters.] It was wonderful talking to you. Now that we can speak, the distance and length of time between visits won't seem so vast.

[Leslie is preparing for a parole hearing in the spring.] It takes a lot of soul-searching to know I believe in myself. All the [D.A.'s] rhetoric [about her involvement with Manson's crime] is going to have to be confronted with simply stated fact, and that is much harder to do than it sounds.

[Recalling her months on bail seventeen years previously, she reminds me of] the farmhouse I fell in love with. It's wonderful we have those [memories] and I use them to know there will be more.

MARCH 26, 1996

I'm going to the Board without an attorney. It seems as good a time as any to try it on my own. I always feel like a piece of merchandise in there. One side says the merchandise has been ruined and will never be repaired. The other side says it is not only fixed but to the point where it is too good to be true. And somewhere in all that, is me. This time, I will simply speak for myself.

MAY 1, 1996

Yesterday was the hearing. I received a two-year review. With the political climate what it is, I am pleased it wasn't longer. It goes without saying that parole hearings are difficult. I know I will be coming home. The question is when.

JUNE 12, 1996

It's interesting that you mentioned Sister Helen Prejean [activist opponent of capital punishment]. I sent her a note, inviting her to come and spend some time with us here if she's in Los Angeles. I think she would find the spirit we have managed to maintain here refreshing—and in her we would certainly find a friend.

SEPTEMBER 30, 1996 (AGE 47):

I loved my birthday card. I am 47 and looking forward to 50. I'm stunned I made it this far. [I guess] I hadn't [expected] to live so long. I have a tendency to pull in when I am blue and wait until I am grounded to present myself. I'm trying not to do that any more. I'm trying to share my unhappiness. It is hard to let go of feeling responsible, to make things OK.

• • •

[In May 1997 I visited Leslie at CIW.]

JULY 28, 1997

It was more than wonderful to see you. Our phone has been out of order for close to a month now. I will phone you as soon as I am able.

OCTOBER 14, 1997 (AGE 48):

Thank you so much for my new books. They will be great winter reading.

[Reflecting on the lack of solitude:] I was thinking of years ago when they started double-bunking, and how, at first, I did not believe I could deal with it. Now it is odd not having that person there [in the cell with her]. A change can become a new way of living rather than a loss.

JANUARY 28, 1998

[Referring to her prison job and volunteer activity:] I work at slowing my pace, to give whatever I am doing my full attention, and it gives me more pleasure and I get more done this way. I take tasks at small increments. I feel that I am doing much better with the pressure.

I have a Walkman to listen to cassettes. This way I can check out Books on Tape. I am enjoying the books you sent. I read a short story before I go to sleep. The book edited by Paula Gunn Allen is particularly good. Things are good for me right now.

Notes

NOTES TO INTRODUCTION

1. Anne Near, *Dubious Journey: From Class to Class* (Oakland: Hereford Publishing, 1993); Anne Near, "The Wisdom of a Child: The Long Journey from One Class to Another," in *Downwardly Mobile for Conscience Sake,* ed. D. N. Anderson (Tucson: Tom Paine Institute, 1993).
2. Penelope J. Hanke, "She Kills Everyone: A Research Note on Homicide Victims," *Sociological Focus* 26, no. 4 (October 1993): 365–68.
3. Karlene Faith, ed., *Soledad Prison: University of the Poor* (Palo Alto: Science & Behavior Books, 1975).
4. Margaret Thaler Singer with Janja Lalich, *Cults in Our Midst: The Hidden Menace in Our Everyday Lives* (San Francisco: Jossey-Bass Publishers, 1995); Flo Conway and Jim Siegelman, *Snapping: America's Epidemic of Sudden Personality Change,* 2d ed. (New York: Stillpoint Press, 1995).
5. Karlene Faith, *Inside/Outside* (Los Angeles: Peace Press, 1976).
6. Leslie Van Houten, correspondence with author, 3 September 1997.

NOTES TO CHAPTER ONE

1. Conway and Siegelman, *Snapping,* 226–27.
2. Jeff Bravin, *Squeaky: The Life and Times of Lynette Alice Fromme* (New York: Buzz Books, St. Martin's Press, 1997), 188–89.
3. Virginia Carlson, quoted in Susan Atkins with Bob Slosser, *Child of Satan, Child of God* (Plainfield: Logos International, 1977), 184.
4. All quotes from Anne Near are from the author's tapes of dialogues between the author and Anne Near, 1980–81.
5. Conway and Siegelman, *Snapping,* 88–90.
6. Charles "Tex" Watson with Chaplain Ray Hoekstra, *Will You Die for Me?*

The Man Who Killed for Charles Manson Tells His Own Story (Old Tappan, N.J.: Fleming H. Revell, 1978), 22.
7. Singer with Lalich, *Cults in Our Midst,* 132–34.
8. Robert Jay Lifton, *Thought Reform and the Psychology of Totalism: A Study of "Brainwashing" in China* (New York: W. W. Norton, 1961); Allyn Rickett and Adele Rickett, *Prisoners of Liberation: Four Years in a Chinese Communist Prison* (New York: Doubleday, 1973).
9. Karlene Faith, "The Santa Cruz Women's Prison Project," in *Schooling in a "Total Institution": Critical Perspectives on Prison Education,* ed. H. S. Davidson (London: Bergin & Garvey, 1995), 173–201.
10. Karlene Faith, *Unruly Women: The Politics of Confinement and Resistance* (Vancouver: Press Gang Publishers, 1993).
11. Van Houten, correspondence with author, 3 September 1997.

Notes to Chapter Two

1. Van Houten, correspondence with author, 3 September 1997.
2. Conway and Siegelman, *Snapping,* 20–30.
3. Ibid., 58; Singer with Lalich, *Cults in Our Midst;* Ted Patrick with Tom Dulack, *Let Our Children Go!* (New York: Thomas Congdon Books/E. P. Dutton, 1976).
4. All quotations attributed to Leslie Van Houten, unless otherwise noted, are from conversations with the author.
5. Leslie Van Houten, interview by Diane Sawyer, taped 15 November 1993, aired on *Turning Point,* ABC-TV, 9 March 1994.
6. Bravin, *Squeaky,* 47.
7. Ibid., 53.
8. Ibid., 47–48.
9. Atkins with Slosser, *Child of Satan,* 2–10.
10. Ibid., 81.
11. Ibid., 115.
12. Watson with Hoekstra, *Will You Die?* 50.
13. Ibid., 12.
14. Ibid., 32.
15. Ibid., 12.
16. Leslie Van Houten, interview by attorney Marvin Part, tape recording, 1969, played in court 18 May 1976.
17. Al Rose and David Smith, quoted in Bravin, *Squeaky,* 87.
18. Watson with Hoekstra, *Will You Die?* 67–68, 74–75.

19. Singer with Lalich, *Cults in Our Midst*.
20. Conway and Siegelman, *Snapping*, 151, 225.

Notes to Chapter Three

1. Vincent Bugliosi with Curt Gentry, *Helter Skelter* (New York: W. W. Norton, 1974), 42.
2. Watson with Hoekstra, *Will You Die?* 132–33.
3. Bugliosi with Gentry, *Helter Skelter*, 424.
4. Watson with Hoekstra, *Will You Die?* 135.
5. Ibid., 148.
6. Ibid., 150.
7. Ibid., 148–50.
8. Van Houten, correspondence with author, 3 September 1997.
9. Stephen Holmes, Eric Hickey, and Ronald Hinch, "Female Serial Murderesses: Constructing Differentiating Typologies," *Journal of Contemporary Criminal Justice* 7, no. 4 (December 1991): 253–54; Ronald Hinch and Hannah Scott, "Explaining Female Serial Murderers: Theoretical Issues" (paper presented to the American Society of Criminology, Boston, 1995), 13–14.
10. Hinch and Scott, "Female Serial Murderers," 14.
11. Watson with Hoekstra, *Will You Die?* 162.
12. Atkins with Slosser, *Child of Satan*, 165.
13. Bugliosi with Gentry, *Helter Skelter*, 341–42.
14. Richard Yarvis, "Patterns of Substance Abuse and Intoxication among Murderers," *Bulletin of the American Academy of Psychiatry and Law* 22, no. 1 (1994): 144.
15. Maxwell Keith, quoted in Bugliosi with Gentry, *Helter Skelter*, 404.
16. Bugliosi with Gentry, *Helter Skelter*, 311.
17. Vincent Bugliosi, quoted in Bravin, *Squeaky*, 127.
18. Bugliosi with Gentry, *Helter Skelter*, 213, 450.
19. Bugliosi, quoted in Conway and Siegelman, *Snapping*, 218, 200.
20. Paul Krassner, *Confessions of a Raving Unconfined Nut: Misadventures in the Counter-Culture* (New York: Simon & Schuster, 1993), 207.
21. Bravin, *Squeaky*, 139.
22. "Deep Trouble," *Crawdaddy*, December 1976, 11.
23. Bravin, *Squeaky*, 88–89.
24. "Bartek Frykowski: Seeking Dollars from a Killer Named Manson," *People*, 3 April 1995, 43.

25. *San Francisco Chronicle*, 22 May 1981, 30.
26. Anne Lamott, *Bird by Bird: Some Instructions on Writing and Life* (New York: Anchor Books, 1995), 25.
27. Vincent Bugliosi, interview by Larry King, *Larry King Live*, CNN-TV, aired August 1994.

Notes to Chapter Four

1. Richard Alatorre, chairman, Assembly Select Committee on Corrections, *The California Institution for Women: One Year Later* (report to the California Legislature, Sacramento, 21 July 1977), 159.
2. Ibid., 156.
3. Ibid., 166.
4. All lyrics from Charles Manson's penned songs are taken from a handmade book given to the author by Leslie Van Houten, Patricia Krenwinkel, and Susan Atkins.
5. Conway and Siegelman, *Snapping*, 152.
6. Ibid., 227, 257.
7. Bugliosi with Gentry, *Helter Skelter*, 132–35.
8. Patricia Krenwinkel and Leslie Van Houten, interview by Diane Sawyer, taped 15 November 1993, aired on *Turning Point*, ABC-TV, 9 March 1994.
9. "Timothy Leary Is Dead," *The Passionate Eye*, Northwest TV (30 November 1997).
10. Singer with Lalich, *Cults in Our Midst*, xii.
11. Frantz Fanon, *The Wretched of the Earth* (New York: Grove Press, 1965).
12. Manson, song lyrics, collection of the author.
13. Bravin, *Squeaky*, 49–53; John Gilmore and Ron Kenner, *The Garbage People: Story of Charles Manson* (Los Angeles: Omega Press, 1971), 22.
14. K. Kennedy, "Manson at 50," *California Magazine*, May 1985, 78.
15. John Godwin, *Murder USA: The Ways We Kill Each Other* (New York: Ballantine Books, 1978), 82.
16. Jeanne Gallick, correspondence with author, July 1998.
17. Bravin, *Squeaky*, 73.
18. Watson with Hoekstra, *Will You Die?* 70.
19. Ibid.
20. Ibid., 73.
21. Ibid., 94.
22. Van Houten, correspondence with author, 3 September 1997.

23. Bravin, *Squeaky*.
24. "Manson's Views on an Ex-Follower," *San Francisco Chronicle*, 10 July 1978, sec. A, p. 3.
25. Van Houten, interview with Marvin Part, 1969; emphasis added.
26. Lawrence Schiller and Jerry Cohen, *The Killing of Sharon Tate* (New York: Signet, 1970).
27. Watson with Hoekstra, *Will You Die?* 21.
28. Atkins with Slosser, *Child of Satan*.
29. Bill Farr, "Still Haunted, Miss Van Houten Says," *Los Angeles Times*, 17 February 1977, part I, pp. 24–26.
30. Author's notes from Leslie Van Houten's second trial, 25 April 1977.
31. *Santa Cruz Sentinel*, 9 September 1975, sec. B, p. 8.
32. Atkins with Slosser, *Child of Satan*, 185.
33. Bugliosi with Gentry, *Helter Skelter*, 417.
34. Ibid., 162.
35. Leslie Van Houten, conversation with author.
36. Manson, song lyrics, collection of the author.

Notes to Chapter Five

1. *Los Angeles Times*, 19 July 1977, sec. A, p. 4.
2. Ibid.
3. Ibid., 3.
4. Leslie Van Houten, quoted in her hearing with the California Board of Prison Terms, 1996.
5. All quotes from the trial are from the author's notes from Leslie Van Houten's second trial, 1977.
6. Mae Brussels, quoted in Krassner, *Confessions*, 200.
7. Bugliosi with Gentry, *Helter Skelter*, 237.
8. Watson with Hoekstra, *Will You Die?* 123.
9. Smith, quoted in Bravin, *Squeaky*, 408–9 n. 95.

Notes to Chapter Six

1. From "Native Dancer," by Cris Williamson. Copyright © 1980 Bird Ankles Music (BMI). All rights reserved. Used by permission.
2. Bugliosi and Gentry, *Helter Skelter*, 41, 336, 340.
3. Bill Farr, "Van Houten Lawyer, DA Confer on Case," *Los Angeles Times*, 12 August 1977, part I, p. 12.

4. Bill Farr, "Miss Van Houten Convicted Again for Two Slayings," *Los Angeles Times*, 6 July 1978, part I, pp. 26–27.

Notes to Chapter Seven

1. Gallick, correspondence with author, July 1998.
2. Kathleen Hendrix, "Leslie Van Houten: 'In Touch' with the Guilt She'll Always Feel," *Los Angeles Times*, 14 December 1980, sec. C, pp. 20–25.
3. Walter Gibson, *Hypnotism: Theory and Practice* (Toronto: Coles Publishing, 1979), 119.
4. Frank Earl Andrews, ed., *Prose and Cons* (New York: Pyramid Books, 1976).
5. Editorial, *Friends of Leslie* newsletter, March 1985, 3.
6. Editorial, *Friends of Leslie*, June 1981.
7. Paul Fitzgerald, Editorial, *Friends of Leslie*, June 1980, 1.
8. Leslie Van Houten, Letter, *Friends of Leslie*, November 1981, 3.
9. Van Houten, interview on *Turning Point*, aired 9 March 1994.
10. Leslie Van Houten, taped interview by Larry King, *Larry King Live*, CNN-TV, aired August 1994.
11. Editorial, Fitzgerald, *Friends of Leslie*, June 1980, 2.
12. Conway and Siegelman, *Snapping*, 223.
13. *Sybil*, a four-hour TV movie, *The Big Event/NBC World Premiere Movie*, NBC-TV, 1977. Based on the book by Flora Rheta Schreiber, *Sybil* (1973; rept. New York: Warner Books, 1989).
14. Van Houten, hearing with the Board of Prison Terms, 1996.
15. Ibid.
16. *Biography*, Arts & Entertainment TV, 23 January 1996.
17. Van Houten, hearing with the Board of Prison Terms, 1996.
18. *National Enquirer*, 30 March 1999, 37.
19. Van Houten, correspondence with author, 6 August 1999.

Notes to Chapter Eight

1. D. Hominik and J. Perry, "Cults in American Society: A Legal Analysis of Undue Influence, Fraud, and Misrepresentation," *Cultic Studies Journal* 12, no. 1 (1995): 1–48; S. Van Hoey, "Cults in Court," *Cultic Studies Journal* 8, no. 1 (1991): 61–79.
2. Singer with Lalich, *Cults in Our Midst*, 245.
3. Conway and Siegelman, *Snapping*, 249.
4. Watson with Hockstra, *Will You Die?* 54.

5. Leslie Van Houten, Letter, *Friends of Leslie*, March 1985, 2.
6. Ibid.
7. Van Houten, correspondence with author, 3 September 1997.
8. Van Houten, interview on *Turning Point*, aired 9 March 1994.
9. Dwight R. Blackstock, "Paying a Debt to Society That Will Cost Society," *Los Angeles Times*, 20 August 1978, sec. A, p. 8.
10. Ibid.

Works Cited

Alatorre, Richard, chairman, Assembly Select Committee on Corrections. *The California Institution for Women: One Year Later.* Report to the California Legislature, 21 July 1977. Sacramento, 1977.
Andrews, Frank Earl, ed. *Prose and Cons.* New York: Pyramid Books, 1976.
Atkins, Susan, with Bob Slosser. *Child of Satan, Child of God.* Plainfield: Logos International, 1977.
"Bartek Frykowski: Seeking Dollars from a Killer Named Manson." *People,* 3 April 1995, 43.
Bravin, Jeff. *Squeaky: The Life and Times of Lynette Alice Fromme.* New York: Buzz Books, St. Martin's Press, 1997.
Bugliosi, Vincent, with Curt Gentry. *Helter Skelter.* New York: W. W. Norton, 1974.
Conway, Flo, and Jim Siegelman. *Snapping: America's Epidemic of Sudden Personality Change.* 2d ed. New York: Stillpoint Press, 1995.
"Deep Trouble." *Crawdaddy,* December 1976, 11.
Faith, Karlene. *Inside/Outside.* Los Angeles: Peace Press, 1976.
———. "The Santa Cruz Women's Prison Project." In *Schooling in a "Total Institution": Critical Perspectives on Prison Education,* edited by H. S. Davidson, 173–201. London: Bergin & Garvey, 1995.
———. *Unruly Women: The Politics of Confinement and Resistance.* Vancouver: Press Gang Publishers, 1993.
———, ed. *Soledad Prison: University of the Poor.* Palo Alto: Science & Behavior Books, 1975.
Fanon, Frantz. *The Wretched of the Earth.* New York: Grove Press, 1965.
Friends of Leslie newsletter, June 1980–March 1985.
Gibson, Walter. *Hypnotism: Theory and Practice.* Toronto: Coles Publishing, 1979.

Gilmore, John, and Ron Kenner. *The Garbage People: Story of Charles Manson.* Los Angeles: Omega Press, 1971.

Godwin, John. *Murder USA: The Ways We Kill Each Other.* New York: Ballantine Books, 1978.

Hanke, Penelope J. "She Kills Everyone: A Research Note on Homicide Victims." *Sociological Focus* 26, no. 4 (October 1993): 365–68.

Hinch, Ronald, and Hannah Scott. "Explaining Female Serial Murderers: Theoretical Issues." Paper presented to the American Society of Criminology, Boston, 1995.

Holmes, Stephen, Eric Hickey, and Ronald Hinch. "Female Serial Murderesses: Constructing Differentiating Typologies." *Journal of Contemporary Criminal Justice* 7, no. 4 (December 1991): 246–56.

Hominik, D., and J. Perry. "Cults in American Society: A Legal Analysis of Undue Influence, Fraud, and Misrepresentation." *Cultic Studies Journal* 12, no. 1 (1995): 1–48.

Kennedy, K. "Manson at 50." *California Magazine,* May 1985, 78–81, 103–4, 113–16, 121–26.

Krassner, Paul. *Confessions of a Raving Unconfined Nut: Misadventures in the Counter-Culture.* New York: Simon & Schuster, 1993.

Lamott, Anne. *Bird by Bird: Some Instructions on Writing and Life.* New York: Anchor Books, 1995.

Lifton, Robert Jay. *Thought Reform and the Psychology of Totalitarianism: A Study of "Brainwashing" in China.* New York: W. W. Norton, 1961.

Los Angeles Times, 17 February 1977–14 December 1980.

May, Rollo. *Power and Innocence: A Search for the Sources of Violence.* New York: W. W. Norton, 1972.

Morgan, Robin, ed. *Sisterhood Is Powerful: An Anthology of Writings from the Women's Liberation Movement.* New York: Vintage Books, 1970.

National Enquirer, 30 March 1999.

Near, Anne. *Dubious Journey: From Class to Class.* Oakland: Hereford Publishing, 1993.

———. "The Wisdom of a Child: The Long Journey from One Class to Another." In *Downwardly Mobile for Conscience Sake,* edited by D. N. Anderson. Tucson: Tom Paine Institute, 1993.

Patrick, Ted, with Tom Dulack. *Let Our Children Go!* New York: Thomas Congdon Books/E. P. Dutton, 1976.

Rickett, Allyn, and Adele Rickett. *Prisoners of Liberation: Four Years in a Chinese Communist Prison.* New York: Doubleday, 1973.

Rose, Al, and David E. Smith. "The Group Marriage Commune: A Case Study," *Journal of Psychedelic Drugs,* September 1970.

San Francisco Chronicle, 10 July 1978–22 May 1981.

Santa Cruz Sentinel, 9 September 1977.

Schein, Edgar H. *Coercive Persuasion: A Socio-Psychological Analysis of the "Brainwashing" of American Civilian Prisoners by the Chinese Communists.* New York: W. W. Norton, 1961.

Schiller, Lawrence, and Jerry Cohen. *The Killing of Sharon Tate.* New York: Signet, 1970.

Schreck, Nikolas, ed. *The Manson File.* New York: Amok Press, 1988.

Singer, Margaret Thaler, with Janja Lalich. *Cults in Our Midst: The Hidden Menace in Our Everyday Lives.* San Francisco: Jossey-Bass Publishers, 1995.

Skinner, B. F. *Science and Human Behavior.* New York: Macmillan, 1953.

Sybil, a four-hour TV movie, *The Big Event/NBC World Premiere Movie.* NBC-TV, 1977. Based on the book by Flora Rheta Schreiber. *Sybil.* 1973; rept. New York: Warner Books, 1989.

"Timothy Leary Is Dead," *The Passionate Eye.* Northwest TV, 30 November 1997.

Van Hoey, S. "Cults in Court." *Cultic Studies Journal* 8, no. 1 (1991): 61–79.

Watkins, Paul, with Guillermo Soledad. *My Life with Charles Manson.* New York: Bantam Press, 1979.

Watson, Charles "Tex," with Chaplain Ray Hoekstra. *Will You Die for Me? The Man Who Killed for Charles Manson Tells His Own Story.* Old Tappan, N.J.: Fleming H. Revell, 1978.

Wizinski, Sy. *Charles Manson: Love Letters to a Secret Disciple: A Psychoanalytical Search.* Terre Haute: Moonmad Press, 1976.

Yarvis, Richard. "Patterns of Substance Abuse and Intoxication Among Murderers." *Bulletin of the American Academy of Psychiatry and Law* 22, no. 1 (1994): 133–44.

Index

AA (Alcoholics Anonymous), 140, 148, 181, 182, 184
ABC, xxi, 98, 142, 185
Abortion, 28, 107, 148
Acid. *See* LSD
Advertising, 8, 16. *See also* Media
African American(s): death of visiting, at jail, 103–4; violence against, in California, 128–29. *See also* Race war
Alcohol, 111. *See also* AA
Allan Memorial Institute (Montreal), 15
Allen, Paula Gunn, 189
Altamont (California), 55
Amphetamines. *See* "Speed"
Anderson, Cheryl, 78
Andrews, Frank, 169
Antioch College, 159, 169, 175
Applewhite, Marshall, 156
Armageddon. *See* "Helter Skelter"; Race war
Aryan Brotherhood, 74
Atkins, Susan, xv; background of, 77; child of, 60; death sentence for, 3, 21, 49, 53, 76; drug use by, 114; as evangelical Christian, 46, 77, 86– 88, 92; false testimony of, 9, 16, 40, 41–42, 76–77; at first trial, 40– 42, 49, 50–53, 76–77; gifts from, 84; initial impressions of, 5, 74–75; initial lack of remorse by, 47, 49, 79, 133; life sentence for, 4, 13, 21, 75; as "Manson girl," xv, 31– 32, 41, 43, 60, 68–69, 99; as Manson's victim, xviii–xix, 24–25, 39, 62–64, 74–75, 79, 106–7; media attention on, 9, 10, 86, 109; murder participation by, 42, 76–77, 86; in prison, 80–86, 139; remorse of, 47, 75–76, 138; as still in prison, 53, 88. *See also* "Manson family"; "Manson girls"

Bail: Leslie out on, xv, xviii, xxi, 119– 27, 133–34, 142–44, 172; money for Leslie's, 141–42
"Bald Lady" (prisoner), 80
Banana splits party, 82–83, 170
Barlow, Bill, 78
Battered woman syndrome, 61, 106
Be Here Now (Ram Dass), 84
Beach Boys (rock band), 32, 54–55

203

204 — INDEX

Beatles: as influence on Manson, 8, 17, 33, 36, 44, 69, 106, 109, 115. *See also specific Beatles songs*
Beausoleil, Bobby, 30, 41, 69–70, 146
Bible, 17, 36–37, 69, 106, 113
"Big Red Balloon" (song), 78
"Bill" (Leslie's husband), 147, 148, 176–77
Black Panthers, 9
"Blackbird" (Beatles song), 109
Blackstock, David, 162
Boys Town (Nebraska), 66
Brainwashing: concept of, 15–17; deprogramming for, 29; of Leslie, xviii, 50–52, 61–64, 100, 105, 106–7, 111–14, 126, 127, 133, 152; of other "Manson family" members, 11, 44–51, 61–64, 68–73, 86, 90–91, 105–14, 133, 140; of Patty Hearst, 54; by prisons, 109; by U.S. Army, 52. *See also* "Manson girls": reeducation of, in prison
Branch Davidians, 156
Brunner, Mary, 30–32, 41, 53, 88, 90, 92
Brussells, Mae, 109
Buddhism (yogic spiritual communities), 28, 85, 105, 116. *See also* Eastern religions
Bugliosi, Vincent, 41, 44, 187; book on Manson murders by, xvi, 9, 75; on length of time "Manson girls" were apt to spend in prison, 132; on "Manson girls," 61–62, 75; as prosecutor in first trial, 49–52, 105, 116, 126, 128; on recent Leslie Van Houten, 56; on Charles "Tex" Watson, 32

California: average age of prisoners in, 181; "Corrections Valley" in, 3; death penalty abolished in, xv, 3–4, 10, 12; death penalty's reinstatement in, 4, 128; number of women currently incarcerated in, 177; parole policies in, 145, 187; 20th-century crimes committed in, 128–29. *See also names of California cities and prisons*
California Board of Prison Terms. *See* Parole boards
California Court of Appeals, 97
California Highway Patrol, 42
California Institution for Women (CIW) (Frontera): author's work at, xv, 3–6, 13–14, 18, 19–23, 53, 57–59, 78–80, 89–92, 123; conditions in, 21, 58, 159, 167, 177–81, 183–85, 187, 189; location of, 3; main prison at, guards in, 81, 138, 140; main prison at, "Manson girls" transferred to, 11, 77, 85–89, 92, 138, 141, 145, 169, 172–89; main prison at, "Manson girls' " view of, 10, 11, 58, 80–81; main prison at, views of "Manson girls" from, 139–40; psychiatrists employed by, 22, 58–59, 156–57; turnover among wardens in, 14. *See also* Carlson, Virginia; *Clarion;* Long–Termers Organization; Psychiatric Treatment Unit; Special Security Unit
California State Supreme Court, xv, 3–4, 12
Calley, William L., 52–53
Cameron, Ewan, 15
Camus, Albert, 102–3

Canada, 167, 176; brainwashing experiments in, 15
Capital punishment. *See* Death penalty
Carlson, Virginia (CIW warden), xv, 3, 5, 10–15, 18
Carter, Jimmy, 54
Castaneda, Carlos, 162
CBC, 15, 149
CBS–TV, 9
"Cease to Exist" (Manson song), 54, 158
Central Intelligence Agency (CIA), 15, 93
Child care, 105; in "Manson family," 18, 34, 60, 70; in Van Houten family, 27–28
Child of Satan, Child of God (Atkins), 87
Chinese Cultural Revolution, 19
Chino state prison, xix–xx
Christians: brainwashing likened to experience of born–again, 61–62; and false prophets, 156; former "Manson family" members as, 46, 76–88, 92; on good and evil, 45–46; "Manson family" members raised as, 32–33, 71, 161–62
CIA (Central Intelligence Agency), 15, 93
Cinque (Symbionese Liberation Army leader), 54
CIW. *See* California Institution for Women
The Clarion (CIW newspaper), 87, 139, 159, 169
Class: as factor among prisoners, 19, 130, 137; as factor in media treatment of murder, 7, 8; of "Manson family" members, xvi, 8, 72, 150; Manson on, 64, 67, 72
"Clem," 42, 43
CNN, 142
"Conspiracy to murder" charges, 105–6, 127, 128
Conway, Flo, 144
Copeville (Texas), 42
Corporate crimes, 130, 158
Counterculture. *See* 1960s
"Crying Time" (song), 78
Cuba, xix
Cult(s): definition of, 63–64; deprogramming from, 29; lack of knowledge about, during Manson era, 44, 155; Manson as leader of, xv–xvi, xviii–xix, 14–18, 24–25, 29–38, 41–47, 49–53, 60–76, 79, 86–92, 95, 98, 99, 104–8, 111–16, 127, 140, 142, 150, 152; and murder, 155–56. *See also* Brainwashing
Cusic, Catherine, 22, 78, 123

Dass, Ram, 84
Davis, Bruce, 41–42
Death: Manson on, 21–22, 30, 33–35, 46–47, 53, 65, 74, 79, 86, 100, 108–9, 115, 158. *See also* Death penalty; Death row
Death penalty: California's abolition of, xv, 3–4, 10, 12; changed to life sentence for "Manson girls," xv, 4, 10, 13, 21, 75, 135; "Manson girls'" acceptance of, 21, 49, 50, 76, 161; "Manson girls" sentenced to, 3–4, 21, 49, 53, 135; as not applicable to crime Leslie was convicted of in her third trial, 128; premises of, 133, 160–61; rein-

Death penalty (cont.)
  statement of, 4, 128. See also
  Death row; Retribution
Death row: "Manson girls" on, xv, 4–6, 46, 57. See also Special Security Unit
Debs, Eugene, 158
"Diminished capacity" defense, 97, 107, 110–15, 126, 127. See also Brainwashing
Divine Light Mission, 29
Doors (rock group), 31
Dreiser, Theodore, 58
Dreiser, Vera, 58
Drugs: focus on, in second trial, 110–15; persons incarcerated for, 173; in prison, 145; role of, in "Manson girls'" brainwashing, 34, 37, 59, 69, 107, 110–15, 127, 140; use of, in 1960s, xviii, 28, 29, 111, 113. See also LSD; Marijuana; "Speed"

Eastern religions, xviii, 29. See also Buddhism
"Ebb Tide" (song), 78
Ecstasy (drug), 115
Einstein, Albert, 178
Ellis, John, 78–79
Eritrea (Africa), 83
Escher, M. C., 79
Evert, Chris, 53

Faith, Karlene: Anne Near's conversations with, xvii–xix, xxi, 23–25, 47–48, 93–94, 132–33, 136, 138, 156–58; car of, 109; drug experiences of, 111; Leslie's friendship with, xix–xxi, xv, 3–6, 22, 78–86, 97–98, 119–21, 147–48, 188, 189; limitations on prison correspondence of, xix–xx; as Peace Corps worker, 83; prisoner education work by, xv, xvi, xvii, 3–6, 13–14, 18–23, 53, 57–59, 78–80, 89–92, 123; research on women and criminal justice by, xx–xxi, 149; women's movement's influence on, 21, 124
Falk, Candace, 78
"Family." See "Manson family"
Fanon, Frantz, 65
FBI, 155
Feminism. See Women's movement
Fitzgerald, Paul, 141
Folie à famille, 89–90
Folsom prison, 63
Ford, Gerald, 53, 73
Foster, Ellie, 129–31
Foster, Herb, 129–31
Friends of Leslie (support group), 141–45, 162, 181
Fromme, Lynette "Squeaky," 10, 31, 32, 61–62, 78, 88; and Gerald Ford, 53, 73; as still in prison, 53
Fulgoni, Dino, 126

Gabereau, Vickie, 149
"Gail," 30
Gallick, Jeanne, 18, 19, 68, 78, 79, 82, 137
Germany, 93–94, 157
Gino, 123–24
Good, Sandra, 10, 53, 61–62, 78
Grahn, Judy, 78
Grand jury, 76
Gray, Liebe, 121, 167, 180
Grinspoon, Lester, 108, 110–14
Grippi, Linda, xix, 120, 141–42, 152, 167

Guards: in main prison, 81, 138, 140; at Special Security Unit, 4–5, 11, 78–83; at Sybil Brand Institute, 103–4; on women prisoners, 19
Guns N' Roses (rock group), 55
"Gypsy." *See* Share, Catherine "Gypsy"

Haight–Ashbury (San Francisco), 29, 31–32, 34, 114
Hare Krishnas, 29, 61
Hearst, Patty, 54
Heaven's Gate cult, 156
Hellman, Lillian, 102
Hell's Angels, 55
"Helter Skelter" (Beatles song): as Manson code word for Armageddon, 8–9, 36, 37–38, 41, 44, 70–71, 89, 102, 109, 115, 126; "Manson family's" ignorance of details of, 37, 42, 105–6. *See also* Race war
Helter Skelter (Bugliosi), 9
Hinman, Gary, 41–42, 77, 90
Hinz, Edward A., Jr., 107
Hippies ("flower children"): distrust of, after Manson murders, 55, 109–10; "Manson family's" communal life as, 9, 22, 33–34, 36, 59–60; Manson's view of, 108. *See also* 1960s
Hitler, Adolf, 115
Hughes, Ronald, 50
Hugo, Victor, 162

Indonesia, 55
International Society for Krishna Consciousness, 29, 61
Internet: on "Manson girls," xvi; Manson-related web sites on, 53; sales of Leslie's parole board hearings over, 152
Inyo County Jail (California), 42
"Isn't She Lovely" (song), 98

Jagger, Mick, 55
Jaki (prison teacher), 84
Jamaica, 3
James, Henry, 184
Jean (death row resident), 5, 6, 10, 78, 128
Jefferson Airplane, 115
Joan of Arc, 25
Jones, Jim, 61, 115, 142, 155
Jonestown (Guyana), 155. *See also* Jones, Jim
Journal of Psychedelic Drugs, 34

Kasabian, Linda, 10, 42, 43, 86, 104, 105
Katie (Patricia Krenwinkel's nickname), 33
Kay, Stephen, 51, 75; as Leslie's prosecutor, 105–6, 108–12, 115–17, 125–28; at "Manson family" members' parole hearings, 129, 132, 136, 150–52, 184
Keith, Maxwell, 50, 51, 97, 105, 110, 120, 126, 127, 144
Kennedy, John F., 49
Kesey, Ken, 33
King, Larry, 56, 142, 187
Korean War, 15
Koresh, David, 142, 155
Krassner, Paul, 52, 78
Krenwinkel, Patricia: background of, 88–90; death sentence for, 3, 21, 49, 53; at first trial, 49, 50–53;

Krenwinkel, Patricia (*cont.*)
initial impressions of, 5, 74–75; initial lack of remorse by, 47, 49, 79, 133; life sentence for, 4, 13, 21, 75; as "Manson girl," xv, 31, 32, 42–45, 68–69, 99; as Manson's victim, xviii–xix, 24–25, 39, 62–64, 74–75, 79, 106–7; media attention on, 9, 10, 62, 142, 185–86; murder participation by, 42–45, 86, 89; in prison, 3, 80–86, 89, 139, 141, 169, 174; remorse of, 47, 75–76, 89, 137; as still in prison, 53
Ku Klux Klan, 73–74, 128–29

LaBianca, Leno: Susan Atkins not present at murder of, 77; family of, 107, 126, 136, 150, 151–53, 186; Leslie's refusal to profit from murder of, 152; murder of, xvi, 6–8, 40, 43–44, 51, 75, 99–100, 105–6, 110, 116–17, 142, 148–51; question of robbery as motive in murder of, 41, 45, 106, 112, 125–26
LaBianca, Rosemary: Susan Atkins not present at murder of, 77; family of, 107, 126, 136, 150, 151, 186; Leslie unable to kill, 44, 50, 116–17, 142; Leslie's refusal to profit from murder of, 152; murder of, xvi, 6–8, 40, 43–44, 50, 51, 75, 99–100, 105–7, 110, 116–17, 142, 148–51; question of robbery as motive in murder of, 41, 45, 106, 112, 125–26
Lamott, Anne, 55
Lawyers (Leslie's), 50. *See also names of specific lawyers*

Leary, Timothy, 28, 63
Lemonheads (rock group), 55
Lennon, John, 69
Lie (Manson album), 55
Life sentence: Leslie's death sentence changed to, xv, 4, 10, 13, 21, 75, 135; as more frightening than execution, xx, 160
Lincoln Center (New York City), 54
Linda (death row resident), 5, 6, 10, 128
Long–Termers Organization (CIW), 139, 176
"Look at Your Game, Girl" (Manson song), 55
Los Angeles: as location of LaBianca murders, 8, 40, 42–45; Manson in, 31, 32; murders in, 104
Los Angeles Police Department, 8, 9, 42, 49, 104
Los Angeles Sheriff's Office, 8, 42
Los Angeles Times, 106, 140, 161
Los Feliz (Los Angeles neighborhood), 8
LSD (acid): author's experiences with, 111, 113; CIA's use of, in brainwashing experiments, 15; expert witnesses on, 110–14; Leslie's high school use of, 28, 111–13, 116, 148, 150; "Manson family's" use of, 34, 37, 59, 69, 107, 110–15, 127, 140; as "out–of–body" experience, 71, 113
LuLu (Leslie Van Houten's nickname), 33

Magical Mystery Tour (Beatles), 33
Malcolm X, 123
Malm, Aili, 167

Manson, Charles: arrest of, on murder charges, 41–44; background of, xv–xvi, xvii, 32, 38, 66; behavior of, at "Manson girls' " first trial, 49–53, 76, 100; change in personality of, 36, 53, 60, 114–15; as cult leader, xv–xvi, xviii–xix, 14–18, 24–25, 29–38, 41–47, 49–53, 60–76, 79, 86–92, 95, 98, 99, 104–8, 111–16, 127, 140, 142, 150, 152; on death, 21–22, 30, 33–35, 46–47, 53, 65, 74, 79, 86, 100, 108–9, 115, 158; on ego, 16, 30, 33, 34, 70, 106, 111, 116, 158; on fear, 35, 37, 53, 66; as "the Gardener," 30, 31; as God and Devil, 9, 17–18, 24, 25, 32–38, 45, 51, 55, 61, 69, 72, 75, 99, 108; on Leslie, 74, 105; Leslie on, xx, 16, 25, 29–30, 32, 60, 72, 99–100, 106, 117, 140, 142, 150; Leslie's introduction to, 29–30; loss of power of, over "Manson girls," xvi, 22, 23, 59, 75–77, 84, 91–92, 107, 108, 112, 117, 131, 138, 144; as lover, 70, 88–89, 99; marriage of, 63, 66; murder conviction of, xv–xvi, 42–44, 104, 115–16; murder roles of, 41, 42–45, 53, 62, 66–67, 71, 112, 125–26, 132, 140; as musician and songwriter, 30–32, 34, 54–55, 59–60, 65–67, 69, 84, 88, 90, 158; mythologizing of, by young people today, xx, 53–56, 142, 186; power of, over "Manson girls," xvi, xx, 5, 14, 15–18, 21–25, 29–38, 41–53, 59–76, 79, 86–92, 96, 99, 104–7, 111–16, 127, 140; as product of prison system, 38, 51–52, 63–66, 109, 139; as race war proponent, 9, 22–23, 36–38, 45, 68–76, 102, 106, 112, 123, 126, 131, 158; refusal of, to accept responsibility for his crimes, 16, 56, 63, 65; speech patterns of, 17, 31, 37, 65, 68; on women's role, 17–18, 22, 33–34, 62–63, 70, 72–75. *See also* "Manson family"; "Manson girls"

Manson, Marilyn, 55

"Manson family," xvi; as brainwashed, 11, 44–51, 59–75, 86, 90–91, 105–15, 133, 140; desert pit plans of, 36, 71, 102, 131; factors in violent changes in, 114–15; as hippie commune, 9, 22, 33–34, 36, 59–60; ignorance of Helter Skelter details by, 37, 42, 105–6; Manson's power over, xvi, xx, 5, 14, 15–18, 21–25, 29–38, 41–53, 59–76, 79, 86–92, 96, 99, 104–7, 111–16, 127, 140; murder as out of character for members of, 86, 89, 93–95, 102, 112, 116, 126, 133, 149, 157; murders committed by, 7–9, 40–45; number of members of, 67; ordinariness of most members of, 25, 33, 88; scavenging for food by, 17, 34, 60; sexual practices among, 17, 18, 24–25, 34, 62–63, 67, 70, 72, 73, 88, 107; testimony of former members of, at Leslie's trials, 104–5, 115; theft by, 36, 42, 45, 90, 112, 125–26, 150; women's role in, 17–18, 22, 33–34, 62–63, 70, 72–75. *See also* Brainwashing; Cult(s); "Manson girls"

The Manson Family: An Opera (Moran), 54

"Manson girls," 45; assumption of responsibility of, for their crimes, 15–16, 51, 52–53, 75–77, 135, 142, 158–59, 162; carving of "X's" in foreheads of, 52–53, 99, 100; false testimony by, 9, 16, 40, 41–42, 76–77; during first trial, 9–10, 16, 36, 40–42, 49–52, 76–77, 126; gender socialization of, xviii–xix, 11, 18, 48, 72–75, 77, 87, 114; historical period of time of, xviii, 9, 17–18, 22, 28–29, 33, 48, 63–64, 66, 67–68, 88, 95, 107–14; initial impressions of, in prison, 5–6, 68–69; initial lack of remorse by, 47, 49, 79, 116, 133; judged to be sane, 14, 21–22, 51, 62, 73, 110; Manson's loss of power over, xvi, 22, 23, 59, 75–77, 84, 91–92, 107–8, 112, 117, 131, 138, 144; as Manson's victims, xviii–xix, 14, 18, 24–25, 39, 53, 62–64, 68–69, 74–75, 79, 99, 106–7, 115; as model prisoners, 13, 14, 22, 26, 56, 57–59, 80–86; quality of innocence of, 14, 21, 23–24, 133; reeducation of, in prison, 19–23, 57–59, 76, 77–80, 87, 123, 125, 186; remorse felt by, xxi, 26, 47, 56, 75–76, 93, 107, 116–17, 136–37, 142, 145, 148–50, 152–53, 161, 163, 175; shaving of heads by, xvi, 11, 25, 52–53, 100. *See also* Atkins, Susan; Krenwinkel, Patricia; "Manson family"; Van Houten, Leslie

Manson Live at San Quentin (album), 55

Marijuana, 28, 114, 140, 145, 148, 150

May, Rollo, 51

McCabe's (Santa Monica folk club), 124–25

McDonald, Country Joe, 78

Media: interest of, in Leslie, xvi, xxi, 30, 56, 98–101, 112–13, 120, 125, 127, 136, 142, 152, 170, 185–87; on Manson, 73; on "Manson family," xx, 3, 6–11, 24–26, 44, 109–10; on Manson murders, 6–9, 39–40, 45, 49, 53, 128–29; on Manson victims' use of drugs, 115; and murders of African Americans, 104; on Charles "Tex" Watson, 9, 32, 49. *See also* Advertising; Internet; *specific television companies, books, and newspapers*

Melcher, Terry, 67

Men: Leslie's correspondence with, 146–47; in Manson's "family," 63–64, 67, 71–72, 108–9; socialization of, 48–49; women's overdependence on, as factor in women's crime, 19, 45, 48–49, 105–7, 140. *See also specific men*

Merry Pranksters, 33

Milk, Harvey, 128

Miller, Debra, 22, 78, 123

Mind control. *See* Brainwashing

Les Miserables (Hugo), 162

Mojave Desert (near Death Valley), 36, 71, 102, 131

Monroe, Marilyn, 55

Moon, Sun Myung, 29

"Moonies," 29

Moore, Andrea, 123

Moore, Bill, 78, 123

Moorehouse, Ruth, 72, 73

Moran, John, 54

Morgan, Robin, 21

Moscone, George, 128

Mothers of Invention (rock group), 70
Motives: for Stephen Kay's obsession with Manson murders, 131–33; for killing, 48–49, 65, 157–58; Manson's, for Tate and LaBianca murders, 41, 42, 44, 45, 64–67, 100; question of robbery as, for LaBianca murders, 41, 45, 112, 125–26
Murder(s): of African–American jail visitor, 103–4; California requirements for conviction of, 126–27; claims about Manson, as crime of the century, 9, 106, 126, 128–29, 148; and cults, 155–56; drugs associated with, 111, 113; of Fosters' daughter, 129–31; Leslie's participation in, xv, xvi, 8, 23–24, 42–45, 50, 68, 99–100, 107, 135; by "Manson family," xv, xvi, 6–8, 10, 40–44, 51, 66–67, 75–77, 86, 89, 99–100, 105–6, 110, 116–17, 142, 148–51; media's coverage of, 6–9, 39–40, 45, 49, 53, 128–29; as out of character for "Manson family" members, 86, 89, 93–95, 102, 112, 116, 126, 133, 149, 157; recidivism rate for, 10; solving of, 7–8; standard length of time served for, 98, 132, 138; by strangers, xvii, 5, 8, 10, 45; women's involvement in, xvii, 5, 8. *See also* Motives; Parole; Prisons and jails
My Lai massacre, 52

NA (Narcotics Anonymous), 148, 184
National Enquirer, 129, 151
"Native Dancer" (song), 124–25

NBC, 98
Near, Anne: author's conversations with, xvii–xix, xxi, 23–25, 47–48, 93–94, 132–33, 136, 138, 156–58; on Leslie, xvii, 107; on prison wardens, 14; on women's movement, 19
Near, Holly, 78
Neo–Nazis, 128–29
"Never Learn Not to Love" (Beach Boys song), 55
Nieman, Tanya, 78
1960s: as context for "Manson girls," xviii, 9, 17–18, 22, 28–29, 33, 48, 63–64, 66, 67–68, 88, 95, 107–14. *See also* Hippies
Nixon, Richard M., 110

"O Rotten Gotham" (Wolfe), 179
Ouspensky, P. D., 28

Parole: holding out hope of, as possibility for Leslie, 127–28, 145–46, 151, 173; for Leslie's cellmate, 184; Manson's, 63; as matter of politics rather than public safety, 144–45; need of, for Leslie, xvi, 132; of other "Manson family" members, 92; standard length of time served for murder before, 98, 132, 138; of women murderers, 10, 128. *See also* Parole boards; Van Houten, Leslie: as rehabilitated
Parole boards, 39–40, 142–53, 159; changing standards set for Leslie by, 136, 144, 148, 151, 181–82; effects of, on Leslie, 92, 143, 151–52, 174–76, 182–84, 188; frequency of hearings held by, 142–43; Stephen Kay's attendance at

Parole boards (*cont.*)
"Manson family" members' hearings before, 129, 132, 136, 150–52, 184; Leslie's testimony before, 44, 145–46, 148–53, 182; support for Leslie in front of, 141–42, 181–82; Charles Watson's hearings before, 151. *See also* Bail; Parole
Part, Marvin, 50, 74
Patrick, Ted, 29
Pavlov, Ivan P., 16, 173
People magazine, 55
People's Temple cult, 61
Picasso, Pablo, 178
"Pig" (written in blood at murder sites), 8, 40, 41
"Piggies" (Beatles song), 36, 109
Pink Flamingos (film), 54
Plea-bargaining, 117, 171
Polanski, Roman, 40, 67
Poverty. *See* Class; Racism
Prejean, Helen, 188–89
Press. *See* Media
Prisons and jails: alternatives to, 87, 124; Carlson's view of women in, 12–13, 18–20; cells in, 5, 173; characteristics of people in, 19, 47–49, 130, 138; effects of, on prisoners, 13, 26, 81, 121–27, 133–34, 136, 150, 178, 183; increase in, 130, 137; lawlessness in, 104; length of time Leslie has spent in, xv, 5–6, 132, 143, 146, 150, 153; Leslie as model prisoner in, xvi, xx, 6, 13, 14, 22, 26, 56, 80–86, 135, 137, 139–41, 143, 145, 148, 151–53, 159–62, 169, 175–76, 179–80, 184, 187; Manson as product of, 38, 51–52, 63–66, 109, 139; phone use in, xix; as producing violence, 130; purposes of, 79–80, 87, 129, 143, 173; standard length of time served for murder in, 98, 132, 138. *See also* Bail; California Institution for Women; Death penalty; Death row; Guards; Parole; Parole boards; Psychiatrists; Sybil Brand Institute
Psychedelic drugs. *See* LSD
Psychiatric Treatment Unit (PTU), 80–81, 85, 173, 187
Psychiatrists: as expert witnesses, 110–15, 126–27; pre-trial evaluations of Leslie by, 44, 50–51; at prison, 22, 58–59, 156–57
PTU. *See* Psychiatric Treatment Unit

Quakers, 130

Race war: Jim Jones on, 155; Manson on, 9, 22–23, 36–38, 45, 68–76, 102, 106, 112, 123, 126, 131, 158
Racism, 128–29; as factor in who gets imprisoned, 130, 137; Manson's, 23; in media treatment of murder, 7
"Rack" (solitary confinement), 58, 81, 97, 103–4, 139, 162, 170
Ram Dass, 84
Rastafarians, 3
Reagan, Ronald, 110
Recidivism rate (of murderers), 10
Rehabilitation: Leslie's, xvi, 22, 92, 107, 112, 131–32, 136–37, 141–42, 144, 153, 159, 161–62; prison policy makers' views of, 144
Reiner, Ira, 50
Retribution (vengeance): Herb and Ellie Foster's lack of, 129–31; Leno

LaBianca's niece's seeking of, 151–52; Rosemary LaBianca's daughter's lack of, 107, 151; Manson's, 64–67; prosecutors' interest in, 51, 128–33; by society, 136–39, 144. *See also* Death penalty; Prisons and jails
Revelation (Bible), 17, 36–37, 69
"Revolution 9" (Beatles song), 69, 109
Ringer, Gordon, 125, 127, 144, 171–72
Rivera, Geraldo, 98–101
"Roadrunner" (prisoner), 80
Rolling Stone magazine, 155
Rolling Stones (rock group), 55
Rose, Al, 34
Rose, Axl, 55
Rotkin, Michael, 78

San Diego, 156
San Francisco, 29, 31–32, 34
San Francisco Chronicle, 161
San Quentin prison, 10, 187
Santa Cruz Women's Prison Project, 20, 121
Sartre, Jean-Paul, 178
Satanism, 35–36. *See also* Manson, Charles: as God and Devil; Witches
Satan's Slaves, 55
Sawyer, Diane, 30, 62, 142, 185–86
Schein, Edgar, 16
Schweitzer, Albert, 178
Scientology Church, 29
Self-Realization Fellowship, 28, 116
Sexual practices: in Jonestown, 155; Leslie's, in high school, 28; among "Manson family," 17, 18, 24–25, 34, 62–63, 67, 70, 72, 73, 88, 107
"Sexy Sadie" (Beatles song), 86, 109
Share, Catherine "Gypsy," 10, 29–30, 53, 90, 92
Shea, Donald, 42
Siegelman, Jim, 144
Simon Fraser University, 167, 176
Simpson, O. J., 53
Singer, Margaret, 63–64, 152
Sister Carrie (Dreiser), 58
Sisterhood is Powerful (Morgan), 21
Skinner, B. F., 16
Smith, David E., 34, 114
Smith, Mrs. (prison occupational therapist), 13
Soledad state prison, xvii, 3
Solitary confinement. *See* "Rack"
Sonoma State University, 172
Spahn, George, 62
Spahn Ranch: Leslie at, during Tate murders, 105–6; Leslie's introduction to, 30; Manson family at, 17, 33–34, 36, 37, 51, 59, 74, 89, 91, 116
Special Security Unit (SSU) of CIW, 3; atmosphere of, 4–5, 13–15, 20–21; guards in, 4–5, 11, 78–83; letters from, 168–69; "Manson girls'" life in, 10–11, 13, 20–21, 80–86, 89–90, 139; psychiatrists in, 22, 58–59, 156–57; reeducation of women in, 19–23, 57–59, 76, 77–80, 87, 123, 125, 186. *See also* Death row
"Speed" (amphetamines), 114–15
Stoller, Nancy, 22, 78, 167
Straight Satans, 55
Sybil (multiple personality individual), 146, 175

Sybil Brand Institute (Los Angeles women's jail), 6, 10, 42, 50, 127, 169–72; conditions in, 97–98, 102–4, 170; support for Leslie from, 141–42

Symbionese Liberation Army (SLA), 54

"Sympathy for the Devil" (Rolling Stones song), 55

Talbot, Sue, 121, 167, 180

Tate, Doris, 129

Tate, Patty, 129, 187

Tate, Sharon: drug use among friends of, 115; murder of, xv, 7, 8, 10, 40, 42, 51, 66–67, 75, 76–77, 86, 89; murder of, brought up in Leslie's trials, 105–6, 117, 127; murder of, Leslie not present at, xvi, 105–6, 151

Television sets, 13, 178. *See also* Media

Tex. *See* Watson, Charles "Tex"

Theft: by "Manson family," 36, 42, 45, 90, 112, 125–26, 150; as possible motive for LaBianca murders, 41, 45, 106, 112, 125–26

Trial(s): Leslie's first, xviii, 10, 44–45, 49–53, 76, 97, 99, 100, 126, 144, 149, 161; Leslie's second, xviii, 91, 101, 104–17, 132, 141, 161, 170–71; Leslie's third, xviii, 117, 125–28, 132, 141, 144, 161, 171–72; Manson's behavior at Leslie's first, 49–53, 76, 100; possibility of Leslie having, separate from other Manson family members, 44–45, 50–51, 97, 127, 128

Turning Point (ABC show), 142

Unification Church, 29

United States: citizens' complicity with evil doings of, 93–94, 157–58; Manson family perceived as threat to, 131. *See also* Prisons and jails

U.S. Supreme Court, 4, 10, 12

University of California at Berkeley, 30

University of California at Santa Cruz, 3, 20, 22–23, 73, 123, 159, 169, 187

Vacaville maximum–security medical facility, 63

Van Houten, Leslie: advocates for release of, 54, 141–45, 162, 181; anorexia of, 91–92, 123, 135, 150, 172; assumption of responsibility of, for her role in LaBianca murders, 15–16, 52–53, 75, 135, 142, 150, 158–59, 162–63; author's friendship with, xix–xxi, xv, 3–6, 22, 78–86, 97–98, 119–21, 147–48, 188, 189; background of, xvi, 27–38, 48, 93–94, 107; on bail, xv, xviii, xxi, 119–27, 133–34, 142–44, 172; conscience of, 43, 44, 68, 76 (*see also* Van Houten, Leslie: remorse felt by); death sentence for, 3, 21, 49, 53; death sentence for, changed to life in prison, xv, 4, 10, 13, 21, 75, 135; and gifts, 81–84; inability of, to kill, 43–44, 50, 116–17, 142; initial impressions of, 5, 24, 74–75; initial lack of remorse by, 47, 49, 79, 116, 133; letters of, xxi, 167–89; on Manson, xx, 16, 25, 29–30, 32, 60, 72, 99–100, 106, 117, 140, 142, 150; as "Manson girl," xv, xviii–xix, 42–

45, 49–53, 68–70, 99, 104–5, 137, 142, 146, 153, 161; Manson on, 74, 105; as Manson's victim, xviii–xix, 24–25, 39, 49–51, 62–64, 68, 70, 74–75, 79, 99, 105–7, 136, 146; marriage of, 147, 148, 176–77; media attention on, xxi, 9–10, 30, 56, 98–101, 112–13, 136, 140, 142, 143, 170, 185–87; as model prisoner, xvi, xx, 6, 13, 14, 22, 26, 56, 80–86, 135, 137, 139–41, 143, 145, 148, 151–53, 159–62, 169, 175–76, 179–80, 184, 187; murder participation by, xv, xvi, 8, 23–24, 42–45, 50, 68, 99–100, 107, 135; positive attitude of, 26, 80–86, 92, 102, 112, 136, 143, 150, 162, 173, 178, 183; quality of innocence in, 23–24, 93–95, 117; as rehabilitated, xvi, 22, 92, 107, 112, 131–32, 136–37, 141–42, 144, 153, 159, 161–62; rejection of Manson by, xvi, 22–23, 59, 91–92, 99, 107–8, 112, 117, 131, 138, 144, 146, 161; remorse felt by, xvi, xxi, 26, 47, 56, 75–76, 93, 107, 116–17, 135–37, 142, 145, 148–50, 152–53, 161, 163, 175; spiritual search of, 28, 29, 48, 85, 92, 105, 116, 159; as still in prison, 53, 132, 134; vocational training of, 28, 94, 132, 143. *See also* Prisons and jails; Trial(s)

Van Houten, Paul (Leslie's father), 27–28, 85–86, 105, 107, 123, 135–36, 148, 160, 173, 174, 185, 187

Van Houten, Jane (Leslie's mother): Leslie's relationship with, xix, 27–28, 85–86, 101, 105, 107, 119, 120, 122, 123, 135–36, 148, 160, 171, 173–75, 179–80, 185; trial testimony of, 107–8

Vegetarianism, 35, 81

Venceremos Brigade, xix

Vengeance. *See* Retribution

Vietnam War, xviii, 9, 29, 52, 109, 157, 179

Violence: to maintain peace, 133. *See also* Murder; War

Voluntary manslaughter, 127

Voting age, xviii

Waco (Texas), 155

Walters, Barbara, xxi, 98–101, 112–13, 136, 170

War, 45. *See also* Murder; Race war; *specific wars*

War on Drugs, 110

Warden (of CIW). *See* Carlson, Virginia

Waters, John, 54

Watkins, Paul, 108–9, 114

Watson, Charles "Tex": background of, 33; drug use by, 114; as evangelical Christian, 92; flight of, to Texas, 42, 49; on Manson, 32–35, 158; as "Manson family" member, 17, 65, 67, 70–72; media attention on, 9, 32, 49; murder conviction of, xv, 49; as murderer, 32, 40–45, 53, 65, 76–77, 86; parole board hearing of, 151; as still in prison, 49

White, Dan, 128

White, Rory, 78, 86

White Album (Beatles), 8, 36, 69, 109, 115. *See also titles of specific songs*

Williams, Tennessee, 178

Williamson, Cris, 78, 124–25, 174

Wilson, Dennis, 32, 54–55
Wilson, Pete, 145, 187
Witches, 24–25, 36, 149
Wolfe, Tom, 179
Women: battered, 61, 106; characteristics of, in prison, 19, 47–49, 138; discrimination against, in prisons, 187; murder committed by, xvii, 5, 8, 10, 45; overdependence of, on men as crime factor among, 19, 45, 48–49, 105–7, 140; role of, in "Manson family," 17–18, 22, 33–34, 62–63, 70, 72–75; socialization of, xviii–xix, 11, 18, 48, 72–75, 77, 87, 114. *See also* "Manson girls"; Women's movement
Women's movement: Carlson's view of, 12, 14, 18; as crime prevention tool, 19; influence of, on author, 21, 124; "Manson's girls'" exposure to, 17, 18, 21, 76, 87, 185–86
Wonder, Stevie, 98
Woodstock rock festival, 9
The World According to Garp (Irving), 174
Wright, Richard, 65

X, Malcolm, 123

Yogic spiritual community. *See* Buddhism
"(Your) Home Is Where You're Happy" (Manson song), 55, 90

Zappa, Frank, 70